CLASSIC
INDIAN
COOKING

CLASSIC INDIAN COOKING

JULIE SAHNI

DORLING KINDERSLEY · LONDON

A Jill Norman Book

First published in Great Britain in 1986
by Dorling Kindersley Publishers Limited,
9 Henrietta Street, London WC2E 8PS

Illustrations by Lorraine Harrison

British Library Cataloguing in Publication Data
Sahni, Julie
    Classic Indian cooking
    1. Cookery, Indian
    I. Title
    641. 5954 TX724.5.14
    ISBN 0-86318-173-2

Typeset by MS Filmsetting Limited, Frome, Somerset

Printed in Great Britain by Richard Clay (The Chaucer Press) Ltd

CONTENTS

◆

◆

*For Patricia Wells
— for changing my destiny*

◆

INTRODUCTION

◆

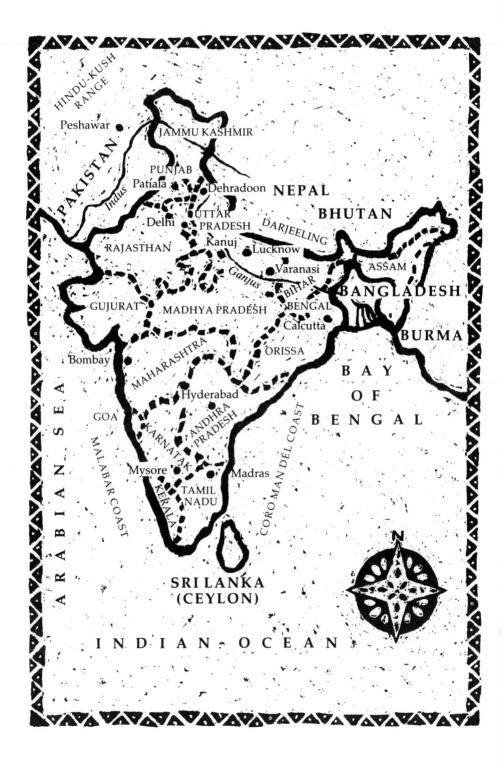

Indian food is the reflection of the heritage of its people. It represents India's historical development, religious beliefs, cultural practices, and above all, geographical attributes. It is, in fact, an amalgamation of the cuisines of many diverse regions. The unifying factor that brings all these varied cuisines under the heading of 'Indian food' is the ingenious way that fragrant herbs and aromatic spices are used in all the regions. Indian food is the most aromatic of all cuisines – it is the cooking of captivating fragrances and intriguing flavours. It is crushed cardamom smothering tender young chickens (*Shahi Murgh Badaami*, p. 163), bruised carom lacing fish fillets (*Bhoni Machi*, p. 184), and pistachios sweetening the cream sauce for foamy cheese dumplings (*Ras Malai*, p. 330).

◆

GEOGRAPHY

India, Pakistan, Bangladesh, Burma, and Sri Lanka (all of which were once part of the single nation of India) occupy the clearly bounded Indian subcontinent. Sri Lanka is a small separate island to the south in the Indian Ocean. Today, Burma is separated from India by the dense mosquito-ridden jungle that is India's modern eastern boundary. Along the southern part of India's eastern boundary is Bangladesh. Pakistan lies along the northwest border. There is no physical boundary separating Pakistan and Bangladesh from India. India is bounded on the north by the mighty ranges of the Himalayas, beyond which lies the Tibetan plateau. These mountains extend all the way northwest to the Hindu-Kush mountains which, although immense, are passable. Most new waves of invaders entered India through these passes (the best-known being the Khyber Pass). Further to the west lies the Afghanistan plateau bordered by Iran, and Turkmeniya and Uzbekistan in the USSR. The remainder of the country is bordered by the sea.

The northernmost part of India, embraced by the snow-dusted peaks of the Himalayas, has a temperate climate. Here lies the Valley of Kashmir with its magnificent Persian gardens and terraced lakes. The brisk, cool fresh air in this region is imbued with the fragrance of pines and saffron flowers. Walnut and fruit orchards dot the countryside, and morels (*gochian*) and black cumin seeds (*kala jeera*) grow wild. The climate is cool enough for the rearing of sheep; thus lamb (*katch*) forms the basis of many Kashmiri dishes.

As one moves south, the landscape becomes flatter and the climate warmer. The world-famous Indian long grain rice known as *basmati* is grown in the foothills of these mountains, where the climate and soil are ideal for growing rice. The northern plains, irrigated by the great rivers Indus and

Ganges, are rich and fertile. The extreme climate variation, from fierce heat (with temperatures rising to 120°F/50°C) to subfreezing cold with dry chilly winds, enables crops of wheat, corn, millet, barley, and innumerable varieties of pulses and vegetables to flourish. Here lie Delhi, Punjab, and Uttar Pradesh, where men are tall and hardy and the diet rich. The cooking fat used here is clarified butter (*usli ghee*). Goat and chicken are the meats eaten here. Even though rice is eaten quite commonly, and with great relish, bread is the primary staple of the people in these regions.

To the east lie the fertile plains of Bengal where the Ganges flows into the Bay of Bengal. The waters here overflow with hundreds of varieties of fish and shellfish, both freshwater and sea. The coastal area is lined with coconut palms, and the fields are covered with the yellow blossoms of mustard plants, looking like golden carpets stretching to the horizon. The climate is hot and humid. Rice grows abundantly here and, together with the abundant fish cooked in mustard oil, forms the daily diet of the people.

Farther to the northeast in the mountains of Assam lies Darjeeling, where the cool air and the seasonal rains that keep the hills perpetually drenched create the ideal conditions for cultivating tea. This is where the famous Darjeeling tea comes from.

Separating the southern regions from the northern plains is the great Deccan plateau. The Deccan is lined on both sides by a chain of hills known as *Ghat* (western *ghats* and eastern *ghats*). The soil along the plateau is not rich and the lack of irrigation further restricts agriculture. The hills taper away to fertile plains near the sea. Gujurat lies to the northwest of the Deccan. Here the soil is rich, which helps the cultivation of cotton, millet, barley, pulses, and many varieties of vegetables. Bread is the staple here. Lentil purées and vegetables cooked in sesame oil are commonly eaten by the primarily vegetarian population.

To the south lie Maharashtra, Goa, and Malabar. In these states tropical conditions prevail, due to their proximity to the equator and because of the monsoon rains. The weather is always warm, wet, and humid. Along the path of the monsoons, rice — the principal staple — is cultivated. The coastal areas yield many kinds of fish. A white non-oily fish called *pomfret*, which tastes like sole, and a small transparent fish, *bombil*, popularly known as 'Bombay duck', which is sun-dried and sold as wafers, are most popular. There is also no limit to the variety of shellfish, including prawns, shrimp, crab, lobster, clams and mussels. In addition, banana plants and different varieties of palm, including the coconut and date palms, line the coastline. Fish and seafood cooked with coconut and rice form the daily diet of the people in these regions.

The eastern plains are much wider, flat, and have highly fertile soil. These areas are abundant in limitless varieties of vegetables and greens. The people here are primarily vegetarians: their diet consists chiefly of vegetables, pulses and rice. Coconut and bananas are used extensively in the preparation of dishes; and coconut or sesame oils are the fats. Here coconut milk substitutes for cow's milk.

◆

CULTURAL INFLUENCE

Even though India is one of the oldest civilizations, it has been enriched over a period of many centuries by the different cultures that were superimposed with each new invasion. These invaders brought with them new ideas and concepts; they introduced new cooking ingredients and techniques which spread to different regions of India, enhancing and refining the local cuisine. However, this influence was concentrated mainly in the North, where the new hordes primarily settled because of the similarity of the climate and landscape to those they came from. Furthermore, the natural barriers and great distances made migration to the South slow and infrequent. Thus northern cooking evolved far more over the centuries than other regional cuisines and attained unparalleled distinction.

◆

RELIGIOUS TABOOS

India is a country of people of varied race, colour, and religion, all bound together by a common culture known as 'Indian Culture'. The religious differences in particular are extreme – and far too many – and their influence on people's lives has been profound, especially in food and eating habits. What is amazing and wonderful is how these people, with their different beliefs, have lived together side by side, tolerating and respecting each other's convictions and practices for so many centuries.

The four major religions that originated and are practised in India are Hinduism, Buddhism, Jainism, and Sikhism (the last three are offshoots of Hinduism). The Moslem religion is also referred to as one of the Indian religions because it was brought to India nine hundred years ago and has since spread over the entire country, with 65 million followers. India has the second largest Moslem population in the world. The other religions include Christianity, Judaism, and Zoroastrianism (the religion of the Parsees, a sect that emigrated from Persia to escape religious persecution). Each of these groups has its own code and methods of cooking and eating.

The Hindus and Sikhs, for example, are prohibited from eating beef because the cow is a sacred animal in Indian mythology. Lord Krishna was a cowherd who saw the whole universe reflected in the cow's body. Also, Lord Shiva's carrier was the bull *Nandi*. Similarly, Moslems and Jews are for different reasons prohibited from eating pork. There are certain Hindus (Brahmins and Jains) who are strict vegetarians, and who number several hundred million. These groups do not eat meat, which in an Indian context means red meat, poultry, fish, shellfish, eggs, and their products. Certain strict vegetarians won't eat food that resembles meat, such as tomatoes, red beetroots, and watermelon, because of their fleshlike colour. Neither do they use seasonings that are strong and generally associated with the cooking of meat, such as garlic and onion.

While most Hindu Brahmins generally follow these rules, there are two exceptions: the Hindu Brahmins from Kashmir, known as Kashmiri Pandits, follow all the general Brahmin codes of cooking and eating, such as refraining from the use of onions and garlic in dishes, but *do* include meat (except of course beef) in their diet. This is because Kashmir for centuries was (and still is) in political turmoil, shifting constantly between Hindu and Moslem rulers. With each new power came mass conversions. The original people, who were Hindus, were forcibly converted during a Moslem reign and reverted back to Hinduism with the coming of a Hindu king. Since they had assumed a Moslem life-style for many centuries, they maintained several Moslem cultural practices, such as the eating of meat, even after finally becoming Hindu. As a result, the Kashmiri Pandits today eat meat but do not use onion or garlic in their cooking. This cooking is distinctly different from Kashmiri Moslem cooking. Both are famous for their exquisite lamb preparations.

The second exception is the Hindu Brahmins from Bengal. These people include fish, shellfish, and their products in their diet, because they consider them to be *Jal Toori*, meaning cucumbers or vegetables of the sea (or river). These Brahmins eat meat on special occasions, such as during the festival of *Durga Pooja* (worship of the Goddess Durga or Kali) in September and October when animals are ritually sacrificed. The meat of these animals, when offered to the Goddess, is considered holy, and thus a sacred privilege to eat.

All these cultural, religious, and geographical factors have played a great role in influencing Indian food and together have shaped and developed it to what it is today.

ABOUT MOGHUL FOOD

The most popular and refined of all regional styles of cooking is the cooking of North India, which is basically Moghul food. This is the style of food served in most better-quality restaurants, here and in India. It evolved with the coming of the Moghuls in the sixteenth century. The Moghuls were Turk-Mongols by origin and Moslem by religion. The culture they admired most was Persian, since they were influenced by it on their way to India. They settled in the northern plains, with Delhi as their centre. This is because Delhi, for strategic reasons (the wide flowing river Jamuna embracing the city, the rich fertile soil surrounding the city, and good landscape providing accessibility and visual security), had for centuries been the capital of the various groups in power. The Moghuls introduced new foods, new ingredients, and new cooking techniques, some of which were their own but most of which were borrowed from the Persians. In time several local herbs and spices found their way into these dishes, thus giving rise to the distinct new style of cooking known as Moghul cooking.

The Moghuls were lovers of nature and the good life, and had a keen sense of beauty, and a passion for elegance. This was reflected in every contribution they made, including art, architecture, painting, landscaping, social attire, mannerism, and most definitely in the presentation of food. For example, elaborate *biriyani* (layered meat and rice pilafs), were put together with meticulous care and presented on three- to four-foot gold and silver platters, garnished with crisp sautéed nuts, crackling onion shreds, and edible pure silver sheets. Many were also given beautiful names.

Moghul food is famous for its mouth-watering meat preparations and rice pilafs. These include braised dishes called *korma*, pot roasts (*dum*), kebabs (*kabab*), kaftas (*kofta*), and pilafs called *pullao* and *biriyani*.

Moghul cooking is also known for its delicate flavourings and superb silky sauces. The dishes thus created are so subtle that many are often mistaken for Persian. Ingredients such as yogurt, cream, fruit, and nut butters are often incorporated into the food to mellow and velvetize the sauces. The dishes are generally flavoured with mild but highly fragrant spices such as cinnamon, cardamom, mace, nutmeg, and clove. There is also extensive use of saffron, especially in the rice pilafs.

The influence of Moghul cooking predominated in the North, especially in Delhi and the areas surrounding it, which are today known as Punjab, Kashmir, and Uttar Pradesh. Moghul cooking also flourishes in Hyderabad, a city in the southern state of Andra Pradesh. It is distinctly different because of regional influences, but is considered just as refined and sophisticated.

All through the centuries, even before the coming of the Moghuls, different cooking styles existed, each highly distinctive and lovely. All these styles flourish today in various parts of the country and each holds a special place in Indian cuisine. The differences among them, however, are great. To describe them would take a volume in itself; such a task is not possible within the scope of this book. What is possible, and what I have tried to do, is to introduce you to most of the important contrasting regional features here and there in the book. This will give you a sense of the fundamental differences that exist in the local cuisines. I want to emphasize that each regional style of cooking is to be appreciated on its own merits, for they all hold a very distinct place in the Indian culinary world.

THE PRINCIPLES
OF INDIAN COOKING

Indian cooking is more of an art than a science. It is highly personalized, reflecting individual tastes. It allows the cook to exercise the full range of her or his creative ingenuity. This is because the foundation of Indian cooking rests not so much on special techniques or expensive ingredients as on the flavourings – specifically, spices and herbs. Their uses, in different permutations and combinations, are what give Indian cooking its distinct character. Just as no two pieces of creative work are alike, so the same dish prepared by different cooks exhibits as many individualized flavours as it has interpreters. I am reminded of James Beard who, in his memoir, *Delights and Prejudices*, emphatically defends his food preferences and makes no bones about the things that never quite suit his fancy. Indian cooks generally follow that mode of thinking. In most instances, the Indian cook will add an ingredient or two beyond what is required in a dish, without deviating from the classic flavour, simply to give it his or her own personal stamp. This is commonly referred to in Indian as *Hath ki bat*, meaning 'one's touch'. These personal touches are what make all the difference and – understandably – are zealously guarded secrets among Indian cooks. That's why a dish never tastes quite the same in any two Indian homes or restaurants, even when it belongs to the same regional style of cooking.

There is no mystical secret behind Indian cooking. It is, in fact, the easiest of all international cuisines; the utensils needed are few and simple and cooking techniques, except for several that are exclusively Indian, are similar to those familiar to Europeans and Americans.

Knowledge of how to use spices and herbs is the key that will unlock the secrets of the seductive flavours and tantalizing aromas in Indian cooking. Knowing the quantities required is only the first step. As you start preparing Indian dishes, you will begin to develop a sense of how the spices and herbs behave with the other ingredients in a dish. Some herbs and spices are used as aromatics, some lend colouring, while others function as souring agents. There are spices that give a hot taste to the food and others that thicken or tenderize a dish. Once you understand the different properties of the various spices and herbs, gain a sense of how they interact, and master the techniques in using them, the classic dishes of India will neither seem a mystery nor be difficult to create yourself.

The role of spices and herbs goes far beyond pleasing the palate and soothing the senses. They have medicinal properties that were known to the ancient Indians. Ayurvedic scripts in the three-thousand-year-old Holy Hindu Scriptures on herbal medicine list the preventive and curative powers of various spices, herbs, and roots in the treatment of common physical ailments. Over many centuries, specific spices were traditionally added to, and thus came to be associated with, certain Indian dishes. Asafetida and ginger root are known to counteract flatulence and colic, so they are added to lentil preparations as a matter of course. Some spices are excellent stimulants of the digestive system, which has a tendency to become sluggish with lack of physical activity. After a meal Indians chew either a betel leaf (*paan*), a betel nut (*Areca catecha*), and lime paste, or a few fragrant spices such as fennel, cardamom, or cloves. These are the Indian substitutes for the Western after-dinner mint. In addition to being wonderfully effective mouth-fresheners, they aid digestion, curb nausea, and provide relief from heartburn and acid indigestion. Cloves also act as an antiseptic. Fenugreek water is used as a tonic for gastritis and other stomach disorders. When soaked in water, the seeds soften and swell, and act as a most effective digestive aid. A few fenugreek seeds are always added to starchy vegetables and hard-to-digest pulses, especially when no asafetida or ginger are present. The North Indian appetizer called *chat* is almost always sprinkled with black salt (*kala namak*) and lemon juice, both of which are well-known for stimulating the appetite and increasing blood circulation.

The Holy Hindu Scriptures also document the effect of spices on body temperature. Spices which generate internal body heat are called 'warm', and those which take heat away from one's system are called 'cool' spices. Bay leaf, black cardamom, cinnamon, ginger powder, mace, nutmeg, and red pepper are 'warm' spices and are recommended for cold weather. All the other spices range from 'very cool' to 'moderately warm' and therefore are suitable at all times in all climates. This is why dishes containing 'warm' spices are instinctively prepared by the Indian cook more often during the winter months and avoided during the summer.

In the state of Kashmir where the climate is cool, spices such as cinnamon, nutmeg, mace, black cardamom, and ginger powder are traditionally used in the local specialities. Tea in Kashmir is also often flavoured with cinnamon and cardamom. In the Plains, especially during the summer, 'cool' spices lace beverages like the delicious cool punch (*Thandai*, p. 350) made with cow's milk, almond milk, sunflower and cantaloupe seeds, fennel, cloves, and green cardamom. The after-dinner spices (fennel, green cardamom, and cloves) are all described as 'cool'.

Spices also induce perspiration, which helps one to feel cool and comfortable. This is why Indians prefer to drink piping hot spice-laced tea in hot weather.

When spices and herbs are added to a dish, they act on the ingredients in many specific and wondrous ways. They don't always make a dish spicy and hot, as is widely believed. Except for a few spices that do impart a hot taste, most act as aromatics (to lace the food with a subtle scent), as colouring agents (to make the classic dishes beautiful to behold), as souring agents (to lend piquancy and tartness), as natural tenderizers for meat, and finally, as thickeners and binders for sauces (to give body and texture).

Most spices and herbs possess several properties. Saffron, for example, lends both a lovely orange-yellow colour and a hypnotizing aroma to a dish. Coriander thickens a sauce at the same time that it imparts a nutty fragrance. Onions both thicken and perfume Moghul gravies. To give a specific example: In the dish Chicken in Onion Tomato Gravy (*Murgh Masala*, p. 157), the cinnamon, cardamom, and cloves aromatize; the turmeric lends yellow colour; the onions, garlic, ginger root, and tomatoes act as thickeners as well as imparting flavour and colour to the dish. The tomatoes also function as tenderizing and souring agents.

The secret to mastering the art of classic Indian cooking, then, lies in developing, until it becomes almost instinctive, a knowledge of the specific properties of each spice, herb, and root, and how they behave with other ingredients. For this purpose, I have described in this chapter the different and important properties of each spice, herb, and flavouring used in Indian cooking. Also for your convenience, there is a ready-reference spice chart on page 22.

To sum up, to become an experienced and creative Indian cook it is essential to feel at home in your kitchen, surrounded by fragrant spices and aromatic herbs. This confidence will come naturally to you when you develop a working knowledge of these ingredients. This is the first lesson in the process of becoming an expert. Learning the use of spices in Indian cooking is somewhat like learning a new language – practice makes perfect.

You should be able to find all of the ingredients you will need for Indian cooking in supermarkets, greengrocers or Asian food shops. This chapter includes a description of all the spices and herbs you will use in Indian cooking, to acquaint you with the multiple roles they play.

SPICES

◆

Except for a few that are highly aromatic in their raw form, most spices have to be cooked before they release any of their fragrance. All spices, however, release more aroma when slightly crushed. And some are more aromatic than others. Cinnamon is more fragrant than cumin; cardamom is more fragrant than coriander; saffron is more fragrant than turmeric. When cooking Indian dishes, you must make sure that no single spice overwhelms a dish, that each harmoniously blends with the others. There are, however, a few exceptions in which the fragrance of a particular spice is emphasized intentionally. The spice whose aroma is meant to predominate is generally added in large quantity, and the number of additional herbs and spices is reduced to a minimum.

Spices are dried organic matter such as roots, leaves, barks of trees, buds, stems, and seeds of plants, all of which are difficult to digest in their raw form. The reason people sometimes have digestion problems after eating Indian food is because they have eaten raw spices. The spices used in Indian cooking should be regarded as vegetables to be cooked before being eaten so that they will be easy on your digestive system and give out their maximum flavour. In Indian cooking, spices are always cooked before they go into a dish. They are generally added to the hot oil at the beginning of preparation and cooked for a moment before other ingredients are added. When the spices are incorporated during the final execution of a dish, or used in cold yogurt salads or appetizers (sometimes finished with a sprinkling of cumin and coriander), they should always be dry-roasted before being added.

Spices should be purchased whole, to be powdered as needed, because freshly ground spices are always more aromatic. Also, whole spices retain their potency and aroma much longer.

All spices should be stored in airtight containers in a cool dry place, or they will become rancid. If properly stored, ground spices will remain fresh up to three months, and whole ones up to one year (some, such as asafetida, mustard seeds, fenugreek, and onion seeds, stay fresh up to three years).

◆

ASAFETIDA *Heeng*

Asafetida is a combination of various dried gum resins obtained from the roots of certain Iranian and Indian plants. It is available in lump or powdered form.

PROPERTIES OF SPICES

WHAT SPICES DO TO FOOD

Spices	Lend Aroma or Fragrance	Lend Taste or Flavour	Lend Colour or Visual Appeal	Act as Thickeners
Asafetida *Heeng*	■			
Bay leaf *Tej Patta*	■			
Cardamom *Elaichi*	■			
Carom *Ajwain*	■			
Cinnamon *Dalchini*	■			
Clove *Laung*	■			
Coriander *Dhania, Sookha*	■			■
Cumin *Jeera*	■			
Fennel *Saunf*	■			
Fenugreek *Methi*	■			
Ginger Powder *Sonth*	■	sour-hot		
Mace *Javitri*	■			
Mango Powder *Amchoor*		sour		
Mustard *Rai*	■			
Nutmeg *Jaiphul*	■			
Onion Seed *Kalaunji*	■			
Paprika *Deghi Mirch*			red	
Pomegranate *Anardana*		sweetish-sour		
Poppy Seed, White *Khas-khas*				■
Red Pepper *Lal Mirch*		hot		
Saffron *Kesar*	■		orangish-yellow	
Salt *Namak*	■	alkaline		
Tamarind *Imli*		tangy-sour		
Turmeric *Haldi*	■		golden yellow	
White Split Gram Beans *Urad Dal*	■			
Yellow Split Peas *Channa Dal*	■			

Asafetida lump, brown in colour (the powder is buff colour), is virtually odourless until it is powdered, when it releases its strong characteristic smell. Asafetida in lump form, its purest state, will keep for years without losing its potency. Yet another reason (though a personal one) for purchasing the lump form: the powerful smell of powdered asafetida takes over the entire kitchen.

For most recipes, you will need a lump of asafetida about the size of a green pea – a size that can easily be crushed. Surprisingly, this strong and overly pungent ingredient, when added to hot oil and fried for five seconds, undergoes a mysterious change: it perfumes the fat with a subtle oniony aroma. Asafetida-flavoured oil is the basic ingredient in the cooking of Hindu Brahmins and Jains, whose strict vegetarian diet forbids them to use onions – a flavouring considered too strong and smelly. The Kashmiri Brahmins, who also abstain from cooking with onions, use asafetida in certain kebab preparations. Since asafetida is used as a substitute for onion flavour, it is logical that in Indian cooking the two are never used simultaneously.

◆

BAY LEAF *Tej Patta*

There are two types of bay leaves commonly available. The type used in Indian cooking, the Indian bay leaf, is the leaf of the cassia tree (*Cinnamomum cassia*), native to China, Southeast Asia and northeastern India. The other, known as sweet bay laurel, is the leaf of the bay tree (*Laurus nobilis*), native to Asia Minor and the Mediterranean. Both trees are evergreen members of the laurel family. The bay laurel leaf, when fully grown, is about 5 in/12.5 cm long, thick, glossy, and dark green. It has a bitterish taste and a pungent, almost lemony aroma. The Indian bay leaf, on the other hand, is almost 7 in/17.5 cm long, thin, dull, and light green, with a sweet taste and a mellow, spicy aroma. Indian bay leaves crumble readily, which is a great asset, as they can easily be powdered and mixed with other spices. One variety may be distinguished from the other in that the Indian bay leaves are broken, dull in appearance, bundled in plastic bags or cardboard boxes, and far less expensive than bay laurel leaves, which are brighter, fresher-looking whole leaves stacked in spice bottles. Indian bay leaves are preferred. If you cannot find them, bay laurel leaves may be substituted. Since bay laurel leaves are much stronger, you will need only half the amount suggested in the recipes. In Indian cooking, the bay leaf is used as a flavouring in preparing meat dishes. It is one of the four essential spices (cardamom, cinnamon, and clove being the others) that give a pilaf the distinctive fragrance associated with Moghul cooking. See Fragrant Pilaf Banaras Style (*Banarasi Pullao*, p. 263).

CARDAMOM *Elaichi*

These are the small, fragrant black seeds of the fruit of the cardamom plant (*Elettaria cardamomum*), which is native to South India and Sri Lanka. Whole cardamom, known as cardamom pods, comes in two varieties – the small green and the larger black.

The green cardamom, known as *Choti* (small) *Elaichi*, is widely available either in its natural green form, or bleached and puffed to give it more aesthetic appeal. This beautifying, however, seems somehow to take away that wonderfully intense cardamom aroma, so I recommend you buy it in its natural green form. Green cardamom, a small, ¼ in/5 mm long pod, has a thin pale-green skin and a powerful aroma, but a delicate sweet taste. Green cardamom is available whole or in powder form. In Indian cooking it is used as a flavouring, in both forms, in puddings, desserts, sweetmeats, conserves, and in some very delicate meat and poultry preparations, such as Moghul Braised Chicken (*Mughalai Korma*, p. 155). It is also one of the chief Indian after-dinner mints (clove and fennel being the others).

The second variety is black cardamom, known as *Kali* (black) or *Badi* (big) *Elaichi*. Black cardamom, a large, 1 in/2.5 cm pod, has a thick, husky dark-brown skin. It has a mellow taste, but a nuttier aroma than the green variety. Black cardamom is available only in whole form. In Indian cooking it is used in meat and vegetable dishes, as a flavouring, whole, or it is ground for use in relishes and sweet pickles, such as Sweet and Sour Tamarind Relish (*Imli Chutney*, p. 315). It is another of the four essential spices (with bay leaf, cinnamon, and clove) that give the Moghul pilaf its distinct aroma. It is also one of the main ingredients of the spice mix known as *Mughal Garam Masala* (p. 41). When a recipe calls for black cardamom, the green or bleached cardamom may be substituted if black cardamom is unavailable.

◆

CAROM *Ajwain*

Carom, also known as lovage, is the seed of the thymol plant (*Carum copticum*), native to the southern regions of India. The seeds resemble celery seeds. Carom seeds have a sharp and piquant taste and give out an aroma much like thyme when slightly bruised. They are used as a flavouring in vegetable preparations, breads, and savoury pastries. Carom is essential in making the delectable biscuits from Punjab called *Matthi* (p. 109). Mixed with garlic and lemon juice, carom transforms simple fillets of fish into mouth-watering *Bhoni Machi* (p. 184). It is also used in many varieties of pickles, both sweet and hot.

CINNAMON *Dalchini*

There are two types of cinnamon that may be used interchangeably. The type used in Indian cooking, the Indian cinnamon, is the bark of the cassia tree (*Cinnamomum cassia*), a member of the laurel family (see Bay Leaf, p. 23). It is generally referred to as cinnamon even though it is technically 'cassia' or 'false cinnamon'. The cassia bark is peeled in long strips and the corky outer layer is scraped off, leaving the bark in 'quills' or 'sticks'. Cinnamon cassia is reddish brown in colour and has a delicate, sweet taste and a captivating aroma.

The other, known as true cinnamon, is the bark of the cinnamon tree (*Cinnamomum zylanicum*), also a member of the laurel family. Since cinnamon cassia and true cinnamon both come from the same botanical family, *cinnamomum*, they are both sold as cinnamon; therefore, it is not always possible to know which you are buying. In any event, it matters little, since both varieties look, smell, and taste almost identical, except that cinnamon cassia quills are coarser, thicker, and have a stronger aroma than true cinnamon quills, which are smooth and slender. The textures are different because the true cinnamon bark is fermented for twenty-four hours after being peeled. This enables the corky layer to be scraped off completely, leaving the bark to curl.

Cinnamon is available in 3 in/7.5 cm long quills or sticks, in broken flat pieces or 'chips', and in powdered form. In Indian cooking both quills and chips are acceptable, except when whole spices are left in special pilafs as garnish. Here the quills are preferred for purely aesthetic reasons; they look handsomer than the broken pieces.

Cinnamon is used as a flavouring, whole as well as in powdered form, in Indian cooking. It is one of the four spices (bay leaf, cardamom, and clove being the others) essential to Moghul pilafs. It is also one of the ingredients of *Mughal Garam Masala* (p. 41). In Indian cooking cinnamon is never used as it is in the West to flavour puddings, desserts, and sweetmeats.

◆

CLOVE *Laung*

Clove is the dried bud of the plant *Syzygium aromaticum*, native to the Molucca Islands in Eastern Indonesia. Cloves are dark brown in colour and have a sharp, pungent taste and fragrant aroma. They are available whole and in powdered form. In Indian cooking cloves are used as a flavouring, whole or powdered, in meat preparations, pilafs, and seafoods. With bay leaf, cardamom, and cinnamon, clove is used to flavour pilafs and is also an ingredient in *Mughal Garam Masala* (p. 41).

CORIANDER *Dhania, Sookha*

Coriander seed is the dried ripe fruit of the coriander plant (*Coriandrum sativum*), an annual herb of the parsley family, which is native to Asia Minor and Southern Europe but is now cultivated around the world. The coriander seed is round, slightly larger than a peppercorn, light brown in colour, and has a strong, nutty aroma and sweetish, piquant taste; it is available whole or powdered. In Indian cooking it is used in both forms. In powdered form it acts as a thickener in sauces and gravies. Roasted ground coriander is frequently added to appetizers called *chat* and yogurt salads known as *raita*, so it is good to keep a small supply of the ground roasted seeds on hand. To roast, grind, and store coriander seeds, follow the instructions on page 62. Coriander is an important spice in cooking throughout India, and an essential ingredient of *Garam Masala* (p. 42).

◆

CUMIN *Jeera*

Cumin, the dried ripe fruit of the cumin plant, is one of the most important spices throughout India, especially in the northern and western regions. No meal is complete without its use in one form or another. There are essentially three varieties of cumin seeds used in Indian cooking. White cumin – *Safaid* (white) *Jeera* – is the most widely used spice in all regional Indian cooking. The other two varieties, which are similar except that one is brownish-black and the other black, are lumped together under the category of black cumin – *Kala* (black) or *Shahi* (royal) *Jeera*.

White cumin (*Cuminum cyminum*), generally referred to simply as cumin (*Jeera*), is widely used in many other cuisines, including Mexican, Spanish, African, and Middle-Eastern. It is yellowish-brown in colour and resembles the caraway seed in shape but is larger. Cumin seed has a nutty aroma and taste. White cumin, though native to upper Egypt and western parts of Asia Minor, is widely cultivated in various parts of Asia, including India. Cumin is available whole or powdered. In Indian cooking it is used in both forms. Many north Indian recipes, including appetizers (*chat*) and yogurt salads (*raita*), call for roasted cumin powder to be sprinkled over the dish. Therefore, keep a small supply handy. To roast, grind and store cumin seeds, follow the instructions on page 62.

Black cumin (*Cuminum nigrum*) is a rare variety that grows in the mountains of southeastern Iran and along the valleys of Kashmir. Black cumin is sweeter-smelling than the white; it too resembles caraway seed but is smaller. Black cumin costs considerably more than the white, but its delicate texture and mellow flavour are unmatched. Because of its mellow aroma, black cumin does not require roasting. It is an important ingredient in the Kashmiri and Moghul styles of cooking.

◆

FENNEL *Saunf*

Fennel refers to the seedlike fruit of the fennel plant (*Foeniculum vulgare*), native to the Mediterranean region. Fennel has been cultivated in India since Vedic times. The greenish-yellow fennel seed resembles the white cumin seed but is larger and fatter. It has a sweet liquorice flavour much like anise, and a very appealing aroma.

Recently a finer grade of fennel called *Lakhnawi Saunf*, or fennel from the city of Lucknow in India, has been made available. It is smaller, thinner, more finely textured, and has a more delicate flavour. It is this variety of fennel which is traditionally served as an after-dinner mint (cardamom and clove being the others). The aroma of this fennel is greatly enhanced when dry-roasted. To roast and store fennel seeds, follow the instructions on page 62.

In Indian cooking fennel is used for its aroma whole as well as powdered in pickles, meat, vegetable preparations, and pilafs. The use of fennel in Indian desserts is rare, with two exceptions: a sweet pastry filled with a mixture of nuts and coconut laced with cardamom, called *Gujjia*, and the wholewheat pancakes studded with pistachio nuts, called *Malpoora* (p. 329).

Anise, also known as *Saunf*, can be substituted wherever a recipe calls for fennel, as both anise and fennel are cultivated in India and are used interchangeably in cooking. Anise seed is slightly dull, almost grey in colour. The seed, small and crescent-shaped, has a texture like fennel's.

◆

FENUGREEK *Methi*

Fenugreek (*Trigonella foenumgraecum*) is an annual herb of the bean family native to India and Asia Minor. It has been cultivated in India since pre-Vedic days. Although both the seed and the leaves of the plant are used in Indian cooking, they are not interchangeable because they have different properties and hence impart different flavours and aromas. The fenugreek seed, rectangular and brownish-yellow in colour, is actually a bean like the mung bean, but because of its extreme aroma and bitter taste, it is used as a spice. In Indian cooking it is used whole as well as powdered. Fenugreek is an important spice throughout India in vegetarian cooking and in pickling. It is an essential spice in the southern lentil-and-vegetable stew called a *Sambaar* (p. 204).

Dry fenugreek leaves (*Kasoori Methi*) are the sun-dried leaves of the fenugreek plant; they are used both as herbs and as dried greens. The leaves have a bitter taste and a captivating aroma. They are generally cooked with starchy vegetables, like potatoes and yams, used as a stuffing for breads, and as flavouring for biscuits such as the delectable Indian Fenugreek Biscuits (*Kasoori Mathari*, p. 111).

◆

GINGER POWDER *Sonth*

Ginger powder is obtained by drying and powdering fresh ginger root, the pungent aromatic root of the tropical ginger plant (*Zingiber officinale*). Good quality ginger is light, airy, and buff-coloured and has a hottish piquant taste and sweet smell. It is used to lend a woody fragrance as well as a sour taste to a dish. Powdered ginger is used primarily in Moghul cooking. It is also used in sweet pickles and relishes such as Sweet and Sour Tamarind Relish (*Imli Chutney*, p. 315).

◆

MACE *Javitri*

Mace and nutmeg are both part of the same fleshy fruit of the nutmeg tree (*Myristica fragrans*), native to the Moluccas. When the fruit is ripe it splits, exposing the brown nut (nutmeg) covered with a brilliant red netty membrane (mace). The membrane is carefully peeled off the nutshell and dried until it turns yellowish-brown in colour and becomes brittle. These dried membranes are commercially known as mace blades. Mace has a pungent aroma much like nutmeg but is stronger and has a bitter taste. Mace is available in blade or powder form. In Indian cooking it is used as a flavouring, powdered, in Moghul and Kashmiri dishes, certain sweet pickles, and relishes. Though mace and nutmeg belong to the same fruit, they have a slightly different taste and should not be used interchangeably.

MANGO POWDER *Amchoor*

Mango, the fruit of the tropical plant *Mangifera indica*, is native to India but is now grown in many tropical regions of the world. Mango is plucked before it ripens, peeled, sun-dried, and ground to produce a pale buff-coloured powder. This mango powder, known as *am* (mango) *choor* (powder), has a pungent aroma and a tangy, sour taste and therefore is used as a souring agent in place of lemon juice. Its primary use is in vegetarian cooking. Because of its dry state, it is preferred over moist souring agents in preparations that will be carried on journeys lasting several days, with temperatures up to 120°F/50°C.

◆

MUSTARD *Rai*

The seed of the mustard plant *Brassica juncea*, an annual herb of the mustard family native to India, is one of the most important spices throughout India. Both the leaves, or mustard greens (*sarsoon*) and seeds (*rai*) are used in Indian cooking, as vegetables and as a spice respectively. Indian mustard seeds are purplish brown, not yellow, and look much like poppy seeds, except larger. They are popularly referred to as black mustard seeds because they look more black than brown. They have a pungent aroma and, when ground and cooked, a sourish, bitter taste. In Indian cooking they are used as a flavouring whole as well as in powdered form. In northern India mustard seed is used primarily as a pickling spice and in vegetable dishes. In the southern and southwestern regions it is as important as cumin is in the North. In the East the mustard seeds are usually roasted and ground to a powder which is used as an important flavouring spice. (To roast, grind, and store mustard seeds, follow the instructions on page 62.) The oil extracted from mustard seeds is favoured over all others for oil-based pickles as well as for deep frying in the northern and northwestern regions of India. Mustard oil is considered an essential ingredient in the famous Goanese dish *Vendaloo* (p. 150), to which it lends its authentic aroma.

◆

NUTMEG *Jaiphul*

As mentioned under Mace (p. 28), nutmeg is the dark brown shell enclosed within the mace membrane. The shell is dried and cracked open and the oil seed inside, known as nutmeg, is removed. Nutmeg has a gentle aroma and a sweet taste, mellower than mace. It is available whole or powdered (grated). In

Indian cooking the reddish-brown powder is used as a flavouring. Nutmeg should be purchased whole and grated as needed. Nutmeg is used primarily in Moghul and Kashmiri cooking. It is one of the ingredients of *Mughal Garam Masala* (p. 41) and is also used in vegetable preparations and relishes.

◆

ONION SEED *Kalaunji*

Onion seed, also known as *Nigella*, actually has nothing in common with the onion plant but does resemble an actual onion seed – hence its name. The satiny-black triangular *Kalaunji* has a sweet taste and an aroma much like oregano. In Indian cooking it is used whole as a flavouring. This spice is used primarily in the northern regions of India, in pickling, vegetable dishes, and for sprinkling on top of the famous *tandoor*-baked bread called *Tandoori Nan*.

◆

PAPRIKA *Deghi Mirch*

Indian paprika or *Deghi Mirch* comes from the mild variety of chili pod of the plant *Capsicum*, grown in the valleys of Kashmir. When ripe, the pod is plucked, sun-dried, and ground to produce a mild-tasting, brilliant red powder. *Deghi Mirch* has a pungent aroma like red pepper but is sweet-tasting like Hungarian sweet paprika. In Indian cooking, *Deghi Mirch* is used primarily to lend its brilliant red colour to the food. It is also extensively used in Kashmiri cooking, specially by Kashmiri Brahmins in making kebabs, kaftas, and other meat preparations.

◆

POMEGRANATE *Anardana*

The brownish-red pomegranate, known as *anar*, about the size of an orange, is the fruit of the tropical tree (or shrub) *Punica granatum*, native to Asia Minor and Mediterranean regions but now cultivated in many warmer regions of the world including India. The thick outer skin is not edible, but the seedlike pulpy interior enclosed in a honeycombed membrane is either eaten fresh as a fruit (see Almond and Rice Dessert, p. 327) or dried and used as a spice called *Anardana*. In Indian cooking it is used in powdered form. Because of their natural piquancy, pomegranate seeds make an ideal souring agent and are frequently used with vegetables and lentils in North Indian cooking. Many chefs prefer pomegranate to mango powder, as pomegranate seeds impart a

SALT *Namak*

Salt in India is used not only as a seasoning but also as a spice to flavour food. This is because many varieties of salt are used in Indian cooking. Especially in the North, different varieties of salt are used to flavour cold appetizers (*chat*), relishes (*chutney*), and cold drinks. These varieties are not the blends of herbs and spices mixed with salt that are known as 'seasoned' salt, but are spicy salts in their natural form, each with a different taste, aroma, and chemical composition. The most extensively used salts are white salt, commonly referred to as table salt (*Sambhar Namak*), black salt (*Kala Namak*), and rock salt (*Sendha Namak*).

The black salt is brownish-black when in lump form but looks pinkish-brown when powdered. Black salt has a tangy taste and smoky aroma. It is an important ingredient in such famous appetizers (*chat*) as *Aloo Chat* (p. 90), and the delicious Sweet and Sour Tamarind Relish (*Imli Chutney*, p. 315).

◆

TAMARIND *Imli*

Tamarind is the pulpy pod, resembling a pea pod, of the tropical plant *Tamarindus indica*, native to India. It is brownish-black in colour and tastes like a sour prune. Tamarind pods, when fully mature, are plucked, peeled, and pitted, and the pulp is compressed into cakes. Tamarind is available in cake or juice form. Only the pulp form is suitable for use in Indian cooking, as the juice is too acidic, yet lacks flavour. To extract juice from tamrind pulp, soak a piece of tamarind cake in boiling water for 15 minutes – the rule is a 1 in/2.5 cm diameter ball of tamarind pulp to 4 tablespoons of water. Then mash with a fork or your fingers, squeezing out as much juice as possible. Strain and reserve the juice, and discard the dry fibrous residue. Tamarind is used as a souring agent. Its use is more extensive in the southern and southwestern regions of India. But in the North, tamarind is used in relishes, the most famous of which is Sweet and Sour Tamarind Relish (*Imli Chutney*, p. 315), and in vegetable, lentil, and bean preparations.

◆

TURMERIC *Haldi*

Turmeric is a perennial tropical herb (*Curcuma longa*) belonging to the ginger family and native to India. Like ginger root, the turmeric rhizome resembles a short finger jutting out of the horizontally growing underground stem of the plant. The roots are cleaned, boiled, dried, and powdered to produce a nutty-tasting, aromatic powder. Turmeric is the main ingredient in commercial curry powder. Good quality turmeric, aside from lending a characteristic yellow colour to a dish, also gives a wonderful woody aroma.

It is used in cooking throughout India, primarily as a colouring agent but also to lend flavour, in various *Dal*, vegetable, meat, poultry, and seafood preparations. However, in the northern and northwestern regions, its use is limited; saffron, and other colour-imparting flowers, generally replace it. Turmeric is never used in dishes containing cream, because its delicate scent gets masked. On the other hand, it blends beautifully with onion and tomato sauces. It is the most important and sacred spice of Hindus and is used in religious and social rituals. The sacred thread, the marriage symbol that is tied around the bride's neck by the bridegroom during the marriage ceremony, is dipped in turmeric paste.

WHITE SPLIT GRAM BEAN *Urad Dal*

The white split gram bean is actually a pulse (see p. 233), but in the southern and southwestern regions of India it is also used as a spice. It is usually cooked in oil with black mustard seeds, and sometimes yellow split peas; it is then added to flavour vegetables and pulse preparations such as Cauliflower and Spring Onions with Black Mustard Seeds (*Gobhi Kari*, p. 218).

YELLOW SPLIT PEAS *Channa Dal*

The yellow split pea is, in fact, a pulse (see p. 233), but in the southern and southwestern regions of India it is also used as a spice. It is generally cooked in oil with white split gram bean and mustard seed, and then used as a flavouring in lentil and bean preparations, in dumplings, and in stuffings for breads and pastries. It is also ground (raw or roasted) to a powder (or flour) and used as a thickener, or in making sweetmeats and fudge preparations.

HERBS AND SEASONINGS

◆

The herbs most frequently used in Indian cooking are coriander, mint, kari, and basil. They are chopped and folded into dishes, or sprinkled over them as a garnish. Herbs may be minced and mixed with ginger root, yogurt, and spices to serve as relishes and dips with appetizers. They are also puréed and cooked with rice to create fragrant herb pilafs, and brewed with ginger root and honey in herbal teas.

Because fresh herbs are essential to vegetarian cooking, they are cultivated all year round in India. Dried herbs are unheard of. I feel there is nothing in the world to compare with the aroma of fresh herbs. Since they are a primary flavouring ingredient in Indian cooking, freshness makes all the difference. Dishes cooked with them are usually more aromatic and flavourful. They have a spring-like bouquet, something always missing in dried herbs.

◆

BASIL LEAVES *Tulsi*

Basil (*tulsi*) is an annual herb of the mint family. The bright leaves have a sharp, biting taste and a distinctly sweet aroma. There are several varieties of basil grown in India. However, three are the most popular: holy basil (*Ocimum sanctum*, known as *Vishnu tulsi*), sweet basil (*Ocimum basilicum*, known as *Biswa tulsi*), and white basil (*Ocimum album*, known as *Ram tulsi*). The three varieties differ in degree of sharpness, holy basil being the sharpest and sweet basil the mellowest; the white basil is somewhere in between. All three can be used interchangeably in Indian cooking and rituals; but sweet basil is the variety most commonly available. This herb must be used in its fresh green form.

Basil is one of the oldest herbs known to mankind and different superstitions are associated with it around the world. In India, Hindus have grown and revered basil as a holy plant since Vedic times. Even today, a pot of growing basil is employed in the daily rituals of many Indian homes. Because of the sacred association of basil with the Hindu God Vishnu, the use of this herb in Indian cooking has been severely limited. However, in many Indian homes a delicious brew of basil leaves, shredded ginger, and honey, known as *Tulsi ki Chah*, is served during the winter.

CORIANDER LEAVES *Hara Dhania*

Coriander leaves, or *Hara* (green) *Dhania*, come from the same plant (*Coriandrum sativum*) as coriander seeds, but they cannot be used interchangeably. Coriander leaves are available in Indian and Cypriot shops. They somewhat resemble flat parsley, except that coriander leaves are thinner, lighter green in colour, and very fragrant. Bunches of coriander with the roots still intact store well in the refrigerator. Untie the bunch and wet a couple of paper towels, or a piece of muslin of about the same size, and wrap the towels or muslin around the roots, enclosing them completely. Place the bunch roots down in a large plastic bag. Tie a cord or elastic around the bag to enclose the wrapped section. This will ensure the retention of moisture in the roots. Place the entire bag in the refrigerator and keep snipping the coriander leaves as you need them. Stored this way, they will keep for eight to ten weeks.

Both coriander leaves and stems (the tender part only) are chopped and used as garnish. In addition to their decorative effect, the leaves lend a very distinct flavour to a dish. If you find it hard to acquire a taste for coriander leaves, omit this herb or substitute parsley, but remember that the taste of the dish will be altered. There is no real substitute for coriander leaves.

GARLIC *Lassan*

Garlic is the edible bulb of the garlic plant (*Allium sativum*), native to India and other Central Asian countries but widely cultivated around the world. The garlic bulb, composed of segments called garlic 'cloves', has a strong, pungent aroma and a sharp, hot taste. In Indian cooking only the fresh garlic clove is used; it is peeled, and either finely chopped or ground to a paste. Garlic powder and garlic salt each has a chemistry of its own quite different from that of fresh garlic, and cannot be substituted.

Garlic keeps well in the kitchen provided it is not too warm and dry and there is sufficent air circulation. If your kitchen is too warm, keep the garlic in the refrigerator, loosely wrapped in a plastic bag, otherwise it will dry out.

In Indian cooking, garlic plays an important role. It is one of the three major seasonings (fresh ginger root and onion being the others) used in making the base for Moghul sauces.

GINGER ROOT, FRESH *Adrak*

Fresh ginger root is the pungent aromatic rhizome of the tropical plant *Zingiber officinale*. Dug up, washed, and scraped, it is sold as fresh ginger root. In Indian cooking the fresh ginger root is first peeled and then either shredded or ground to a paste (one may also finely chop it or grate it) before use. If fresh ginger is unavailable, dry ginger powder may be substituted – 1 teaspoon of dry ginger powder is equivalent to 1 tablespoon of finely chopped fresh ginger root. The powder should be added to the dish with other dry spices. Crystallized ginger and candied ginger are completely different products and cannot be used as substitutes.

To store fresh ginger root, follow the instructions given for garlic above.

Fresh ginger is one of the three major seasonings (garlic and onion being the others) that form the base of most sauces in North Indian cooking. In addition to flavouring and lending a hot taste to the dish, it also acts as a thickener. Actually, fresh ginger root is valued much more than garlic or onion because of its extensive use in Indian vegetarian cooking; garlic and onion are more commonly associated with nonvegetarian cooking. This is particularly true among the Jain and Hindu Brahmins, whose extensive vegetarian repertoire rarely includes onion and totally omits garlic. (See Cauliflower, Green Peas and Potatoes in Spicy Herb Sauce, p. 189.)

◆

GREEN CHILI *Hari Mirch*

Green chili (*Hari Mirch*) is the young pod of the pepper plant *Capsicum*. It comes in a wide range of strengths, from very mild to devilishly hot. The smaller the size of the pod, the more ferocious it is. You should keep away from the very small ones or use them with caution. Green chilies, I have discovered, get hotter near the stem end, i.e., the portion with the seeds. I personally prefer the medium-to-large size; I slit it open with a sharp knife and scrape out the seeds – the hottest part of the pepper; this way I can use a considerable quantity of the pod for flavour without making the dish too hot. If you like a hotter taste, leave the seeds in. Green chilies keep well in the refrigerator for three to four weeks, wrapped loosely in a plastic bag.

Green chili is used primarily in preparing vegetables, lentils, dips, and relishes. It is sometimes used in place of red pepper in other dishes. In Rajasthan, a western region in India, the mildly hot green chilies are turned into a mouthwatering delicacy called *Mirchi ki Bhaji* by cooking them in butter with tomatoes, molasses, and spices. The large variety of chili is slit, stuffed with roasted spices, and pickled in mustard oil to make a pickle called *Mirch ka Achar*, an all-time favourite of the North Indians. This pickle is eaten with Wholemeal Flaky Bread (*Paratha*, p. 285) and a lump of freshly churned butter.

KARI LEAVES *Meethe Neam ke Patte*

Kari leaves, known as *Meethe Neam ke Patte*, come from the kari plant (*Murraya koenigii*), native to South India and Sri Lanka. The bright green leaves of this tall plant, which grows to a height of 6-7 feet (2 m), are full of fragrance. The leaves have a bitterish taste and a sweetish, pungent aroma almost like lemon grass. These leaves are used in southern and southwestern cooking in the same way coriander leaves are used in the North. They are essential to these regional styles, lending the dishes the characteristic southern flavour. Fresh kari leaves are difficult to obtain but the dried variety is readily available and works quite well.

◆

MINT LEAVES *Podina*

Spearmint (*Mentha spicata*) is an annual herb of the mint family that is native to Europe and the Mediterranean but is now grown in countries around the world, including India. Mint has deep green leaves, reddish-brown stems, and a very appealing taste and aroma. Because mint is an essential herb in North Indian cooking, it is cultivated year round in India; dried mint leaves are unheard of. Mint keeps well in the refrigerator for five to seven days, wrapped loosely in a plastic bag.

Mint is used primarily to make relishes (*chutney*) such as Fresh Mint Relish (*Podina Chutney*, p. 309), and cold appetizers such as Cold Minted Potatoes (*Aloo Podina Chat*, p. 88). It is also used in some exceptional lamb preparations, such as Kebab Patties Laced with Ginger and Mint (*Shamme Kabab*, p. 92). Mint has traditionally been preferred over all other herbs to lace pilafs in Moghul cooking, as in the Emperor's Layered Meat and Fragrant Rice Casserole (*Shah Jahani Biriyani*, p. 146) and the famous Mint Pilaf (*Hari Chutney ka Pullao*, p. 270) from the Andra Pradesh, a province in the south.

ONION, SPRING ONION, AND SHALLOT
Piaz, Hara Piaz, aur Chota Piaz

Not much need be said to introduce the onion, the bulbous root of the onion plant *Allium cepa*, belonging to the lily family and used in one form or another around the world. Onion is the most important of the three ingredients (garlic and ginger root being the others) that form the basis of most dishes of North Indian origin. Onions are added to virtually every dish and are also pickled or eaten raw as a relish called *Kachoomar* (p. 304), or in *Kache Piaz* (p. 304). *A word of caution:* Onions available in Great Britain differ from those available in India. Because the Indian climate is warmer, the onion grown there is pungent and less juicy. This is a crucial difference, because Indian recipes specify that onions should be ground to a paste before frying. This is impossible to do with English onions; they become a purée or watery sauce in the process. Therefore, always finely chop the onions or slice them into thin strips (never mash) before frying, so that you do not destroy the fibres that contain the moisture. A second point to note is that Indians, particularly northerners, eat raw onions – the pungent ones – with great relish. This is something you may find hard to do, not because the onions are any sharper but simply because eating onions takes a little learning. Therefore, until you get used to the strong flavour of raw onions, I recommend using large Spanish onions, which are sweet, juicy, and mild, in relishes and cold appetizers.

Spring onions are the young sprouts, that appear before the onion bulbs begin to mature. Shallot, the bulbous root of the plant *Allium ascalonicum*, also belonging to the lily family, is a variety of onion that has a slightly garlicy taste. In North Indian cooking spring onions and shallots are virtually unheard of, but in the other regions they hold high places in the culinary world. They are used not only as flavourings, but are cooked as vegetables in such dishes as Cauliflower and Spring Onions with Black Mustard Seeds (*Gobhi Kari*, p. 218). Shallot is particularly savoured by those vegetarians who are forbidden to eat garlic. The southern vegetable-and-lentil stew called *Sambaar*, p. 204, made with shallots as the only vegetable, is considered a delicacy all over India.

SPECIAL INGREDIENTS

◆

SPICE BLENDS

MASALA

◆

Literally translated, *masala* means a blend of several aromatic spices. *Masala* is usually added to a dish to lend it the distinct flavour characteristic of that dish or of a regional style of cooking. In Indian homes *masala* sometimes refers to a 'wet' blend of spices, i.e., spice paste, which is made by grinding herbs and seasonings along with the spices.

The most important of all spice blends is the *garam* (warm or hot) *masala*. It is not just important − it is absolutely essential to most North Indian preparations (its counterparts are *sambaar podi* in the South, and *punch phoron* in the East). *Garam masala* is usually added to a dish at the end, just before serving, to enhance the flavours of the other ingredients. There are, however, recipes that do call for it to be added at the beginning or during cooking. Even though many dishes contain *garam masala*, the additions of extra herbs and ingredients to one's own classic blend and the way one incorporates it into each dish transform the food and make it the distinctly special creation of the individual cook.

There are two types of *garam masala* used in classic Indian cooking. One is the traditional *garam masala*, a blend of four spices − cardamom, cinnamon, cloves, and black peppers (sometimes a little nutmeg is added). This blend of subtle spices has come to be known as *Mughal garam masala*. It is the hallmark of classic Indian cooking, which originated in the North, in the courts and palaces of the great Moghul emperors. *Mughal garam masala* is used in making the classic Moghul dishes Royal Braised Lamb with Spices (*Shahi Korma*, p. 134) and Royal Roast Leg of Lamb with Saffron Raisin Sauce (*Shahi Raan*, p. 141).

Over the years large quantities of coriander and cumin have been added to the classic blend. The addition of such spices causes the original subtle *Mughal garam masala* to taste sharp and pungent. This spicy version is usually referred to as *garam masala* (or sometimes *Punjabi garam masala*). It is predominantly used in North Indian cooking today, in dishes such as Green Peas and Indian Cheese in Fragrant Tomato Sauce (*Matar Paneer*, p. 196) and Savoury Pastries with Spicy Potato Filling (*Aloo Samosa*, p. 105). This blend of *garam masala* is also used in meat, poultry, and seafood preparations that have a reddish-brown spicy sauce, such as Velvet Butter Chicken (*Makhani Murgh*, p. 170).

Some *garam masala* blends also include other spices, such as cassia, cassia buds, fennel, and bay leaf. This is attributed to the variations introduced by other regional styles of cooking. Commercial blends often include salt, dry ginger, garlic, or other seasonings, and thickening agents such as poppy seeds, which are quite unnecessary. They mask the robust tanginess of the spices.

I strongly advise that you make your own blends of both kinds and keep them ready before you start Indian cooking. In case you are wondering whether it is worth the bother of making two separate blends, let me assure you the answer is yes. This is because each *garam masala* imparts a distinctly different fragrance and is used for different types of dishes; hence they cannot be used interchangeably. (*Mughal garam masala* is a subtle, mellow blend with an accent of cardamom. Its primary use is in cream-, milk-, yogurt-, and fruit-sauce-based dishes. The *garam masala*, on the other hand, is a spicy blend with an accent of roasted cumin and coriander. It is particularly suited for onion and tomato-rich gravies.)

As I mentioned earlier, I love food that is full of aroma and flavour but not hot, and so I have reduced the amount of black pepper in both recipes. This way, each time I sprinkle a little of either *garam masala* in a dish to perk up the flavours (this is especially necessary when reheating frozen food), I do not have to worry about the dish becoming too peppery. If you want, you can always add more black pepper separately.

The following two recipes are my personal blends. The *Mughal garam masala* captures, insofar as possible, the fragrance of the original classic blend that once filled the Moghul courts and perfumed their food. The recipe for the general *garam masala* is popular in Punjab and Uttar Pradesh. Both *garam masalas* will keep fresh for three months in airtight covered containers.

MUGHAL GARAM MASALA

MAKES ABOUT 5 oz/150 g

◆

3 oz/90 g (about 60) black, or 2 oz/60 g (about 200) green cardamom pods
2 cinnamon sticks, 3 in/7.5 cm long
1 tablespoon whole cloves
1 tablespoon black peppercorns
1½ teaspoons grated nutmeg (optional)

Break open cardamom pods. Remove seeds, and reserve. Discard the skin. Crush cinnamon with a kitchen mallet or rolling pin to break it into small pieces. Combine all the spices except nutmeg, and grind them to a fine powder (follow instructions on page 62). Mix in the grated nutmeg, if desired. Store in an airtight container in a cool place.

NOTE The recipe may be cut in half.

GARAM MASALA

MAKES ABOUT 9 oz/270 g

◆

3 tablespoons (about 20) black, or 2 tablespoons (about 75), green cardamom pods
3 cinnamon sticks, 3 in/7.5 cm long
1 tablespoon whole cloves
1 oz/30 g black peppercorns
1½ oz/45 g cumin seeds
1½ oz/45 g coriander seeds

Break open cardamom pods. Remove seeds, and reserve. Discard the skin. Crush cinnamon with a kitchen mallet or rolling pin to break it into small pieces. Combine all the spices, and roast and grind them (follow instructions on page 62). Store in an airtight container in a cool place.

NOTE The recipe may be cut in half.

You may have noticed that the *Mughal garam masala* doesn't require roasting whereas the general *garam masala* does. This is because the *Mughal* blend primarily consists of what are in English known as 'dessert spices' or 'sweet spices'; these are very aromatic in their natural (raw) forms, and are also very easy to digest.

The other all-purpose spice blend that is very popular in India is *Sambaar podi*. It is used exclusively in South Indian cooking. *Sambaar podi* (powder) is a hot and spicy blend of turmeric, coriander seeds, red and black pepper, fenugreek, cumin seeds, and several varieties of pulses. *Sambaar podi* is commercially available under the label 'Sambaar Powder'. It is principally used in flavouring vegetable-and-lentil stews, and in stir-fried vegetable preparations and other delicacies of South India.

You may have noticed that the *Sambaar podi* contains mostly 'cool' spices. In addition, the proportion of red pepper in this blend is usually very high, so that the dishes flavoured with it turn out fairly hot. Since hot food induces perspiration, it is perfectly suited for the hot and humid climate of the South.

There are several other spice blends that are commercially available today, prepackaged mixes of such popular Indian specialities as *Tandoori masala*, *Kabab masala*, *Vendaloo masala*, and *Dhansak masala*. These blends contain all the necessary spices, dehydrated herbs, seasonings, thickeners, and so on. If you want to make *Tandoori* chicken, all you need to do is stir the *Tandoori masala* into the yogurt, marinate the chicken in it, and roast the preparation in the oven. It sounds simple and it is, but bear in mind that there is absolutely no comparison between the fresh blend that you make yourself in your own kitchen with your own spices and commercial varieties that might contain inferior ingredients and have been sitting on a store shelf for months.

Finally, a word about curry powder.

'Curry' is the Western pronunciation of the Indian word *kari*, which can mean one of two things: the sweet aromatic leaves of the kari plant (p. 38) used in southern and southwestern Indian regional cooking, or the southern cooking technique of preparing stir-fried vegetables such as Green Beans with Coconut and Black Mustard Seeds (*Beans Kari*, p. 223). The spice blend used for making kari dishes is called *kari podi* (powder) or curry powder. The South Indian variety is a mixture of several spices varying from one local region to another, but the classic blend essentially contains the following: turmeric, red pepper, coriander, black pepper, cumin, fenugreek, kari leaves, mustard seeds, and (sometimes) cinnamon and cloves – all of which are roasted and ground to a powder.

The earliest British merchants, who arrived with the East India Trading Company, worked and settled along the southeastern coast of India. It is more than likely that they wanted to take back with them to England the familiar aromas, flavours, and colours of the Indian food they had become so passionately fond of. But not having mastered the different Indian cooking techniques or a sense of the spice blends, they in all likelihood just indiscriminately sprinkled *kari podi* over stews and casseroles. This yielded preparations with the familiar golden colour, hot taste, and flavour of the dishes known as 'curries'.

As the British presence spread to the North and East of India, several new spices found their way into the simple *kari podi*. However, the name of the blend, as well as the dishes which contained it, remained the same.

Among the English-speaking Indian middle class, the word 'curry' became so popular that in due course a simple everyday dish called *salan* (spicy thin gravy) was renamed *kari*. As a result, chicken in spice gravy, which for centuries was known as *Murghi ka Salan*, came to be called Chicken Kari (or Curry), and shrimp in spicy gravy, known as *Jheenga ka Salan*, became Prawn Kari. In North Indian cooking, no real equivalent to the Western or English curry powder (or, for that matter, any dish known as a curry) exists.

Mind you, the Indian *kari* bears no resemblance whatsoever to the English curry, which is made without using Indian cooking techniques and with packaged curry powder. The other points of difference are that *salan* dishes often contain cardamom, an essential Indian spice that is never found in curry powder – probably because cardamom is not used in the cooking of savoury dishes in the South. Also, curry powder contains fenugreek, mustard seeds, and turmeric – the first two never and the third seldom found in the spice blends for *salan* dishes. Finally, the spices for these karis (or *salan*) are mixed individually, with the same judicious care that is taken for any other Indian dish. Today, the name *kari* has totally replaced the name *salan* in all of India and is applied to dishes with a wide variety of ingredients.

COOKING FATS AND OILS

GHEE AUR TEL

◆

The two basic fats used in Indian cooking are butter, known as *usli ghee* (*ghee* means fat; *usli* means pure, but in everyday Indian usage the word *usli* refers to butter), and vegetable shortening, known as *vanaspati* (vegetable) *ghee*. There are several different kinds of vegetable oils (*tel*) used in Indian cooking, the popular ones being sesame, peanut, mustard, coconut, corn, and sunflower. Butter and shortening are generally used for all-purpose cooking. Oils are reserved for frying, deep frying, and pickling. Animal fats, such as lard and suet, are *never* used as a cooking medium in India because of the religious convictions of the Hindus and Moslems. They are also unacceptable to vegetarians since they are considered a meat product.

You may wonder how a vegetarian can consider lard and suet meat products and yet accept butter, which is also an animal fat. The explanation is very simple. The vegetarians believe in and practise *A-himsa* (A means no; *himsa* means violence), which forbids the killing of a living creature. To obtain lard or suet, the life of an animal has to be taken. So the vegetarians abstain from eating it just as they do the animal's flesh. Butter, on the other hand, is the gift of the animal, or of nature. To obtain it the animal does not have to be killed. On the same principle, several vegetarians have recently started including unfertilized chickens' eggs (known as vegetarian eggs in India) in their diet, since they contain no life and are therefore a vegetarian product.

Until recently, *usli ghee* was the only cooking medium used in North India. But as the price of butter has rocketed, shortening and oils have replaced it. Indian vegetable shortening, or *vanaspati ghee*, has a light lemon colour, grainy texture, and a faint nutty-lemon aroma. It is almost identical in appearance and flavour to *usli ghee*. Indians have used *usli ghee* for centuries and would never accept a substitute unless it reproduced the good taste of butter as closely as possible. Therefore, Indian vegetable shortening, a product of highly saturated oils such as coconut, cottonseed, rapeseed, and palm, is not only hydrogenated, but is also specially processed to look, smell, and taste almost like *usli ghee*. Those accustomed to its flavour prefer it to *usli ghee*.

In the last decade in India, just as in Western countries, there has been a growing awareness of the possible harm in consuming excessive quantities of highly saturated fats (which includes both butter and shortening). As a result, many Indians today who find that food cooked with fat is too rich, heavy, and difficult to digest have substituted unsaturated oils for saturated fats in much of their cooking. There still exists a segment of the population that feels otherwise. The vegetarians, which include Hindu Brahmins, Jains, and Buddhists, and the people from Kashmir (both Brahmins and Moslems) do not like substitutes. For vegetarians, *usli ghee* is the primary source of nutrition. The Brahmins consider it brain food with supernatural powers, and attribute the development of one's intelligence to it. Even today, young Hindu children, particularly males, are given a spoonful of *usli ghee* every day to sharpen their intelligence. The old Brahmin ritual of feeding a newborn infant a spoonful of *usli ghee* within minutes of his birth is still followed by all Indians. Kashmiri cooking, known for its delicate preparations and haunting flavours, uses *usli ghee* as one of its chief ingredients.

Many parts of India have used oil in general cooking for centuries, except for flavouring pulses and desserts. In the southern and southwestern regions, many foods are traditionally cooked in sesame or coconut oil, and mustard oil is used in the central and eastern regions of India.

I personally prefer to use such light vegetable oils as sunflower and soybean for most of my cooking, because they are easy to digest and impart a mellow taste – they do not subdue or overwhelm the subtle flavours of herbs and spices. There are, however, a few Moghul and Kashmiri dishes where *usli ghee* is one of the primary flavouring elements and for these dishes nothing but *usli ghee* should be used. I make a special mention in the recipe when such a situation arises. I am also particularly fond of Indian vegetable shortening, especially for vegetarian main dishes and bread preparations in which it acts as one of the ingredients rather than just as a cooking fat. For deep frying, I use peanut or corn oil because they withstand heat well without burning (the boiling temperature of these two oils is high). To bring out authentic flavours in regional specialities, I like to use the oils popular in those regions, for example, light sesame oil in *Sambaar* (p. 204) from the South, and mustard oil in *Vendaloo* (p. 150) from Goa in the Southwest.

Usli (butter) *ghee*, and *vanaspati* (vegetable) *ghee*, and different *tel* (oil) are commercially available. For those who would like to make *usli ghee* at home, see instructions on page 52.

MEAT BROTH

YAKHNI

◆

The highly aromatic broth used in the cooking of Indian dishes plays an important role in the creation of captivating flavours. The meat broth *yakhni* is made by simmering meat and chicken parts and a few vegetables with several fragrant spices and seasonings. It is used primarily in making pilafs, and enriching sauces for meat and poultry dishes. The practice of using meat broth is common among the Moslems, especially in the region of Kashmir, where a robust broth is almost essential to several of the regional specialities. In other parts of India, a cook may simply add a few meaty bones or some boned meat directly to a dish during cooking rather than preparing a meat broth.

Meat broth is extremely simple to make. It is not essential to make it only when you have a quantity of fresh bones on hand. The bones can be kept frozen until you have the time and the inclination to make the broth. The broth itself may be kept indefinitely in the refrigerator, provided it is boiled for five minutes every four days, or it may be stored in the freezer.

MAKES 2½ pints/1½ litres

◆

2-3 lb/1-1.5 kg lamb bones or chicken parts, or a combination of them, cut into 2-3 in/5-7.5 cm pieces
1 small unpeeled onion, quartered
1 large unpeeled garlic clove, crushed
1 slice fresh ginger root, ¼ in/5 mm thick
1 cinnamon stick, 3 in/7.5 cm long
8 whole cloves
½ teaspoon black peppercorns
1 bay leaf
1 teaspoon coarse salt

Place all of the ingredients in a large stockpot or any deep saucepan with a lid. Add enough cold water to cover the bones by at least 1 in/2.5 cm. Bring to the boil over medium heat. Lower heat so that the liquid is barely simmering, and for the next 5 minutes, skim off the scum that rises to the surface. Then cover the pot partially with the lid and let simmer for at least 2 hours, preferably 4.

Keep adding boiling water as the liquid in the pot evaporates so that the bones are fully immersed throughout cooking. When cool, strain the broth through several layers of muslin into a container and refrigerate for 2 hours, or until the fat on the surface solidifies. Scoop off the fat, leaving perhaps a teaspoon, and check broth for taste. If desired, add more salt.

NOTE The longer the simmering, the richer the broth; 2 hours of simmering I have found to be the bare minimum required to produce a rich and flavourful broth. An additional 2 hours of simmering, as well as enriching the broth further, mellows the flavours of the spices and blends them with the flavour of the meat.

VEGETABLE BROTH

AKHNI

◆

Vegetable broth, commonly used by vegetarians, evolved mainly as a base for the vegetarian counterparts of the famous Indian meat and poultry preparations. The vegetable broth contains the same ingredients as the meat broth except that additional spices and vegetables are added to replace the bones.

MAKES 2½ pints / 1½ litres

◆

3 tablespoons usli ghee or light vegetable oil
2 small unpeeled onions, quartered
1 carrot, cut into 1 in / 2.5 cm slices
1 large unpeeled garlic clove, crushed
1 slice fresh ginger root, ¼ in / 5 mm thick
1 teaspoon cumin seeds
2 teaspoons coriander seeds
1 cinnamon stick, 3 in / 7.5 cm long
3 black (or 6 green) cardamom pods
8 whole cloves
1 teaspoon black peppercorns
1 teaspoon coarse salt

Heat butter or oil in a large stockpot or deep saucepan, and add all other ingredients. Fry the vegetables and spices over medium heat for 10 minutes, or until the onions are wilted and begin to brown. Add 3¼ pints/2 litres of cold water and bring to the boil. Lower heat, cover the pot partially with the lid, and let simmer for at least 1 hour, preferably 2. When cool, strain the broth through a double layer of muslin into a container, and refrigerate or freeze as described under meat broth.

COCONUT

NARIAL

◆

Coconut, the fruit of the coconut palm tree (*Cocos nucifera*), growing along the coastal regions of many parts of India, is commercially available all-year-round. The edible white meat is enclosed in a hard, brown, husky shell.

BUYING A COCONUT Care must be taken when you select a coconut for freshness because, externally, fresh and stale ones look alike. A fresh coconut is usually heavy because of the liquid inside it. This may be checked by shaking it. Also, the shell should not have cracks, because they expose the meat inside and cause it to rot.

OPENING A COCONUT To get to the meat of the coconut, you must first crack the outer shell. The common way to do this is to whack the coconut with a cleaver or a hammer until the shell cracks open, then scoop out the meat with a curved knife. This procedure is tricky and can be dangerous. It should be done only by those who are veterans at coconut cracking. I suggest you follow this simple and safe technique:

Preheat oven to 375°F/190°C/Gas 5. Pierce the 'eyes' of the coconut with a knife or a sharp pointed object such as an ice pick or skewer, and drain off the liquid. Taste the liquid – it should be sweet-tasting and pleasant-smelling. (It is a favourite drink of Indian children.) If it tastes sour and smells oily, the coconut is rotten. Place the coconut in the oven for 25 minutes or until the shell cracks. Remove the coconut from the oven and tap it all around with a kitchen mallet or hammer to release the meat from the shell. Then give it a hard whack to crack open the shell. The white meat with its brown skin should fall away from the shell. If it doesn't, use a sharp knife to release the meat.

GRATING A COCONUT Peel the brown skin off the coconut meat. Cut the meat into 1 in/2.5 cm pieces. Grate the coconut, about 3 oz/90 g at a time, in a blender or food processor, or simply use a hand grater. An average-sized coconut will yield about 10 oz/300 g grated coconut.

The dry, grated, unsweetened coconut that is commercially available in plastic bags can be substituted in an emergency, but remember that it will not be as delicate, moist, and aromatic as freshly grated coconut.

MAKING COCONUT MILK To each 3 oz/90 g of coconut, add 8 fl oz/2.5 dl of boiling water (or milk if you want it richer). Cover and soak for half an hour. Pour the coconut pulp, along with the water it's soaking in, into the container of an electric blender or food processor and purée for 1 minute. (This will extract every speck of juice from the coconut pulp, thus making the coconut milk much richer and more flavourful.) Strain the liquid through a double layer of muslin, squeezing the pulp as much as possible. (In India, to economize, this process is repeated over and over with each new batch yielding thinner, less aromatic milk. The different batches of milk are then mixed together and used in cooking.) An average-sized coconut will yield 1¼ pints/¾ litre of milk.

The use of coconut is more extensive along the coastal regions of India where coconut trees grow. In the South where there is a lack of cow's (or buffalo's) milk, coconut milk is used as a substitute in general cooking as well as in desserts and sweetmeats. One of the delicacies from the coastal area of Malabar is prawns simmered in fragrant coconut-milk sauce laced with fresh herbs called *Yerra Moolee* (p. 181). In the North it is used in certain famous lamb dishes, pilafs, and to make relishes, the most famous of which is Coconut Relish (*Narial Chutney*, p. 311). It is also used in the preparation of the delectable Foamy Coconut Fudge (*Narial Barfi*, p. 339).

MILK AND MILK PRODUCTS

DOOTH AUR OSKE OP-PHUL

◆

Of all the wonderful gifts of nature, there is none more important or more sacred to an Indian than cow's (or buffalo's) milk. The ancient Vedic literature lists milk and clarified butter as the principal foods of an Aryan. In a country of 675 million people, where more than half are vegetarians, milk and milk products comprise the chief source of protein and energy. The five main products of milk are yogurt (*dahi*), Indian clarified butter (*usli ghee*), Indian cheese (*chenna or paneer*), thickened milk sauce (*rabadi*), and milk fudge (*khoya*). Although these products are all derived from the same source, their flavours, textures, and uses are distinctly different.

Milk is often drunk straight in India, but it is always drunk warm and sweetened with a little sugar or honey. Milk is frequently used in cooking vegetables, *dal*, and meat, and in making puddings, desserts, and sweetmeats.

YOGURT

DAHI

◆

Yogurt is indispensable to Indian cooking. It is a staple, especially among India's hundreds of millions of vegetarians. In Indian households, yogurt is made every day with fresh milk purchased in the morning. Only when one runs out of the homemade supply does one buy the commercially made yogurt from the local pastry shop.

To describe the multitude of ingenious ways yogurt is used in Indian cooking would take volumes, but this brief list points out some of the important uses: it is used in making yogurt salads (*Raita*, p. 245) and yogurt drinks (*Lassi* p. 348), as a meat tenderizer, thickening agent, souring agent, and flavour enhancer. It is added to special pilafs, such as Chicken Pilaf (*Murgh Biriyani*, p. 172), and to various relishes and dips, including Mint Coriander Dip (*Dhania-Podina Chutney*, p. 310). It is used in preparing gravies for lentils and vegetables and sauces for fish and shellfish. Mixed with dried fruits and honey, it makes delicious desserts.

The yogurt used in India is made with buffalo's milk, which is richer than cow's milk because of the full fat content. Indian yogurt is therefore thick, sweet, and rich-tasting. The common commercially available yogurt made with low-fat or skimmed milk is thin and watery. It lacks the creamy consistency of whole-milk yogurt and, as a result, Indian sauces made with it do not have enough body and flavour. I have come up with a minor modification: A mixture that is ¾ yogurt and ¼ sour cream.

You may prefer to make your own full-fat yogurt as I do. It is very simple to make – all you need is a thermometer to measure the temperature of the milk, some whole milk, and some plain yogurt. If you are making yogurt for the first time, you will have to use a small container of commercial plain yogurt as a starter. Once you have made your own yogurt, you can use a bit of your first batch as a starter. Always save a few tablespoons to make the next batch. The quality of the first starter is clearly crucial, since it will eventually control the quality of all your future batches, so take particular care while buying the plain yogurt. Read the expiry date on the container and make sure you are buying the freshest yogurt possible. Also, when you've brought it home, smell it to make sure that it is sweet, or you may end up with an entire batch of sour yogurt.

MAKING YOGURT Bring 1½ pints/1 litre of milk to the boil in a heavy-bottomed pan, stirring constantly to prevent a skin from forming on the surface. Let it come to a warm temperature, about 130°F/55°C is the ideal temperature for the yogurt culture to work. If the milk is less warm the yogurt will set but it will take much longer, allowing time for the yogurt to turn sour. If, on the other hand, the milk is too hot it will kill the yogurt culture altogether. If a skin forms on the surface, carefully remove it with a spoon. Add 2 tablespoons of plain yogurt; stir well with the same spoon and transfer it to a bowl. Cover the bowl closely with a piece of muslin or a kitchen towel and set it in a warm place that is at least 80°F/26°C but not more than 115°F/45°C. If the temperature is too low the yogurt will not set. On the other hand, if the temperature is too high the milk will turn sour before the yogurt is set. It will take anything from 10 to 16 hours for the milk to thicken into yogurt, depending upon the surrounding temperature. Once it thickens, transfer it to the refrigerator. The longer you let the yogurt stand, the thicker and more tart it will be. For some reason yogurt made in unglazed clay pots has the best texture and also picks up the earthy aroma that Indians love. However, yogurt can be made in any glass, china, Pyrex, stainless steel, or enamel-coated bowl, or in a commercial yogurt-maker. Yogurt keeps well for several days in the refrigerator but tends to get tangy and sour with time. That's why yogurt should always be tasted before use. For best results, yogurt should be used within 72 hours of making it.

INDIAN CLARIFIED BUTTER

USLI GHEE

◆

Usli ghee is made by separating the clear butterfat from the milk solids and moisture. Even though *usli ghee* is referred to as clarified butter, it is quite different from the French version. The French clarified butter is made by melting fresh butter, then straining the clear butter off from the milk residue that has settled at the bottom of the pot. *Usli ghee* is also begun by melting fresh butter, but it is then kept at a simmer for a long time, to allow the moisture present in the milk solids to evaporate. This process gives it its characteristic nutty aroma. Sometimes coriander, kari, or basil leaves are added at the end to further perfume the *ghee*. *Usli ghee* is a popular cooking medium in India. In addition it is used to light holy lamps in temples and homes and as an offering to the fire (*Agni*) during religious ceremonies invoking the gods.

MAKING INDIAN CLARIFIED BUTTER In a heavy-bottomed large pan heat 1 pound/500 g of unsalted butter (preferably cut into tiny pieces) over low heat – it should not sizzle – until it melts completely. This will take anywhere from 5 to 15 minutes, depending upon the size of butter pieces. Increase heat

to medium. A thin layer of white foam will form on the top and the butter will begin to crackle as moisture is released from the milk solids. Let it simmer, crackling, for about 10 minutes. It is not necessary to stir during this period. The crackling will gradually stop and the foam will subside, indicating that there is no more moisture left in the milk solids. From this point on it must be watched carefully and stirred constantly, because the foam will once again cover the liquid, making it difficult to see the butter fat as it is browning. As soon as the solids turn brown (push aside the foam to see), turn off the heat and let the brown residue settle on the bottom. When the melted butter is cool enough to handle, pour the clear liquid into a jar, taking care that none of the residue gets in, or strain it through a double layer of muslin. Let it cool completely; then cover the jar tightly. To ensure freshness, *usli ghee* should be kept in the refrigerator. It keeps in the refrigerator for 4 months; and indefinitely in the freezer.

INDIAN CHEESE

CHENNA YA PANEER

◆

Homemade Indian cheese is similar to commercially available Italian ricotta, except that the curd is much drier. Indian cheese is one of the primary sources of protein among Buddhists and Jain and Hindu Brahmins, who follow the principles of nonviolence and adhere to a strict vegetarian diet. It is used extensively in cooking throughout India, except in the South where cow's milk is scarce.

Indian cheese in curd form is called *chenna*; when *chenna* is compressed into a cake and cut into small rectangular pieces, it is called *paneer*. *Chenna* is the basis for many of the famous desserts from Bengal, an eastern region of India. It is used in making the famous dessert Cheese Dumplings in Pistachio-Flecked Cream Sauce (*Ras Malai*, p. 330). *Paneer* is used in the preparation of many savoury dishes, such as Green Peas and Indian Cheese in Fragrant Tomato Sauce (*Matar Paneer*, p. 196). Indian cheese is not available commercially, but you can easily make it in your own home.

MAKING INDIAN CHEESE Bring 3 pints/2 litres of milk to the boil in a deep heavy-bottomed pan, stirring often to prevent sticking. Reduce heat and add one of the following starters: 4 tablespoons lemon juice, or 3 tablespoons cider vinegar mixed with 3 tablespoons water, or 8 oz/250 g plain yogurt. (I tend to use lemon juice more often than the other starters because I have found the curd produced is much more soft and delicate). Stir gently until the white curd

forms and separates from the greenish-yellow whey (about 10 seconds if you are using lemon juice or vinegar and 30 seconds to a minute if you are using plain yogurt). Once the curd begins to form, the contents of the pot should be stirred very slowly and gently, as though stroking it, so that the freshly formed fragile curds do not disintegrate into small pieces. The curd should be in lumps. Immediately turn off the heat. Pour the cheese and whey through a colander or large sieve, lined with a thin fabric or four layers of muslin and placed in the kitchen sink. (If you intend to make the cheese again within 24 hours, save the whey to add to the next batch of boiling milk instead of using lemon juice, vinegar, or yogurt; cheese made with whey has a softer curd and a more authentically Indian aroma. This is what the pastry shops in India use as a starter, day after day.) Hold the colander or sieve under the tap and let cold water run, at a medium flow, through the curds for 10 seconds – to wash away whatever remains of the smell of lemon juice, vinegar, or yogurt. Bring up the four corners of the muslin and tie them together. Gently twist to extract as much water as possible, and hang the cheese to drain for 1½ hours.

This drained, crumbly, slightly moist cheese is *chenna*. To make the cheese into cakes (*paneer*), set the cheese – still in the muslin – on a clean flat surface and place a weight (such as a large pot filled with water) on it for half an hour. Remove the weight, take the compressed cheese out of the muslin, and place it back on the flat surface. With a sharp knife cut the cheese into neat rectangles. *Paneer* keeps well in the refrigerator for 4 days.

NOTE Even though exact amounts of lemon juice, vinegar, and yogurt are specified here, you will sometimes find that the curd forms before all the starter has been incorporated. If that happens, do not add the full amount of the starter, as that will only harden the curd. This is a serious matter, especially in delicate desserts such as *Ras Malai*, where soft, moist curds are essential for the dumplings to be soft and fragile.

Or you may find that after you have added the entire suggested amount of starter, the curd still has not formed or has only partially formed and the whey remains milky. There is no need for alarm. All it means is that your starter is not potent enough to do the job. Therefore, add a little more of the same starter until lumps of snow-white curd separate, leaving behind a clear greenish-yellow whey.

THICKENED MILK SAUCE

RABADI

◆

Rabadi is milk that has been cooked down to about a quarter of its original volume. The distinct aroma and pale beige colour characteristic of *rabadi* are developed by boiling the milk slowly over low heat. *Rabadi* is essential in making the delectable *Ras Malai* (p. 330). *Rabadi* is also served as a dessert sauce for fruits, and is sweetened and sprinkled with nuts as a pudding called *Basoondi* (p. 323). It is also thinned with water or milk to the consistency of regular milk, sweetened, and served as aromatic milk (*Rabadi doodh*) for a beverage. Except for the time involved it is very easy to make *rabadi* at home.

MAKING THICKENED MILK SAUCE Bring 3 pints/2 litres of milk to the boil in a heavy flat-bottomed pan, preferably one with a non-stick surface, stirring constantly with a steel or aluminium spatula, or a large metal spoon. This will take about 15 minutes and needs very careful attention so that the milk doesn't stick to the bottom of the pan. Lower heat and simmer 45 to 55 minutes, stirring constantly and scraping down the sides until the liquid is reduced to about 1 pint/½ litre. Cool for 5 minutes. The consistency will be that of a thick, lumpy cream sauce. Transfer to a bowl and refrigerate.

MILK FUDGE

KHOYA

◆

Khoya is the next stage of *rabadi*. When *rabadi* is cooked further and reduced by half, it turns into *Khoya*, a thick mass resembling fudge.

MAKING MILK FUDGE Follow the preceding recipe for making *rabadi*, but turn down the heat and continue cooking for an additional 15 minutes or so, stirring constantly to keep it from sticking and burning, until the entire mixture resembles a thick paste and comes away from the bottom of the pan when stirred. It will be grainy and very sticky. When cool, this paste develops a fudgelike texture and consistency, and loses its stickiness. Refrigerate after it cools, in a bowl or wrapped in aluminium foil. 3 pints/2 litres of milk will produce ½ pint/30 dl of pure milk fudge weighing about 12 oz/375 g. *Khoya* is used in making a variety of nut fudges, sweetmeats, and other delicacies such as Almond Milk Fudge (*Badaam Barfi*, p. 342). In the valley of Kashmir, milk fudge grains are fried until they resemble meat and then cooked with green peas in a spicy tomato gravy. This vegetarian dish, called *Matar Shufta*, resembles its meat counterpart, *Keema Matar* (p. 125).

FLOWER ESSENCES

RUH

◆

Flower extracts are used to perfume many of the classic Moghul dishes. The two most popular are Screw-pine Essence (*Ruh Kewra*) and Rose Essence (*Ruh Gulab*). Screw-pine essence is extracted from the thick, leathery, yellow-green flower petals. It is used mainly in meat and poultry preparations, in certain Moghul pilafs, in such meat and rice casseroles as Emperor's Layered Meat and Fragrant Rice Casserole (*Shah Jahani Biriyani*, p. 146), and in some desserts and sweetmeats. You can find it commercially under the labels 'Kewra Water' or 'Kewra Essence'.

Rose essence (*ruh gulab*) is extracted from small deep-red roses, famous for their fragrance and cultivated solely for this purpose. It is primarily used in flavouring desserts, puddings, sweetmeats, and cold drinks. Rose essence is available commercially in three forms.

Rose water, known as *ruh gulab* or *gulab jal*, is the diluted version of rose essence. It is used, just as rose essence is, in making the Rose-flavoured Yogurt Drink (*Lassi*, p. 348) and the luscious Almond and Rice Dessert (*Firni*, p. 327). In India it is considered a good omen to sprinkle rose water on guests arriving at weddings and other religious ceremonies. It is also used as an air-freshener in many Indian homes.

Rose syrup, known as *Gulabe Sharbat*, is made by adding rose essence to a heavy sugar syrup. In India it is diluted and served as a cool, refreshing rose drink. The syrup is ideal for making rose ice cream (*Kulfi Ruh Gulab*) and the yogurt beverage *lassi*.

Rose preserve, known as *gulkand*, is made by preserving whole rose petals in heavy syrup. *Gulkand* is an important accompaniment to the betel leaf (*paan*) for cutting bitter aftertastes.

SILVER FOIL

VARK

◆

Silver foil, known as *vark,* is silver dust pressed to form a foil sheet. Its sole purpose is to adorn sweetmeats, kebabs, and special pilafs. Moghuls used it to decorate their elaborate food preparations. Today *vark* is used on special occasions such as wedding buffets and religious festivals. I like to use *vark* on nut fudges like Almond Milk Fudge (p. 342) and Cashew Nut Fudge (p. 341), and on special Moghul preparations, including *biriyani* (p. 146). *Vark* is perfectly safe to eat. It is tasteless and odourless.

Vark is made by heating and beating pure silver until it resembles cotton candy. A very thin layer of it is then spread on a sheet of paper. Another sheet of paper is placed over that to compress the silver dust into a single long sheet.

To apply *vark,* first peel off the top layer of paper. Lift the bottom sheet, with the silver foil still attached to it, and invert it over the dish to be garnished. Gently peel away the paper. The silver foil will stick to the food.

Two words of caution: Do not work with *vark* in a breezy area, as it may blow away. And, because *vark* is pure silver, store it tightly covered in plastic film or in an airtight container, or it will tarnish.

EQUIPMENT

◆

There are no special cooking utensils or tools that are absolutely essential to Indian cooking. To give you a sense of things, let me describe the humble setting of the traditional Indian kitchen (*rasooi*). It is really just another room in the house. It is starkly empty and has no counters, cupboards, electrical appliances, or fixtures of any kind – not even a kitchen sink. When a family moves in, it builds a wood- or coal-burning stove (*choolha*) in one corner, which is ritually broken down when the family moves out. The cooking on this stove is done from a squatting position on the floor, or while sitting on one of the low stools.

There is a tap in or outside the kitchen, or water is brought from the centre of town in jugs called *ghara*, and stored. Meat, fish, and vegetables are bought the same day they are cooked. This is because there is no refrigeration, and in the hot climate the meat and fish are apt to spoil, and vegetables wilt in a matter of hours. It is a blessing in disguise, for the meat used in cooking is still warm and sweet-smelling, its juices fully intact, and the vegetables fresh, crisp, and full of their delicate fragrance. The cooked dishes have the wonderful flavour that comes with the freshest of ingredients. This is how food is meant to taste and, therefore, should.

Given this unpretentious set-up, it follows that the cooking equipment will also be simple. The genius of Indian utensils lies in their adaptation to a multitude of functions, thus reducing their number to a bare minimum. These tools are made of metal, stone, wood and pottery, and include the following:

◆ Handleless saucepans with rim (*pateela*) for general cooking
◆ A handleless flat lid for a saucepan (*dhakkan*)
◆ Spoons for stirring (*karchi*)
◆ An Indian wok (*kadhai*) for frying (Indian kitchens usually have two types: one deep, and narrow across the top, used for deep frying; the other shallow, and broad across the top, used for stir-frying)
◆ A shallow, flat-bottomed platter (*paraath*), 12 to 24 in/30 to 60 cm diameter with a 3 in/7.5 cm high rim. This all-purpose utensil is used for preparing vegetables for cooking, cleaning rice and *dal*, and, most importantly, for mixing and kneading bread dough
◆ A flat round marble or wooden board (*chakla*)
◆ A wooden rolling pin (*belan*) for rolling bread

◆ A handleless iron griddle (*tava*) for making bread
◆ Tongs (*chimta*) for lifting the *tava*
◆ A flat grinding stone (*sil*) with a triangular stone (*batta*) for grinding herbs and wet seasonings
◆ A grain-mill (*chakki*) for grinding spices, *dal*, grain, and other dry ingredients
◆ Long, sharp knives (*chakoo*)
◆ A sieve (*chalni*) for cleaning and sifting ingredients
◆ A vegetable grater (*kaddoo-kas*)
◆ A coconut grater (*narial-kas*)
◆ A pottery or brass jug (*ghara*) used for storing water
◆ Dinner plates (*thali*) and bowls (*katoori*) for serving the meal, made of brass, stainless steel, silver, and even gold

In India almost all cooking is done on top of the stove. In classic Indian cooking there is no equivalent to the Western-style oven. There is, however, the *tandoor*, clay oven, a giant barbecue with a small narrow opening at the top, built into the ground. The sides are lined with a special smooth clay and used for baking many kinds of Indian breads. The pit of the *tandoor* itself is used for roasting the meat.

The *tandoor* is not a feature of most Indian households because it is expensive to build and operate. It is used for bulk cooking, and is found in the ordinary restaurants of North India and in smart restaurants throughout India and in other parts of the world.

EQUIPPING YOUR KITCHEN FOR INDIAN COOKING

◆

POTS AND PANS

Enamel-coated, heavy-bottomed casseroles and frying pans are best suited to Indian cooking. They retain and distribute heat evenly, and you do not have to worry about the ingredients reacting with the metal. They can go directly from the stove top or oven to the table, into the refrigerator, and then into the dishwasher.

A couple of saucepans or casseroles with non-stick surfaces are a worthwhile investment. They are especially good for frying onions, garlic, and ginger; cooking with dried fruits and nut butter; or cooking down milk for milk fudge, as all these substances have a tendency to stick to the bottom of the pan. They are also ideal for pot-roasting dishes that have very little liquid.

The Indian wok (*kadhai*), which looks like a round-bottomed casserole, is immensely useful for deep frying and stir-frying vegetables. It requires much less oil than a deep-fryer or a frying pan because of its shape. But I have found that non-stick frying pans are just as useful for stir-frying; for deep frying, a large pan works well. If you are interested in investing in a *kadhai*, I suggest you buy a heavy cast-iron one that can withstand high heat. A cast-iron *kadhai* needs to be seasoned before being used for the first time.

To season a *kadhai*: The *kadhai* usually has a protective coating to prevent rust. Wash the *kadhai* thoroughly with dishwashing detergent and warm water, scrubbing it with a steel-wool pad. Wipe dry, and place over medium heat for 1 minute in order to dry it completely. After it has cooled, brush the inside with a little oil (peanut or corn oil will do), and heat again over medium heat until the oil is hot and smoking. Turn off the heat and sprinkle about 2 tablespoons of salt inside. When the *kadhai* is cool enough to handle, rub the salt around the inside with a kitchen towel or a piece of muslin. Wash thoroughly, dry, heat over medium heat for one minute, then let cool. The *kadhai* is now ready for use. This final step (heating over medium heat) ensures thorough drying; it should be followed after every use in order to prevent the *kadhai* from rusting.

TOOLS
◆

Aside from the usual tools found in the average kitchen – an assortment of knives, spatulas, peeler, grater, sieve, colander, and beater – you will need a sugar thermometer for making yogurt, sugar syrup, and in heating oil for frying. You will also need a coffee grinder for grinding spices, and electric blender or a food mill for grinding and puréeing.

I have found that if a single coffee grinder is used for grinding coffee beans as well as spices, it is the coffee whose flavour is altered. This is because the coffee-grinder blades take on the aroma of the spices and not of the coffee beans. Therefore, unless you are willing to drink spice-laced coffee, I recommend keeping a separate grinder for spices.

I have also found a small mortar and pestle – preferably made of marble – ideal for pulverizing small quantities of spices.

Since I discovered the virtues of the food processor, I have become a total addict. If properly used, its versatility knows no bounds. Most Indian dishes call for chopped onion, garlic, and fresh ginger. The chopping takes considerable time by conventional methods, but with a food processor the job is done in seconds. A good food processor chops fresh herbs to perfection, powders nuts, and purées fresh tomatoes (with the skin, as I prefer). With a little experience and caution on your part, it will even slice onions to the wafer-thin shreds called for in many Indian dishes. And to my ultimate delight, it mixes and kneads the dough for Indian breads, pastries, and biscuits.

TECHNIQUES

◆

In the following pages I have explained the basic techniques used in classic Indian cooking to prepare spices and seasonings, meats and vegetables, and I refer to them again and again in the recipes. You need to understand and master these methods which, coupled with a knowledge of the special spices, herbs, and seasonings, form the backbone of Indian cooking. Once you learn them, you can think, plan, and cook Indian meals with the natural flair of an Indian cook. This means that eventually you will be able to put away this book and start cooking Indian food guided solely by the wealth of your experience, employing your own developed creative skill, improvising confidently and brilliantly where needed. And most important of all, you will know how to rescue dishes when they meet with disaster, which occasionally happens to me. You will be cooking the classic dishes with your own personal touch, tailored to suit your individual taste. This is the essence of becoming a master Indian cook.

ROASTING AND GRINDING SPICES

MASALA BHOONANA AUR PEESANA

◆

Spices are roasted in an Indian wok (*kadhai*) or a frying pan on top of the stove, and ground by one of the following methods:

TO ROAST SPICES Heat a *kadhai* or a heavy frying pan, preferably an iron one, for 2 minutes over medium heat. Add the spices and roast over medium heat, stirring and shaking the pan constantly in order to prevent burning. For the first minute or two, nothing will happen – the spices are losing their moisture during this time – and then all of a sudden they will start to brown. This is a crucial period: If you don't watch them carefully and stir them constantly, they will burn almost instantly. As the spices brown they will begin to smoke, releasing the sweet fragrance of roasting spices. Roast them until they turn dark brown. Turn down the heat a little if they seem to be browning too fast. The time will depend upon the spice and the amount of it being roasted in relation to the size of the pan – the larger the surface area of the pan, the faster the spice will brown. In a *kadhai*, 4 tablespoons of coriander seeds will take about 6 minutes, 4 tablespoons of cumin seeds will take about 8 minutes, and 10 oz/300 g of the spice mixture *garam masala* will take about 10 minutes. Take the browned spices out of the pan immediately, and put them into a clean dry bowl to cool completely before using.

TO GRIND SPICES Put the spices in a coffee grinder, a spice mill, or an electric blender, and grind them to a fine powder. The food processor is not suitable for grinding a blend of spices of varying hardness and size. It works well for spices that crumble easily, such as roasted cumin seeds.

For powdering small quantities of spices, such as ½ teaspoon of fennel seeds or a small lump of asafetida, it is best to use a mortar and pestle, a kitchen mallet, or a rolling pin. If you use a mallet or rolling pin, place the spice in a small plastic bag between two sheets of greaseproof paper or plastic film before grinding it; otherwise the instrument will permanently take on the smell of the spice. Store in airtight containers in a cool, dry place so that the spices do not lose their fragrance.

CRUSHING SPICES

MASALA MUSULANA

◆

There are several recipes in Indian cooking which call for crushed, rather than ground, spices because a certain amount of the texture of the spice is desired, as in Crab Malabar (p. 87) and Fried Fillet of Sole Laced with Carom (p. 184). Crushed spices are usually prepared just before the cooking, not too far in advance, because they lose their fragrance. Spices can be crushed between finger and thumb, or with the thumb while holding the spices in the palm of the other hand. To crush spices in a mortar or with a kitchen mallet or rolling pin, follow the instructions above for powdering small quantities, but pound or crush only until they look broken and release their fragrance.

FRYING SPICES

SOOKHA MASALA BHOONANA

◆

An indispensable process in Indian cooking is the frying of spices in a little hot fat or oil, to release their flavour prior to adding the other ingredients. The secret of success lies in having the fat hot enough so that a green cardamom pod will sizzle gently when put into the pan and will puff and brown in a few seconds. At this temperature most spices will brown almost instantly; watch carefully that they do not burn. It will take a little practice to learn exactly how to fry spices in your own pan on your own stove. Be prepared to lose a few batches and keep trying until you learn how high to turn the heat, how long to heat the oil, and how to lift the pan away from the heat before the spices start to burn. And you must have the next batch of ingredients ready, so that they may be added without interrupting the process. Lift the pan away from the heat and lower the temperature a little before you add more ingredients, and stir rapidly to keep them from burning in the extremely hot oil.

This technique is vital to the flavour of the dish: it removes the raw flavour from the spices at the same time that it perfumes the fat with their sweet scent. As a result, the aromas of the spices penetrate the meat and vegetables much more thoroughly than if the spices had been added after the liquids.

Whole spices, which take longer to brown, should always be added before the ground ones. In dishes that call for ground spices only, the fat should be moderately hot (350°F/175°C) so that the ground spices, when added, get a chance to brown without burning.

Whole spices that take a little longer to fry than others should always be added *first*, separately. These include black mustard seeds, sesame seeds, fenugreek, and various pulses used as spices. If a combination of spices includes black mustard seeds, the seeds should be added first and fried until they pop like popcorn. The seeds will not pop evenly if there are other spices present, causing the temperature of the fat to drop. The popping of the seeds is very important: it releases their flavour. Also unpopped seeds are chewy and bitter. A word of caution: Keep a lid handy, since the mustard seeds may fly about when popping.

PREPARING ONION, GARLIC, AND GINGER FOR COOKING

GEELA MASALA TAYYAR KARANA

◆

Onions, garlic and ginger are the essential ingredients of most Indian main dishes, particularly those of North India. There, the gravies and sauces characteristic of the classic Moghul dishes were created. Onions are usually chopped or finely sliced; garlic and ginger root are usually finely chopped or ground to a paste before they are added to a dish. The texture of each dish, from coarsely grained and crunchy to smooth and velvety, is determined by the degree of fineness of the chopped ingredients.

TO SLICE ONIONS Peel, and cut the onion in half vertically, beginning at the top end. Place halves on a cutting board, flat side down, and cut off about ½ in/5 mm from the root end, making sure to cut away all of the tough solid stem portion. Slice them lengthwise from top end to root end into paper-thin slices, about ¹⁄₁₆ in/1.5 mm thick. With your fingers, separate the slices.

TO CHOP ONIONS Follow the instructions given for slicing onions, but do not slice them quite as thin – about ¼ in/5 mm thick. Then gather the slices and dice them across, into small cubes.

TO CHOP GARLIC AND GINGER ROOT Peel, and slice into thin slices, about ¹⁄₃₂ in/.75 mm thick. Then stack the slices together, a few at a time and cut into thin strips. Gather the strips and dice across into tiny cubes. You can also crush them to a coarse pulp with a mortar and pestle.

TO GRIND GARLIC AND GINGER ROOT TO A PASTE Peel, place in a mortar, and crush or pound with the pestle until the ingredients are reduced to a fine paste. To ensure smooth texture of the paste, crush garlic and ginger root separately.

TO CHOP FRESH HERBS Wash and thoroughly dry the herbs. Gather the herbs, and, holding them by the stems, slice across the leaves with a sharp knife to achieve the desired size, discarding the stems.

TO CHOP GREEN CHILIES: First cut them in half, lengthwise. If you want the chilies to be mild, scrape off the seeds and discard. Gather the halves into a bunch and cut across into thin slices about ⅛ to ¹⁄₁₆ in/3 to 1.5 mm thick. If chilies are hot, wear rubber gloves to protect your hands.

USING THE FOOD PROCESSOR

◆

TO SLICE ONIONS Peel, and cut the onions in half from top end to root end. Cut off the solid stem portion. If the onions are very large, cut into quarters. Attach the serrated slicing disc, preferably fine, on the food processor, and cover the container. Fill the feed tube with onions, standing them on their sides. Slice, using a little pressure on the pusher (you will be able to process 1 or 2 onion halves at a time). When onion slices fill up the workbowl, transfer them to another bowl. Continue with the remaining onions.

TO CHOP ONIONS Attach the metal cutting blade and add 2 or 3 onion halves at a time to the workbowl. Process, turning the machine on and off rapidly until the onions are finely chopped (about 15 seconds). Transfer the onions to another bowl, and continue with the remaining onions.

TO CHOP GARLIC, GINGER, CHILIES, AND HERBS Attach metal cutting blade, begin processing, and gradually drop peeled garlic, peeled ginger root, green chilies (cut chilies in half; if desired, scrape away the seeds), and clean, dry, fresh herbs (with the coarse stems snipped off) through the feed tube separately, in that order. (If each has to be prepared separately, then remove one from the workbowl before adding the next.) Stop processing as soon as the ingredients are chopped and cling to the sides.

For recipes where several herbs and seasonings are combined with onions and cooked together, it is logical (and easier) to chop all the ingredients at the same time. But always make sure that you chop the garlic, ginger root, and green chilies *before* processing the onions. A little extra processing will not affect the herbs, but it will be disastrous on the onions; they will become a purée and be unsuitable for frying.

BROWN FRYING ONION, GARLIC, AND GINGER ROOT

GEELA MASALA BHOONANA

◆

An important technique in frying the aromatic seasonings is the brown frying of onions, garlic, and ginger root, or sometimes only one or two of them. My research has turned up no equivalent process in French or other Western schools of cooking. The process of brown frying lies somewhere between sautéing and deep frying.

Most lamb, beef, and chicken dishes, particularly those with golden-reddish gravies, start off with the technique of frying finely chopped or sliced onions in a small amount of fat until they lose most of their moisture and turn caramel-brown. Brown frying the onions, garlic, and ginger, is intrinsic to Moghul cooking; these seasonings add both colour and fragrance to the dish, and act as thickeners, creating the most wonderful gravies imaginable.

TO BROWN FRY 2 LARGE ONIONS, THINLY SLICED Heat 4 tablespoons of oil over medium-high heat in a heavy-bottomed pan. Add the sliced onions and stir to coat the slices with oil. Fry the onions, stirring constantly. For the first 5 minutes the onions will steam vigorously, losing much of their excess moisture. As the steam begins to subside, the onions will wilt and begin to fry. In the next 5 minutes they will lose the rest of their excess moisture and turn limp and golden yellow. The oil will now start to separate from the onions, an indication that they are ready to brown. Keep stirring the onions constantly. They will begin clumping together, and in about 5 minutes they will turn light brown. Continue frying until they turn caramel-brown and look shrivelled up (about 5 minutes more). Add chopped garlic and ginger midway during the last 5 minutes of frying (or when the onions are 95 percent browned), since they take a very short time to brown. In certain recipes in which the quantity of onions is small, the three seasonings are often combined and fried together.

NOTE

1 When onions are added to the hot oil, they often burn unevenly before they finish cooking. To prevent such a disaster, start frying on a lower heat. Heat the oil for ½ minute over medium high heat, and add the onions. In a couple of minutes the oil and the onions will gradually heat up.

2 The onions must be stirred constantly during the entire process to ensure that they brown evenly, or else they will not impart the appropriate caramel colour and sweet fried-onion flavour to the sauce. In addition, partially cooked onions will not dissolve into the sauce, thus affecting its texture and consistency.

3 If the onions stick, or fry too rapidly and burn, a little cold water should be added, 1 tablespoon at a time, to slow down the cooking. You should never lower or turn off the heat during the frying process.

4 The last 10 minutes, and particularly the last 5 minutes, of cooking time is a very crucial period in this process. This is because the onions have lost just about all their moisture by this stage, and brown very rapidly. If they are not watched and stirred constantly, without interruption, they burn almost instantly and lend a bitter burnt taste to the dish.

5 To stop any further frying of onions once they are done, add a tablespoon of cold water and stir in.

6 Brown-fried onions can be prepared in large batches and refrigerated, or frozen and defrosted as needed. Be sure to freeze them in small portions based on your need. Once defrosted they must be used; they cannot be refrozen.

SPECIAL FRIED GARNISHES

TADKA AUR BHONE PIAZ KE LACHE

◆

Fried garnishes are as important to Indian dishes as the dishes themselves; they form an integral part of the preparation they adorn. In several dishes, particularly pulse preparations, they are considered part of the cooking ingredients and should never be omitted.

In addition to making the dish look attractive and appetizing, fried garnishes lend a very distinct and special aroma, taste, and texture. The two important fried garnishes in Indian cooking are Spice-Perfumed Butter (*Tadka*) and Crispy Fried Onions (*Bhone Piaz ke Lache*).

SPICE-PERFUMED BUTTER

TADKA

◆

This is an age-old technique, used since the Vedic times for flavouring all varieties of *dal*, yogurt salads, vegetables, relishes, and meat preparations. *Tadka*, also known as *baghar* and *chaunk*, is the simplest and most effective way of aromatizing food. It is prepared by heating Indian clarified butter to a very hot point (375°–400°F/190°–205°C) and frying certain fragrant spices and seasonings, such as asafetida, cloves, cumin, black mustard seeds, ginger root, garlic, onions, or green chilies, to imbue it with fragrance. This perfumed butter is then folded into the dish with the fried ingredients.

There are regional traditions governing the various combinations of spices that can flavour *tadka*, a different one for each *dal*. In northern cooking, the *tadka* for lentils consists of garlic and red pepper; for mung beans and split peas, cumin and onions; for white split gram beans, asafetida or onions and cloves. Similarly, different combinations of spices and seasonings are used for different pulse preparations in all the other regions of India. Recipes for *tadka* can be found as part of each *dal* recipe.

TO PREPARE TADKA First prepare the dish, such as pulse (*dal*) purée, and transfer to a serving bowl. In a frying pan, heat the Indian clarified butter, or *ghee* (oil or vegetable shortening may be used), almost to the smoking point (375°–400°F/190°–205°C). Add the whole spices first, and fry until they release their fragrance (about 5 seconds). Add onions, garlic, ginger root, etc., and fry, stirring constantly, until they turn brown. The time will depend upon each seasoning and the quantities used. It can take anything from 30 seconds for a few cloves of sliced garlic to 15 minutes for 2 large onions, sliced. Now add the ground spices. Immediately turn off the heat and pour the entire contents of the frying pan over the *dal* in the serving bowl. Serve immediately.

CRISPY FRIED ONIONS

BHONE PIAZ KE LACHE

◆

These crunchy fried onions are a delicacy all by themselves. They are primarily used for garnishing pilafs, and meat and rice preparations. This is another Moghul contribution. There are a great many meat dishes in which these fried onions, also known as *barista*, are crumbled or ground, and folded in just before serving. This is done to keep the flavour of fried onions more distinct in the dish and to lend a sweet flavour to the sauce. In addition, meat cooked with fried onions often turns dark. Therefore, to keep the meat lightly-coloured, especially in pilafs, the fried onions are added at the end, after the meat has been cooked.

The process of preparing crisp fried onions is simple to learn. First, slice the onions into thin shreds following the instructions on page 65. Heat vegetable oil in a *kadhai* or frying pan over medium high heat until very hot but not smoking (375°–400°F/190°–205°C). Add the onion slices and fry, stirring constantly, until they turn dark brown (watch carefully that they do not blacken and burn, which will make them taste bitter). The time will depend on the quantity of onions being fried. Two large onions, thinly sliced, will take about 25 to 30 minutes.

Drain them on paper towels for 5 minutes, and they will turn crackling crisp. These fried onions keep well for a day if kept in a tightly covered container. If left uncovered, collected moisture will cause them to go limp.

MOGHUL AND NORTH INDIAN COOKING

◆

There are several Indian cooking techniques similar to the ones most of us in the West are familiar with, such as boiling (*oobalana*), stewing (*salan ya kari*), frying (*bhonao aur bhoonana*) and deep frying (*talana*). The braising (*korma*) and pot-roasting (*dum*) are also very similar to familiar methods, with the few minor exceptions that I discuss below. The techniques that owe their origin to the Moghuls are named after the specific method of preparation, or the cooking equipment used to make them. These include kebab (*kaba*), kafta (*kofta*), and the Indian clay-oven-cooked dishes (*tandoori khana*).

BRAISING

KORMA

◆

Braising (*korma*) is an important technique in Moghul cooking. It was initially used in cooking meat and chicken dishes, but the technique later found its way into innumerable vegetable preparations, particularly those imitating their nonvegetarian counterparts.

The process of braising is very similar to the Western method, with one difference. The braising liquid used in *korma* is much thicker: it includes yogurt, cream, fruit purées, and nut butters.

With a few exceptions, *korma* dishes are begun by marinating the meat in the braising liquid together with the spices and seasonings. The meat is then cooked in the marinade itself, by a slow, prolonged simmering over very low heat on top of the stove. Often a little cream and spice-perfumed butter are incorporated at the end so as to velvetize and aromatize the sauce further.

Korma dishes are generally made with the choicest cuts of meat, because they are traditionally served on special occasions. Furthermore, the *korma* dishes usually contain a very few subtle spices, so as to allow the flavour and texture of the meat to come through and enrich the sauce. A good heavy-bottomed pan with a non-stick surface is essential to successful *korma*. Some examples of classic braised dishes are Lamb Braised in Aromatic Cream Sauce (*Rogani Gosht*, p. 127), Royal Braised Lamb with Spices (*Shahi Korma*, p. 134), and Royal Braised Vegetables in Cardamom Nut Sauce (*Shahi Sabz Korma*, p. 198).

POT-ROASTING

DUM

◆

Dum is the Indian method of pot-roasting food in a charcoal-burning stove. I have adapted the method for cooking *dum* dishes on top of the stove. *Dum* dishes generally call for a large amount of fat (usually butter) since the basic ingredients (meat, poultry, fish, or vegetables, left whole or cut into large chunks) are literally steamed in the vapour of the butter. A good heavy-bottomed, well-greased pot (such as a heavy casserole with non-stick surface) with a tight-fitting lid is essential to *dum* cooking. To cook any food by the *dum* process, the spices and seasonings must be fried in the butter at the start. The ingredients to be pot-roasted are then added, and lightly browned. (They are often pricked well before being added, to allow the flavours to penetrate fully.) The heat is momentarily increased to high, to create steam (often a little water is sprinkled over the ingredients to speed up this process, especially if they look dry). The lid is placed on and sealed, the heat reduced to the lowest point, and the *dum* cooked slowly in the aromatic vapour.

Traditionally, the pot is sealed with a little dough to prevent the escape of any vapour and the pot is placed over hot ashes and the lid is covered with live charcoal. The pot is opened only when the cooking is completed. To keep the food from sticking and browning unevenly, the ingredients are stirred by lifting and shaking the entire pot in a circular motion. I've devised a simpler and more efficient substitute for the dough seal. I cover the pot with a piece of foil before putting the lid on. The foil hanging over the lid is then crumpled and pressed against the pot to form a tight seal. The advantage of this method is that the foil can be lifted off, the food stirred with a spoon, and the foil resealed, which is far easier and safer than lifting and shaking the pot. It also allows you to check the *dum* so that there won't be any danger of your overcooking it. (In a sealed pot, you have no way of knowing exactly when the ingredients are done. As a result, you frequently end up with an overcooked dish.)

A classic example of *dum* cooking is Whole Potatoes in Spicy Yogurt Gravy (*Dum Aloo*, p. 191).

The *dum* process is also used extensively in the final execution of Moghul rice pilafs (*pullao*), layered meat and rice casseroles (*biriyani*), and certain braised dishes (*korma*). This is the process that causes grains of rice to develop the exquisite texture and elasticity characteristic of classic Moghul pilafs. It also enhances the flavours of braised dishes, making the meat melt-in-your-mouth tender, and at the same time improves the overall appearance of the dish. These dishes, when 95 percent done, finish their cooking by steaming in their own vapour. *Dum* simply slows the cooking process without stopping it. As a result, meat, chicken, rice, and so on begin to relax in the vapour-filled pot. The juices in the meat and chicken begin to settle, thus making them plump and moist. The starch in the rice forms a permanent bond that enables the grains to expand without breaking or cracking. And the fat mixes with the sauce to give it a velvet glaze and a lovely texture.

KEBAB

KABAB

◆

There are special techniques for preparing the cooking meat. *Kabab* generally refers to small pieces of meat that are grilled or fried. *Kabab* is prepared either with minced lamb flavoured with spices, herbs, and seasonings and shaped into sausages, patties, or croquettes, or with small chunks of lamb which are marinated in a spicy, fragrant marinade. There are innumerable varieties of kebabs popular in India. Seven (four made with minced lamb, and three with chunks) are considered classics.

SEEK KABAB These kebabs are made with minced lamb, fresh herbs, and only a few spices. The meat is shaped into patties, then wrapped in thin layers around a metal skewer and grilled over a charcoal grill. These soft and moist kebabs are by far the most popular. They are frequently served in restaurants where they are cooked in the Indian clay oven, *tandoor*.

SHAMME KABAB These kebabs contain a large quantity of yellow split peas – a distinctive feature of *shamme kabab* – in addition to spices, herbs, and seasonings. The minced lamb is shaped into patties and shallow fried. *Shamme kababs* are generally very spicy and fragrant with cardamom.

HUSSAINI KABAB These kebabs are made with minced lamb and several highly aromatic spices, and are often stuffed with dried fruit and nuts. The meat is shaped into thin sausagelike rolls and panfried or grilled. The flavour is very mild and the texture juicy.

CHAPLI KABAB These are very similar to *shamme kabab*, but do not contain yellow split peas and are spicy hot.

BOTI KABAB These kebabs are traditionally made of boneless lamb pieces, usually from the rib. The meat is coated with a thin layer of aromatic yogurt mixture and marinated before being grilled. Kebabs are often sold as roadside snacks in the northernmost regions of India during the cold winter months.

TIKKA KABAB These kebabs are made with lean boneless chunks of lamb, chicken, large pieces of liver, and shellfish. These are the kebabs you see in most Indian restaurants. The meat or fish chunks are marinated in a spicy, ginger-laced yogurt marinade and then grilled. In restaurants they are cooked in the *tandoor*. Their colour is usually brilliant orange-red – the characteristic colour of all *tandoor*-cooked food (a colouring dye is usually added to the marinade).

PASANDA OR BARRA KABAB *Pasanda* or *Barra* means fillet. These kebabs are made with the choicest cuts of lamb (usually from the loin or rib) which are cut into thin strips and pounded until they are reduced to almost paper-thin fillets.

(Often lamb breast is substituted for reasons of economy.) The fillets are marinated in a mild fragrant marinade, threaded on bamboo skewers, and grilled over a charcoal grill.

KAFTA

KOFTA

◆

Kofta are very similar to the kebabs that are made with minced meat except, after being grilled or fried, they are simmered in rich sauces and turned into lovely main dishes. The kebabs for kafta dishes are usually shaped into round meatballs. Of the many different kinds of *kofta* preparations commonly served in India, the following two are the most popular by far and are considered to be classics:

MALAI KOFTA In this dish the meatballs are usually flavoured with mild spices and herbs. They are then simmered in butter and cream in an enriched aromatic tomato sauce.

NARGISI KOFTA This *kofta* preparation is somewhat elaborate. First, whole hard-boiled eggs are enclosed in a thin layer of spice-laced ground-lamb mixture and deep fried (they very closely resemble Scotch Eggs at this stage). The stuffed meatballs are neatly sliced to expose the egg, and then simmered in a fragrant onion gravy. The combination of meat and egg looks like a narcissus flower (which, in Indian, is called *nargis*), hence its name.

INDIAN CLAY-OVEN COOKING

TANDOORI KHANA

◆

In India the processes of baking, roasting, and grilling are all achieved by *tandoori* cooking. This is because the food is prepared in a *tandoor*, which simultaneously bakes, roasts, and grills.

The *tandoor* is believed to have originated in the northeastern part of Persia (present-day Iran). Its use spread to different parts of the continent with migrations, and as a result, today the *tandoor* is used in all of Central Asia. It is, of course, known by different names, such as *tanoo* in Iran and *toné* in southeastern Georgia in the U.S.S.R.

In India the *tandoor* was initially built for the purpose of baking breads (still its main use). The dough is stretched and shaped into flat breads and smacked onto the sides of the pit, to which it adheres. It puffs up and bakes in 7 to 10 minutes. The cooked breads are then peeled off gently with long metal skewers specially designed for this purpose.

In the earlier part of the nineteenth century, in Peshawar, a city in the northwest frontier region of Pakistan (then part of India), an ingenious method for cooking meat was invented and introduced. In this process, whole chickens and large chunks of lamb were threaded on specially designed long skewers, lowered into the *tandoor* pit, and cooked. Any food thus cooked was referred to as *tandoori* food. Today, it has become one of the most popular cooking methods in India.

The meats cooked in a *tandoor* are generally more moist, and tender (but not dripping juice) than those cooked by any other method. In addition, they have a special earthy aroma absorbed from the clay lining of the oven.

Just about any meat that can be threaded on skewers can be cooked in a *tandoor*. The most popular is the chicken, called *Tandoori Murghi* (p. 168). The others include *Seek Kabab, Tikka, Boti, or Barra Kabab* and *Jheenga* (prawn) *Tikka Kabab*. Chunks of liver and whole fish are also cooked this way. After the main roasting has been finished, the leftover heat in the *tandoor* is used to prepare wonderful delicacies like the pot-roasted leg of lamb with pistachio and raisin-laced saffron sauce, called *Shahi Raan* (p. 141) and Buttered Black Beans (*Kali Dal*, p. 242).

All dishes cooked in a tandoor are first marinated in a spiced yogurt marinade for a long period, to flavour and tenderize the meat. Chicken is usually coated and marinated in special tenderizers before marinating in a yogurt-spice mixture. (See below.)

The lamb or beef used should always be very lean so that it can be generously basted with butter (*usli ghee*) during cooking. This is because the smoke created by the butter dripping on the charcoal imparts a distinctly sweet aroma, very different from the smoke created by any other fat or oil, and essential to the authentic *tandoori* flavour.

All meats cooked in a *tandoor* have a characteristic bright reddish-orange colour, lent by a natural dye called *tandoori rang* that is added to the marinade, so as to give the dishes a strong aesthetic appeal and to distinguish *tandoori* food from all others. Since *tandoori* colouring is a product of nature, it is possible there will be variations in colour. Such variations are perfectly acceptable. The colouring of *tandoori* food is not essential to the flavour. You may substitute a little paprika in its place. Some use saffron, but in my judgement it is not a good choice for colouring *tandoori* chicken because its powerful aroma often interferes with and masks the subtle fragrance of the herb marinade. Besides, it is too expensive to waste on colour alone.

Unfortunately, there is no way to duplicate the *tandoor* process. Until someone comes up with a modified version of this gigantic clay pit – which is more like a furnace than a barbecue pit – *tandoori* cooking, with its unique flavour, cannot be reproduced in your home. You can, however, get very good results in the meantime by using a charcoal grill, an electric grill, or the grill part of a conventional oven. The recipe for *Tandoori* Chicken is on p. 168.

MEAT TENDERIZERS

◆

In Indian cooking the most common method of tenderizing tougher cuts of meat is by marinating them in a spice-laced yogurt mixture. Another traditional Indian method is to add to the meat, while it is cooking, 1 or 2 betel nuts (*sopari*), known to contain enzymes that break down the muscle fibres of protein. (The tradition of chewing betel leaf [*paan*] with betel nut [*sopari*] among other digestives is common after a heavy meal, and the betel nut performs the same function.) Fillets, chops, and cutlets, which are generally deep fried or grilled, are tenderized by pounding the fibres with a heavy tool until they are broken.

Chicken is usually tenderized with the green papaya (*kacha papeeta*), the unripe fruit of the papaya plant (*Carica papaya*). The papaya is usually ground and rubbed onto the pieces of meat to marinate before the grilling process. The enzyme papain, present in the green papaya, breaks up the muscle fibres and makes the chicken tender. This is the source of the special plump, moist, and elastic texture of *tandoori* chicken, which cannot be produced by any other culinary process.

One of the limitations of the enzyme papain is that it does not penetrate deeply enough into the flesh of the chicken (on average, it penetrates about ⅛ in/3 mm into the surface of the meat). In order for the tenderizer to be effective, the meat should not be very thick. This is why very young chickens, weighing less than 2 lb/1 kg, are chosen for *tandoori* cooking. In addition, they are pricked thoroughly and slashed every 1–1½ in/2.5–4 cm to allow the tenderizer to penetrate as deeply as possible.

ABOUT SALTING FOOD

◆

Salt has been used in food since the beginning of time, not just as a preservative, but to perk up the hidden flavours of other ingredients and to improve the overall taste of the dish. When salting food, two factors must be considered: the strength of the salt itself and individual taste.

Most Westerners find Indian dishes, especially those with sauces, somewhat oversalted. This is because they often eat them straight. This is a mistake. Indian dishes (both main and side) are meant to be eaten with a staple – rice or bread – whose blandness mellows and counteracts the saltiness of the dishes, creating a proper balance. Another factor worth noting is that salt works to subdue the peppery taste in any particular dish. So you must be careful when omitting or drastically reducing the amount of salt in any Indian dish, because you may end up with food that's too hot. For this reason, in every recipe in this book I suggest that you check for salt just before serving.

In Indian cooking, especially in stir-fried vegetable preparations, salt is always added in the beginning of, or during, the cooking process. This allows the flavours to penetrate and distribute evenly. Salt is either omitted or added sparingly in the bread doughs because it produces a tough texture. In yogurt salads salt is always stirred in last, just before serving, because it tends to separate and thin the yogurt.

I always use coarse salt in all my cooking, because it is milder and more flavourful than other salts. It is, however, perfectly acceptable to use other salt, as long as you adjust its quantity in the recipe.

REFRIGERATING AND FREEZING

◆

One of the wonderful things about Indian food is that a great many dishes can be prepared well in advance, refrigerated or frozen, and reheated just before serving without losing the main flavouring or original texture.

Almost all the dishes that have gravies or sauces, as well as soups, most puréed vegetables, certain herb relishes, and certain breads can be frozen successfully. The secret of success lies not so much in the freezing as in the defrosting and reheating. One rule for successful defrosting that applies to all dishes is that you must not be in a hurry. The defrosting process needs to be carried out slowly, preferably overnight in the refrigerator. Only when the food has been thoroughly defrosted should it be reheated. In most instances you will find that the liquid has separated and has collected at the bottom of the container in the form of a gelatinous mass. No need for alarm. Do not rush to stir it all up and mix it in; this is a sure way to destroy the fragile texture of the meat and vegetable pieces. Begin by placing the pan on very low heat. When the liquid comes just to a simmer, gently stir the mixture with a fork. This method of slow heating allows the food pieces to absorb the moisture back into their tissues, thus restoring their firmness and body. It is essential that the meat be stirred with a fork, and not a spoon, because it is gentler.

One drawback to freezing food is that most of the fresh herbs, some spices, and salt lose part of their fragrance and potency. Therefore, be sure to taste the dishes and readjust the salt and seasonings before reheating. Usually, a pinch of *Mughal garam masala, garam masala,* or some powdered roasted cumin seeds, and some chopped fresh herbs folded into the dish just before serving, do the trick in reviving all the flavours.

Most fried, grilled, and roasted foods, yogurt salads, puddings, and rice preparations do not freeze successfully; they lose both flavour and texture in the process. Therefore, I caution against freezing them. They can, however, be refrigerated successfully.

THE SENSES

◆

Of the human senses, the visual sense and the sense of smell are the most important in Indian cooking. They are what Indian cooks rely upon most often. This is because Indian chefs, unlike most others, never taste a dish while it is cooking or, for that matter, even after it is cooked, to check for flavours and 'doneness.' This is because in most parts of India there are religious or social taboos against putting food in one's mouth while it is cooking. Among certain sects the food has to be offered to the gods for their blessings before mortals can consider themselves worthy of putting it in their mouths. Therefore, out of sheer necessity, Indian cooks develop a greater sensitivity to and a deeper understanding of the relationships between aromas, textures, and flavours from a very early age. Indian cooks believe that if a dish looks and smells right, then it has got to taste good. An experienced eye can often gauge exactly whether the onions are fried to the correct degree of brownness, whether the sauce has achieved the appropriate glaze, and if the colour and consistency of the gravy are in proper balance. So, too, can a sensitive Indian nose tell whether the spices are cooked and if they are harmoniously blended together in the dish.

Equally important is the sense of feel, especially in kneading bread dough and in making sweetmeats, fudges, and meat dishes. With the touch of a finger an Indian cook can tell if enough liquid has been incorporated into the dough and if it has been kneaded enough. Or with a gentle stir of a spoon, know if the pieces of meat are cooked to perfection. (When fully cooked, they move like marshmallows or float like dumplings in the sauce, without any resistance.)

Before you start exercising and relying upon the judgement of these senses, you must first familiarize yourself with the dishes and the techniques for cooking them, and develop the tactile ability to know what to expect at the end of any process. In other words, what the dish should smell, look, and taste like. To help you reproduce the dishes exactly as I have prepared them, I have given detailed explanations of each process for each recipe in this book wherever necessary. After you create the dish a few times in your own kitchen, the flavours and the details of the process should register in your mind. Then you will find yourself relying more and more upon your senses, and beginning to cook with the same spontaneity that I do.

A final word of advice: if you are well prepared, with all the ingredients measured and ready to be added at a moment's notice, the whole process of Indian cooking will be much simplified. Read the recipes carefully and fully. Many recipes call for preliminary procedures, such as soaking, resting, and marinating. Therefore, be sure to notice these considerations and make allowances for time.

The lengths of time suggested in all the recipes are approximate. They will vary depending upon the stove, the burner, the type and size of the pan you are using, and also the temperature of the ingredients. Therefore, you should look for the suggested texture, colour, or consistency indicated in the recipe.

PLANNING AND SERVING INDIAN MEALS

◆

There is one fundamental difference between the Western and Indian styles of planning and serving meals. A typical Western meal consists of several courses planned around a main course and served in several stages. A traditional Indian meal, on the other hand, consists of several courses which are all served at once and has no such thing as a main course. There is, however, a main dish. This status is given to a particularly elaborate preparation that is a culinary creation in and of itself.

Most nonvegetarian dishes are considered main dishes simply for economic reasons. The cost of meat in India is about five times that of vegetables; poultry and shellfish cost twice as much as meat. The quantity of the main dish is thus based not upon the number of people to be served, as in the West, but upon the family's budget. All the dishes are either placed at the centre of the table, so that everyone can help himself to each dish, or served in the classic manner in a *thali*. A *thali* is a large, rimmed metal plate containing several small metal bowls (*katoori*). The various dishes, including soup and dessert, are served in these small bowls. The wafers, relishes, and pickles are put directly in one corner of the plate and the centre of the plate is reserved for the staple rice or bread.

Indian food is traditionally eaten with the fingers. In urban homes, however, spoons and forks are widely used especially in eating rice and soupy dishes. Indians believe that food does not taste quite the same when eaten with a fork or spoon, and using bread as an eating utensil really does seem logical, because Indian breads are highly pliable. It is, therefore, easy to tear a piece of the bread and use it as a scoop or to wrap it around a piece of meat or vegetable. Eating rice with one's fingers, especially when it is mixed with soupy sauces, is a different matter, however. Even experts would agree that it is a very tricky affair for which a long apprenticeship is a prerequisite. I personally prefer to use a fork or spoon. Traditionalists, however, would argue to the contrary.

MENU PLANNING

◆

An Indian meal essentially consists of three dishes: a main dish, a side dish, and a staple. Of course there is nothing to prevent you serving more than one dish from each category – particularly several side dishes – as is commonly done at parties and feasts. You can also omit a main or side dish altogether for light meals. The important thing to remember is that a staple must accompany an Indian meal.

A *main dish* can either be nonvegetarian or vegetarian. The nonvegetarian main dish can consist of meat, poultry, fish, shellfish, or eggs. A vegetarian main dish, on the other hand, consists of vegetables, *dal* of all varieties, or Indian cheese.

A *side dish* can either be vegetables or *dal* or yogurt salads. These vegetable preparations differ from the vegetable main dishes in that they are usually stir-fried and require very little time to prepare. *Dal* preparations are basically soupy purées flavoured with fragrant spices and herbs. They are usually used for dipping breads, or they are poured over rice, mixed, and eaten. Yogurt salads consist of various ingredients – such as raw or cooked vegetables, fruits, nuts, dumplings – all or some of which are folded into the yogurt. These salads are very light and can serve as simple unfilling meals, especially good during the summer.

An accompanying staple can be either rice or bread. An Indian meal is not complete without a bread or a rice dish. This actually makes a lot of sense, because the consistency of many Indian dishes is much like a thick soup or a stew; both are difficult to eat with a fork. Also, without a staple, you cannot do full justice to the wonderful sauce, which is the best part of the dish. Generally rice is served with the soupier dishes, and bread with the drier ones. Rice acts as a sponge to soak up the juices of the sauce, making the dish much easier to handle and eat. A fairly dry piece of meat or vegetable can be scooped up with a piece of bread, but if the sauce is too thin, the bread may fall apart when manoeuvred and dipped. This is why most dishes, including the pulse preparations served in areas where bread is the staple, as in the North, are much drier and have thick, almost nonexistent gravies. In the South, where rice is the staple, the dishes are soupy and much like broth.

In order to simplify menu planning, the recipes in this book are organized by categories of dishes, as described above: main dish, side dish, accompanying staple, and so on. To plan a meal, simply pick a dish from any category and follow the menu planning suggestions given at the end of the recipe. Or pick a dish from each category, taking particular care to ensure diversity in flavour, colour, and texture, yet choosing the dishes so that they blend and complement each other.

NOTE In Indian cooking, potatoes, sweet potatoes, yams, and other starchy roots are treated as vegetables; they are not categorized as starches and grouped with rice and bread as in Western cooking. Therefore, an Indian meal may very well be composed of the main dish Whole Potatoes in Spicy Yogurt Gravy (*Dum Aloo*, p. 191), the side dish Lucknow Sour Lentils (*Lakhnawi Khatti Dal*, p. 241), and the accompanying staple Fragrant Pilaf Banaras Style (*Banarasi Pullao*, p. 263). This is definitely not an example of a well-balanced diet, because all the dishes are high in carbohydrates, but as far as taste, texture, and aroma are concerned, they blend exquisitely.

There are a few general rules worth noting when planning an Indian menu. If the main dish is a *dal*, the side dish should be a vegetable. However, if the main dish is a vegetable, then the side dish could be either a *dal* or vegetables. In other words, it is perfectly acceptable to serve two vegetable preparations, but not two *dal* dishes, as this would make the meal very heavy.

If the main dish is an elegant pilaf, no additional accompanying staple is necessary, because the pilaf contains rice.

If the main dish contains both meat and vegetables, the side dish may be omitted, but increase the quantity of the main dish to compensate for the omitted dish.

Traditionally in India, appetizers and sweetmeats are eaten like snacks, with a beverage, at just about any hour of the day. Among the more affluent Indians, however, appetizers are now served with cocktails. There are several appetizers that make an excellent first course. And, even though serving a beverage with sweetmeats at the end of an Indian meal is unconventional, I prefer to do so because it makes a perfect ending to the meal.

WHAT TO DRINK WITH AN INDIAN MEAL

◆

The drink most commonly served with an Indian meal is ice-cold water. Sometimes fresh lemonade, fruit punch, or yogurt drinks are served instead. The tradition of serving wine with a meal does not exist in India. This by no means suggest that there is no liquor in India. On the contrary, India has been producing alcoholic beverages since Vedic times. The ancient Indians brewed and drank *Vasa*, a liquor made from fermented rice. The holy priests and the noblemen drank a more refined brew called *Soma Rasa* (*Soma* means moon;

Rasa means juice) which was made from the Moon Creeper plant that once grew in the Himalayas. India today produces several varieties of alcohol, including whisky, gin, vodka, and rum. These are consumed primarily by men, because Indian women have, for the most part, traditionally abstained from alcoholic beverages.

What India does not have is good quality wine. This is because vineyards need high altitudes and a cool dry climate to flourish – and both are in limited supply in India. Whatever vineyards did exist were originally brought by the Moghuls from Persia; they planted grapes in the cool hills of the North. Unfortunately, the venture was not much of a success, since the wine had often turned to vinegar by the time it reached the Moghul courts in the arid city of Delhi. Also, the Moghuls found that the subtle bouquet of their wine was easily overpowered by the fierce Indian spices. They gradually gave up wine and settled for the cool *Sharbat* (fruit drinks) and fruit punches. Today, with the aid of modern farming techniques and storage equipment, India is producing all varieties of wine, although Indian viticulture has a long way to go.

I have found that beer, ale, and certain wines go well with Indian food. Beer and ale are excellent served with lunch, particularly on hot summer afternoons. In addition to being good thirst quenchers, they add a slight bite and bitterness which is a perfect complement to the spicy food. Sangria is also ideal as a luncheon drink, if you like a fruity taste. For a nonalcoholic drink there is nothing better than a homemade punch made with the fruits of the season; this is the official drink served at presidential dinners in India.

For suppers and formal dinners, I prefer to serve wine: chilled rosé with *tandoori* food and dishes that have cream, yogurt, and nut sauces; and hearty reds for dishes in onion and tomato gravy. I accompany fish and shellfish, no matter how they are prepared, with a chilled dry white wine.

Appetizers, Snacks, and Soups

In an Indian meal there is no equivalent to the Western starter. Appetizers are traditionally eaten the way *Dim Sum* are eaten in Chinese tea houses – as a snack, at any time of the day, and usually accompanying a beverage. But with the rise of an affluent middle class, appetizers have begun to find their way into Indian meals. Because of this new and great demand, many main course dishes have been modified slightly and served as first courses.

Indian snacks are traditionally eaten with a relish. There are different relishes to accompany different appetizers. Although not essential, they do provide an interesting contrast: tangy sweet or soothingly mellow against peppery hot or spicy food. They also perk up rather bland tasting snacks.

Until recently, a separate soup course would have been completely unthinkable as part of an Indian meal. Today, however, there are several soups, not to mention the famous Mulligatawny, that are often served as a separate first course. In fact, many new soups have been created for just this purpose.

APPETIZERS AND SNACKS

NAMKEEN

◆

CRAB MALABAR

KEKADA CHAT

◆

Crab Malabar, as the name suggests, is a speciality of Malabar, a coastal region in southern India known for the wealth of its shellfish. Traditionally, the dish is fairly hot and contains a lot of gravy so as to increase the number of servings. My recipe yields just enough fennel-laced, garlicky tomato gravy to coat the shellfish. This way, the crab meat may be enjoyed to its fullest. The crab must be sweet and succulent and the coriander utterly fresh and fragrant for this dish to taste perfect. For a variation, you may substitute cooked lobster meat, which is also very good.

FOR 6 PERSONS

◆

1 lb/500 g fresh or frozen cooked crab meat
3 tablespoons light vegetable oil
4 oz/125 g finely chopped onions
1 tablespoon finely chopped garlic
¼-½ teaspoon red pepper
1½ teaspoons paprika
⅓ teaspoon thyme (or ¼ teaspoon carom seeds, crushed)
¼ teaspoon fennel seeds, crushed
1½ lb/750 g peeled ripe tomatoes, cut into 1 in/2.5 cm cubes
Coarse salt
4 tablespoons finely chopped spring onions, including the green part
4 tablespoons coarsely chopped fresh coriander leaves

1 Pick over crab meat thoroughly, and cut into large pieces. If using frozen crab meat, thaw following directions on the package. Drain and reserve the juices. Set aside.

2 Heat the oil in a frying pan (one with a lid) and add onions. Cook onions over medium heat until wilted and lightly coloured, but not browned (about 5 minutes).

3 Add garlic and cook for an additional minute. Add red pepper, paprika, thyme (or carom), and fennel, stirring rapidly. Cook for 2 more minutes. Add ⅓ of the tomatoes and the reserved juices from crab meat (if using frozen crab meat). Lower heat and simmer, covered, until the sauce is reduced to a thick pulp (about 15 minutes). Turn off heat.

4 Fold in the crab meat. Add salt to taste. When cool, carefully fold in remaining tomatoes and spring onions, making sure not to break the fragile crab pieces.

5 Cover and refrigerate for at least 4 hours or until thoroughly chilled. Just before serving, fold in chopped coriander leaves, and serve over a bed of shredded lettuce.

NOTE The *chat* may be made a day ahead and kept refrigerated. In that case, the chopped coriander leaves should be folded in just before serving.

This exquisite first course must be followed by an equally subtle main dish. I prefer to serve yogurt- and cream-based Moghul dishes to contrast with this southern speciality. Examples include Lamb Braised in Aromatic Cream Sauce (p. 127), Yogurt-Braised Chicken (p. 159), Creamed Prawns (p. 182), and Royal Braised Vegetables in Cardamom Nut Sauce (p. 198). This also makes a marvellous light lunch or late supper main course, served hot.

COLD MINTED POTATOES

ALOO PODINA CHAT

◆

Chat is Indian salad; it is usually eaten by itself, as a snack or appetizer. There are two types of *chat*: one made with vegetables such as potatoes or *arbi*, a variety of starchy root; the other made with fruits such as bananas, guava, papaya, apples, or *chikoo*, an Indian fruit that resembles a kiwi in its shape. Its flesh, however, is sugar-sweet, and light brown in colour.

Of the many varieties of *chat*, the most popular are two *Aloo Chats*, one flavoured with mint and the other with spices. *Chat* is traditionally served on a flat serving plate accompanied by tooth picks for easy buffet serving with cocktails. *Chat*, as a general rule, is eaten cooled – never chilled, because chilling dims the fragrances of spices and herbs.

Waxy potatoes are best for making *Aloo Chat*, because when cooked and while still warm, they retain a tight-grained texture. When salad dressing is poured over these potatoes, they do not become mushy and fall apart, and they remain firm after being sliced.

FOR 8 PERSONS

◆

6 medium-sized potatoes
2 small cucumbers, 5-6 in/ 12.5-15 cm long
2 teaspoons coarse salt
2 tablespoons lemon juice
1 teaspoon ground roasted cumin seeds (p. 62)
1 teaspoon ground roasted coriander seeds (p. 62)
¼ teaspoon each of black and red pepper
½ teaspoon black salt (optional)
4 tablespoons chopped mint leaves

1 Boil potatoes in their jackets in water to cover until tender but firm. Drain and peel them. While still warm, cut them into cubes of uniform size, about ½ in/ 1 cm.

2 Peel cucumbers, and cut them in half, lengthwise. If the seeds look mature and hard, scrape them out and discard. Cut the cucumbers into the same size cubes as the potatoes.

3 Put potatoes and cucumbers in a bowl. Add coarse salt and lemon juice. Toss briefly to coat all the pieces. Add the remaining ingredients and toss again, carefully, so as not to break the pieces of potato. Cover the bowl and place it in the refrigerator to cool thoroughly (it should not be chilled). Check for salt, and serve heaped on lettuce leaves.

NOTE The *chat* may be made several hours ahead and kept refrigerated. Remove from the refrigerator about 15 minutes before you are ready to serve. To perk up flavours, sprinkle on a little ground roasted cumin seed.

This appetizer may be followed with any main dish except, of course, those containing potatoes. Try Chicken in Onion Tomato Gravy (p. 157), or Prawns with Mild Spices (p. 179).

COLD POTATO APPETIZER

ALOO CHAT

◆

FOR 8 PERSONS

◆

1 tablespoon Chat Masala, *(see recipe below)*
3 fl oz/ 10 cl cold water
6 medium-sized potatoes
1 lb/ 500 g ripe tomatoes, cut into ½ in/ 1 cm cubes
4 tablespoons finely chopped onions
3-4 tablespoons coarsely chopped coriander leaves
1 teaspoon ground roasted cumin seeds (p. 62)
Coarse salt
Juice of ½ a medium-sized lemon

1 Mix the *chat masala* with the water and set aside.

2 Boil potatoes in their jackets, in water to cover, until tender but firm. Drain and peel them. Cut the potatoes into ½ in/1 cm cubes, put them in a bowl, and while still warm, pour the *masala* mixture over them. Mix the potatoes, carefully, to distribute the spices. Let rest, uncovered, at room temperature, until potatoes have had time to absorb the spices (about 10-15 minutes), stirring a few times.

3 Add chopped tomatoes, onions, and coriander leaves to the potatoes but *do not stir the mixture.* Cover the bowl and place it in the refrigerator until the potatoes are fully cooled – they should *not* be chilled. This will take 30 minutes.

4 Take the bowl from the refrigerator and gently stir to mix all the ingredients. Sprinkle the cumin, salt, and lemon juice to taste. Toss and serve over lettuce leaves.

NOTE The *chat* may be made several hours ahead and kept refrigerated. Remove from refrigerator about 15 minutes before you are ready to serve. To perk up flavours, sprinkle on a little ground roasted cumin seed.

CHAT MASALA To make homemade *chat masala*, mix ¾ teaspoon ground roasted cumin seeds with ¼ teaspoon each of red pepper, black pepper, ground asafetida, mango powder, ½ teaspoon black salt, and ¾ teaspoon coarse salt.

MOGHUL KEBABS WITH RAISIN STUFFING

HUSSAINI KABAB

◆

These kebabs, fragrant with a subtle blend of Moghul spices, are a classic example of Moghul cooking. They are shaped like small sausages, stuffed with raisins and almonds, and cooked in a frying pan. To serve these kebabs as hors d'oeuvres, roll them into small, cocktail-size sausages and cook them for about 8-10 minutes. And if you finely crush the stuffing, you will find it much easier to stuff the kebabs.

FOR 8 PERSONS (MAKES 16 KEBABS)

◆

THE KEBABS
1 lb/ 500 g minced beef or lean minced lamb
2 teaspoons finely chopped garlic
1½ teaspoons finely chopped fresh ginger root
1 teaspoon black cumin seeds, crushed (or substitute 1 teaspoon ground cumin)
1 teaspoon ground coriander
1 teaspoon paprika
1 teaspoon Mughal garam masala (p. 41)
½ teaspoon black pepper
⅛ teaspoon ground asafetida
4 tablespoons bread crumbs
1 tablespoon sweet butter
1 large egg, lightly beaten
1¼ teaspoons coarse salt
THE STUFFING
2 tablespoons blanched chopped almonds
2 tablespoons seedless raisins
2 tablespoons light vegetable oil for frying

1 Put all the ingredients for the kebabs in a bowl, and mix thoroughly. Cover, and let the mixture rest for ½ hour. (The kebab mixture may be made ahead and refrigerated for up to 2 days, or frozen. Defrost thoroughly before proceeding with the recipe.)

2 Mix almonds and raisins together for stuffing.

3 Divide the kebab mixture into 16 equal portions. Shape each into a 'sausage'. Make a lengthwise depression in the centre of each kebab, and fill with stuffing (about ¾ teaspoon). Pinch meat closed over the stuffing, reshaping each sausage as you go along. Continue with the rest of the meat mixture the same way. (The stuffed kebabs can be shaped several hours ahead and kept covered and refrigerated until you are ready to fry them.)

4 When ready to fry, heat the oil in a frying pan – preferably a non-stick one – for a minute, and add the kebabs in one layer. Repeat the cooking process if the pan is not large enough to accommodate all the kebabs. Fry the kebabs over medium heat, turning them often, until they are cooked and browned all over (about 15 minutes for beef, 25 minutes for lamb). The kebabs may also be grilled. Serve these kebabs accompanied by Raw Onion Relish (*Kache Piaz*, p. 304) or Roasted Onions (*Bhone Piaz*, p. 227).

These kebabs are fairly substantial; therefore the main dish that follows should be very light and contain a lot of sauce. You might try light fish or shellfish dishes such as Prawns Poached in Coconut Milk with Fresh Herbs (p. 181), or Fish in Velvet Yogurt Sauce (p. 187), or for a vegetable dish, try Mixed Lentils and Vegetable Stew (p. 208). You can also serve these kebabs as a main dish (this recipe will serve 3-4 persons). To keep the meal light, pair them with a simple lentil purée, such as Lentils with Garlic Butter (p. 238), and plain cooked rice (p. 256).

KEBAB PATTIES LACED WITH GINGER AND MINT

SHAMME KABAB

◆

Shamme Kabab, bursting with the fragrance of mint and ginger, is the most exquisitely flavoured of all kebabs. Beef cannot be substituted for lamb in this kebab, because the taste of lamb is essential in creating the authentic flavour of this dish.

AN IMPORTANT POINT The cooked kebab mixture should be fairly thick, like bread dough, before you form it into patties. Before they are fried, the kebabs are coated only with a thin film of egg white to impart a shiny glaze. If the meat mixture is not dry enough to hold its shape, it will spatter and scatter into the oil.

FOR 8-12 PERSONS (MAKES 24 KEBABS)

◆

FOR COOKING THE MEAT
1 lb/500 g lean minced lamb
3 oz/90 g yellow split peas (channa dal)
2 oz/60 g finely chopped onions
2½ tablespoons finely chopped garlic
1 tablespoon finely chopped fresh ginger root
1 teaspoon ground cumin
½ teaspoon ground cardamom
¼ teaspoon ground cloves
1 teaspoon black pepper
½ teaspoon red pepper
1½ teaspoons coarse salt
½ pint/30 cl cold water
FOR FLAVOURING THE MEAT
1 tablespoon peanut oil
1 medium-sized onion, finely chopped
1-2 green chilies, seeded and coarsely chopped
1 oz/30 g mint leaves, coarsely chopped
1 teaspoon lemon juice
Peanut or corn oil, to fill a frying pan to a depth of ¾ in/2 cm
Whites of 2 medium-sized eggs, lightly beaten

1 Put all the ingredients for cooking the meat into a heavy saucepan. Over medium-high heat bring the mixture to the boil. Lower heat to medium and cook, covered, until the meat is fully cooked and the water totally absorbed into the meat (about 45 minutes). If there is still liquid remaining, uncover, and cook briskly over medium-high heat until the moisture evaporates and the meat mixture looks dry. (It is essential that the meat mixture be very dry; otherwise the patties will disintegrate during frying. If, for any reason, your meat mixture does not dry during brisk cooking, add about 1 oz/30 g of dry breadcrumbs to it and mix well. The crumbs will soak up the excess moisture.)

2 In a small frying pan, heat the oil and add onions. Over medium-high heat, fry the onions until they turn caramel brown (about 10 minutes), stirring constantly to prevent burning.

3 Add the fried onions along with the green chilies, mint, and lemon juice to the meat mixture. Grind the mixture in a meat grinder with the fine blade attachment or in a food processor. *Be careful not to make a paste of this.* It should have a coarse grainy texture, yet be smooth enough to be shaped into patties and fried. (The kebab mixture can be made ahead and refrigerated up to 2 days, or frozen. Defrost thoroughly before proceeding with the recipe.)

4 Divide the meat mixture into 24 equal portions. Shape the pieces into 2 in/5 cm round patties. (The kebabs can be shaped several hours ahead and kept covered and refrigerated until you are ready to fry them.)

5 When ready to fry, heat the oil in a *kadhai* or frying pan until hot (350°F/175°C). Dip kebabs in beaten egg whites and slip them into the oil. Add no more kebabs than can easily be accommodated in one layer in the pan. Brown them evenly on both sides (about 1 minute for each side). Take them out with a slotted spoon and drain on paper towels. Continue with the remaining patties. Serve hot accompanied by Roasted Onions (*Bhone Piaz*, p. 227).

NOTE The kebabs may be made several hours ahead and, just before serving, reheated, loosely covered with foil, in a preheated 375°F/160°C/Gas 5 oven for 12-15 minutes.

These fritters blend with just about any main dish, though a lamb or beef dish might seem a little redundant. To keep the meal light, try serving a vegetarian main dish, such as Cauliflower, Green Peas, and Potatoes in Spicy Herb Sauce (p. 189). You may also serve these kebabs as a main dish (this recipe will serve 6) over a bed of vegetable pilaf, such as The Emperor's Pilaf with Black Mushrooms (p. 268).

FRITTERS

◆

Indian fritters are in a class by themselves. What distinguishes them is their spicy coating of chick-pea flour (*besan*) batter. They are made with vegetables, such as broccoli, cauliflower, aubergine, onions, plantain (green bananas), potatoes, spring onions, shallots, spinach, tomatoes, and courgettes; with Indian cheese (*paneer*); and with chicken, prawns, and fish.

Fritters are either batter-dipped or spoon-fried. Batter-dipped fritters are made by dipping the pieces of vegetables, cheese, meat, or fish in batter, dropping them in hot oil, and frying. Spooned fritters are made only with vegetables, which are folded into a thick pastelike batter and then spooned into hot oil and fried slowly over low heat, which enables them to become crisp and crunchy.

Sometimes a little baking soda is added to fritter batter to give the coating a light and fluffy texture; sometimes the fritters are refried to give them an even crisper texture.

A crucial ingredient in successful fritters is the oil. *It must be fresh and sweet-smelling so that it will not mask the subtle flavour of the food.* I never use the same oil twice for frying fritters, because it loses its gentle flavour when exposed to prolonged high heat. After frying the fritters, I strain the oil through a double layer of muslin and use it for cooking robust-flavoured dishes that contain onions or tomatoes. Always store used oil in a cool place.

ONION FRITTERS

PIAZ PAKODE

◆

These fritters have a crunchy texture on the outside and are soft inside. They are also wonderful when made with shallots.

FOR 6-8 PERSONS

◆

THE BATTER
4 oz/ 125 g unsifted chick-pea flour (besan)
2 teaspoons peanut or corn oil, or melted vegetable shortening
2 medium-sized onions
Peanut or corn oil, enough to fill a kadhai *or large casserole to a depth of 2 in/ 5 cm*
1 teaspoon ground cumin
1½ teaspoons coarse salt
1-2 green chilies, seeded and minced
4 fl oz/ 12.5 cl warm water

1 Sift the flour into a large bowl. Rub the 2 teaspoons oil or shortening into it with the fingers until the dough resembles breadcrumbs. Stir in cumin, salt, and chilies. Add water in a thin stream, constantly beating the mixture with an electric beater, wire whisk, or with your hands. The batter should be very thick and smooth. (To make the batter in a food processor or in an electric blender, put all the ingredients into the container of the machine and process until thoroughly blended and smooth. Then transfer the mixture to a bowl.)

2 Beat the batter vigorously for 10 minutes or until it turns pale, light, and fluffy. Cover the bowl and let the batter rest in a warm place for ½ hour. (This resting is essential because, in addition to fermenting the batter, it lightens it to the almost foamy consistency that is necessary if the fritter is to be spongy.)

3 While the batter is resting, peel and thinly slice the onions. When ready to fry, add sliced onions to the batter and mix thoroughly. The mixture will look coarse and lumpy.

4 Heat oil in a *kadhai* or frying pan until very hot but not smoking (375°/190°C). Gently drop the onion batter mixture, in 2-tablespoon amounts, into the oil. Make about 6-8 fritters at a time. When the fritters are added, the temperature of the oil will drop automatically to around 300°F/150°C. Keep the temperature of the oil at this low point by regulating the heat between medium-high and medium-low (the oil should be bubbling gently). This will allow the fritters to cook thoroughly before browning. Also the slow frying enables the fritters to develop a crackling crisp texture. Fry, stirring and turning them, until they are golden brown all over (about 10 minutes). Take out the fritters with a slotted spoon, and drain them on paper towels. Continue with the rest of the onion batter mixture the same way. Serve hot or warm, accompanied by Fresh Mint Relish (p. 309).

NOTE The fritters may be made several hours ahead, and reheated just before serving, by refrying them briefly (about 1 minute) in hot oil (375°F/190°C), providing the fritters are a little underdone and pale brown. This last frying will thus both warm and brown them.

There is no appetizer more authentically Indian than these crisp fragrant fritters. The only thing to remember is not to serve too many of them; they are very filling and can ruin a perfectly planned meal. These fritters can precede almost any main course, and also make an ideal dish for high tea.

CAULIFLOWER FRITTERS

GOBHI PAKODE

◆

These crisp fritters studded with coriander seeds are a sure winner. Only use a cauliflower that is young and fresh. The fritters may also be served in place of a side dish, especially with other fried food.

FOR 8 PERSONS

◆

1 large head, or 2 small heads, cauliflower
THE BATTER
6 oz/180 g unsifted chick-pea flour (besan)
2 teaspoons peanut or corn oil
2 teaspoons coriander seeds, crushed
¼ teaspoon red pepper (optional)
2 teaspoons coarse salt
½ pint/30 cl cold water
Peanut or corn oil, enough to fill a kadhai *or large casserole to a depth of 2 in/5 cm*

1 Break and separate the cauliflower into florets. Wash them under running cold water, drain, and set aside.

2 Sift the flour into a large bowl. Rub oil or shortening into it. Stir in coriander, red pepper (if you are using it), and salt. Gradually add water in a thin slow, steady stream, beating the mixture all the while with an electric beater, wire whisk, or with your hands. The batter should be thin and smooth. To make the batter in a food processor or in an electric blender, put all the batter ingredients into the container of the machine and process until thoroughly blended and smooth. Transfer the batter to a large bowl.

3 Cover the bowl and let the batter rest for at least ½ hour in a warm place. This will ferment it slightly, and make it light and fluffy. (The batter may be made a day ahead and kept refrigerated. Remove from refrigerator and bring to room temperature before use.)

4 Heat the oil in a *kadhai* or large casserole, until very hot but not smoking (375°F/190°C). Dip a piece of the cauliflower into the batter, and slip the coated floret into the hot oil. When several batter-coated florets have been added, the temperature of the oil will automatically drop to around

300°F/150°C. Keep the temperature of the oil at this low point by regulating the heat between medium-high and medium-low (the oil should be gently bubbling). This will allow the fritters to cook slowly and brown gently, thus developing a golden, crackling crisp crust. Fry, stirring and turning the fritters until they are pale golden all over – they should not get brown – about 10-12 minutes. Transfer the fritters with a slotted spoon to a baking sheet lined with several sheets of paper towel, to drain. Continue with the rest of the cauliflower pieces the same way. Serve hot.

NOTE The fritters may be made several hours ahead, and reheated just before serving, either in a 375°F/190°C/Gas 5 preheated oven, uncovered, for 5-7 minutes, or by refrying in hot oil (375°F/190°C) for one minute. If refried, they must once again be drained on paper towels before serving.

PRAWN FRITTERS

JHEENGA PAKODE

◆

Fragrant with ginger root, garlic, and a hint of green chili pepper, these fritters are among my very favourites. The coating is light, and fluffy, it gets its unusual flavour and texture from a batter made with cornflour, chick-pea flour, and baking powder. The prawns get their piquant flavour from long marination in a blend of ginger root, garlic, green chilies, and a good dose of lemon juice.

NOTE This batter is equally suitable for use with crab meat, lobster meat, and firm fleshed fish.

FOR 6-8 PERSONS

◆

1 lb/500 g large prawns
1 teaspoon minced garlic
1 tablespoon grated or finely chopped fresh ginger root
1-2 green chilies, seeded and minced
½ teaspoon coarse salt
Juice of ¼ lemon

THE BATTER
3½ oz/ 100 g cornflour
3 tablespoons unsifted chick-pea flour (besan) or plain flour
3 tablespoons peanut or corn oil
¼ teaspoon red pepper
1 teaspoon coarse salt
1 tablespoon baking powder
2 large eggs
3 tablespoons cold water
Peanut or corn oil, enough to fill a kadhai or large casserole to a depth of 2 in/5 cm

1 Shell (leaving the tail part on) and devein the prawns. Rinse under cold water and pat dry with kitchen towels.

2 Place the prawns in a bowl. Add garlic, ginger root, chilies, salt, and lemon juice. Mix thoroughly to distribute the marinade evenly over them. Cover and marinate for 2 hours at room temperature, or overnight in the refrigerator, turning from time to time. A longer marinating time is better for flavour.

3 Put all the ingredients of the batter into a bowl and beat, using an electric beater, whisk, fork, or your hands, until thoroughly blended and free of any lumps. (The batter may be mixed in an electric blender or food processor.) Cover and let the batter rest for ½ hour.

4 When ready to fry the fritters, heat the oil in a *kadhai* or casserole until very hot (350-375°F/175-190°C). Hold each prawn by its tail and dip it into the batter. Hold it briefly over the bowl to let excess drip off, and gently drop the prawn into the oil. Fry only 6-8 at a time, so that there is ample room for them to float easily on the oil.

Fry the prawns for 3 minutes, then flip them over with a slotted spoon or tongs, and continue frying until they are light golden on both sides. Take the fritters out with a slotted spoon, and drain on paper towels. Continue with the remaining prawns the same way. Serve hot, accompanied by Sweet Tomato Relish (p. 313).

These fritters may be followed by any main dish. Try Beef in Fragrant Spinach Sauce (p. 138), or, for a complete seafood dinner, Prawns with Mild Spices (p. 179). For a light meal, omit the main dish, and serve these fritters with a pilaf such as Saffron Pilaf with Peaches (p. 266), or Indian Fried Rice (p. 261).

DUMPLINGS

◆

Dumplings originated to transform the everyday mundane *dal* into something different and interesting. The results were so good that today dumplings are an important part of Indian cooking. They are made by soaking dried peas and beans until soft and grinding them into a fine thick paste that looks almost like soft dough. The paste is then set to rise in a warm place. When risen, light and fluffy, it is scooped up with the fingers, shaped into different forms, dropped into the hot oil, and fried. This whole process, a traditional one, is somewhat tedious and time-consuming. For this reason, dumpling making in India is not an everyday affair.

Dumplings can be made quite effortlessly in less time (cutting down on the soaking and grinding, and totally eliminating rising time) by using a food processor. The machine not only grinds the beans in a matter of minutes to a smooth, silky, light-textured paste, it also warms the batter, thus aiding the dumplings to puff up while frying. You can use an electric blender to grind the beans, but since it does not beat in the air as well as a food processor does, you will need to beat the batter first and then allow it to rise by resting before making the dumplings.

These two dumpling recipes take a little time and effort to make, but the results will prove worthwhile.

SPINACH AND MUNG BEAN DUMPLINGS

MOONG BADIAN

◆

These golden mung bean dumplings, streaked with shreds of spinach leaves, are absolutely irresistible. A delicacy from the State of Uttar Pradesh, they can be served as a snack at any time of the day.

FOR 4-6 PERSONS (MAKES 24 1½ in/4 cm

DUMPLINGS)

◆

6 oz/180 g yellow split mung beans (moong dal)
4 oz/125 g fresh spinach, stemmed, washed and shredded
1 tablespoon finely chopped coriander leaves
1-2 green chilies, seeded and thinly sliced
⅛ teaspoon baking powder
¾ teaspoon coarse salt
Peanut or corn oil, enough to fill a kadhai *or large casserole to a depth of 2 in/5 cm*

1 Pick over, clean, and wash mung beans, following the instructions given for cleaning *dal* on p. 235.

2 Put the mung beans in a bowl and add enough water to cover the beans by at least 1½ in/4 cm. Let them soak for 4 hours. Drain and rinse.

3 TO MAKE THE PASTE IN A FOOD PROCESSOR Attach metal cutting blade. Put the drained beans in the container with 4 fl oz/12.5 cl water and process for 5-6 minutes, turning the machine on and off every 15-20 seconds and scraping down sides of container from time to time. Paste made in a food processor is extremely light and fluffy; there is no need to beat it or let it rest before frying.

IN A BLENDER It is more difficult to make the bean paste in a blender, but it can be done. Whether you grind the drained beans first and then gradually add 4 fl oz/12.5 cl water to make a paste, or put the water in the blender container and gradually add the beans, you will have to run the blender off and on every few seconds, scrape down the sides, and push the paste from the blade with a rubber spatula. Blend until the paste is perfectly smooth (about 4-5 minutes). Do not add any more liquid than necessary, as the paste should be fairly thick. Transfer to a clean bowl and beat, using an electric beater or a wire whisk, until very pale, light, and fluffy (at least 5 minutes). Cover, and let the paste rest in a warm place for at least 2 hours. (The beating and resting steps are not essential but are recommended because they will ferment the paste and cause it to rise, producing an even lighter and fluffier texture.)

4 When ready to fry the dumplings, stir the remaining ingredients, except for oil, into the paste. *Do not overblend or the mixture will become dense, which will in turn make the dumplings hard and chewy.*

5 Heat the oil in a *kadhai* or frying pan until very hot but not smoking (375°F/190°C). Drop a heaped teaspoon of the bean mixture into the hot oil. Fry 8-12 dumplings at a time, making sure not to overcrowd the frying pan. Fry, stirring and turning, until dumplings are light golden (about 4-5 minutes). Take them out with a slotted spoon, and drain on paper towels. Continue with the rest of the bean mixture the same way. Serve hot accompanied by Fresh Mint Relish (p. 309) or Mint Coriander Dip (p. 310).

NOTE These dumplings can be made several hours ahead and, just before serving, reheated, loosely covered in a preheated 350°F/175°C/Gas 4 oven for 12-15 minutes.

The dumplings should be followed by a main dish containing a spicy sauce, such as Green Peas and Indian Cheese in Fragrant Tomato Sauce (p. 196).

SILKY BEAN DUMPLINGS

BADE

◆

These dumplings have a silky and fluffy interior. The beans are soaked and puréed to a thick paste, which is then formed into small patties with holes in the centre. When they are fried, they puff up and look like doughnuts. The shaping of the bean dumplings takes a little time and effort; a simpler method, followed by many Indian cooks as well, is to dip your hand in cold water, scoop up 2-3 tablespoons of bean paste, shape it into a rough ball, and drop it into the hot oil, and fry. They are good to eat by themselves, or soaked in spice-laced yogurt and served as a salad.

FOR 8-12 PERSONS (MAKES 24 DUMPLINGS)

◆

6 oz/180 g white split gram beans (urad dal)
2 tablespoons finely chopped onions
1 tablespoon finely chopped fresh ginger root
2 green chilies, seeded and chopped
1 tablespoon ground coriander
⅛ teaspoon baking soda
1⅓ teaspoons coarse salt
2 tablespoons peanut or corn oil
Peanut or corn oil, enough to fill a kadhai or large casserole to a depth of 2 in/5 cm

1 Pick, clean, and wash gram beans, following the instructions for cleaning *dal* on p. 235.
2 Put the beans in a bowl, add enough water to cover by at least 2 in/5 cm, and let them soak for 4 hours. Drain and rinse the beans.
3 TO MAKE THE PASTE IN A FOOD PROCESSOR Attach metal cutting blade. Put the drained beans in the container with 4 fl oz/12.5 cl water and process for 5-6 minutes, turning the machine on and off every 15-20 seconds and scraping down sides of container from time to time. Paste made in a food processor is extremely light and fluffy; there is no need to beat it or let it rest before frying.

IN A BLENDER It is more difficult to make the bean paste in a blender, but it can be done. Whether you grind the drained beans first and then gradually add

4 fl oz/12.5 cl water to make a paste, or put the water in the blender container and gradually add the beans, you will have to turn the blender off and on every few seconds, scrape down the sides, and push the paste from the blade with a rubber spatula. Blend until the paste is perfectly smooth (about 4-5 minutes). Transfer the bean paste to a clean bowl and beat with an electric beater, wire whisk, or fork until light and fluffy. (It will take at least 10 minutes of beating with wire whisk or fork, and 5 minutes with the electric beater.) Cover and let the paste rest in a warm place for at least 4 hours. (The beating and resting steps are not essential, but are recommended, because they ferment the batter, causing it to become even more light and foamy.)

4 When ready to fry the dumplings, stir all the remaining ingredients except any of the oil into the paste. Do not overblend, or the paste will become dense and the finished dumplings hard and tough.

5 Cut 6 squares of greaseproof paper, 6 × 6 in/15 × 15 cm. Put the 2 tablespoons of oil in a small bowl, fill another small bowl with cold water, and keep these three items close to where you will fry the dumplings.

6 Make one at a time. Place one piece of greaseproof paper on the work board and brush it with some of the oil. Then, first dipping your fingers in the cold water, scoop up enough of the bean mixture to form a ball the size of a golf ball. Drop it onto the oiled paper. Using your fingers, flatten the ball into a 2 in/5 cm round patty. With your forefinger make a hole in the centre of the patty. The patty should now resemble a small doughnut. Make 5 more patties. When you have formed all 6 patties, you are ready to fry the first batch. (You will make 4 batches altogether.)

7 Heat the large quantity of oil in a *kadhai* or large pan until moderately hot (325°–350°F/165°–175°C).

8 Lift one piece of greaseproof paper at a time, with the patty on it, and hold it right over the hot oil. Using a rubber spatula or a wide knife to guide it, slide the patty gently off the paper and into the hot oil. Slide the remaining five patties into the oil the same way. Fry on one side for 3 minutes, then very carefully flip them over with a slotted spoon, and continue frying until the dumplings are light golden on both sides. Drain the dumplings on paper towels. Continue with the remaining bean mixture the same way. Serve hot with Coconut Relish (p. 311), or Sweet and Sour Tamarind Relish (p. 315).

NOTE These dumplings can be made several hours ahead and just before serving, reheated, loosely covered, in a preheated 350°F/175°C/Gas 4 oven for 12-15 minutes.

SAVOURY PASTRIES WITH SPICY POTATO FILLING

ALOO SAMOSA

◆

Samosas are the most traditional snacks of India. They are so delicious that Indians often make a meal of them. *Samosas* are stuffed with either potatoes or minced meat (*keema*), but *Aloo Samosa* is the more popular. *Samosas* take some time to make, since both the filling and the dough have to be prepared before rolling, filling, shaping, and frying.

MAKES 32 SAVOURY PASTRIES

◆

THE PASTRY DOUGH
6 oz/180 g plain flour
1 teaspoon coarse salt
4 tablespoons vegetable shortening
6-7 tablespoons cold water
THE SPICY POTATO FILLING
4 tablespoons vegetable shortening, or light vegetable oil
2 teaspoons coriander seeds
3 oz/90 g finely chopped onions
1½ teaspoons finely chopped fresh ginger root
7 medium-sized potatoes, boiled till soft, peeled, and cut into ½ in/1 cm cubes
3 oz/90 g cooked shelled green peas
2-3 green chilies, seeded and chopped, or ¼ teaspoon red pepper
1¼ teaspoons garam masala (p. 42)
2 teaspoons ground pomegranate seeds, or 1 tablespoon lemon juice
2 teaspoons coarse salt
5-6 tablespoons flour for dusting
Peanut or corn oil, enough to fill a kadhai or large casserole to a depth of 3 in/7.5 cm

1 Mix flour and salt in a large bowl. Rub shortening into the flour with your fingertips, until the mixture resembles breadcrumbs. Pour 6 tablespoons water over the flour, and mix. Add the remaining tablespoon in droplets, until all the flour adheres together in a mass that can be kneaded.

2 Place the dough on a marble or wooden board. Coat your fingers with a little oil to prevent the dough from sticking, and knead the dough for 10 minutes. This will be a firm but pliable dough, not at all sticky. Cover with a towel or plastic film, and let the dough rest for half an hour. (The dough may be made a day in advance and kept refrigerated, tightly sealed in foil. Remove from refrigerator about 30 minutes before you are ready to roll it out.)

TO MAKE THE DOUGH USING A FOOD PROCESSOR Put the flour and salt into the container of the food processor, with steel cutting blade attached. Process for a few seconds to mix them. Add shortening, and process, turning the machine on and off, until the fat is well distributed through the flour. Add the water through the feed tube, with the motor running, until ball of dough forms on blades (about 15 seconds). Take out the dough and gather it into a smooth ball. Coat the ball with a little oil and place it in a bowl. Cover with a moist towel or plastic film, and let it rest for ½ hour.

3 To make the filling, heat the shortening or oil over medium-high heat in a frying pan for two minutes. Add coriander seeds and fry until they turn dark brown (about 15 seconds). Add onions and ginger root, and continue frying until the onions turn light brown (about 4-5 minutes). Add potatoes and peas, stir rapidly, and fry until the potatoes begin to become dry and look fried (about 10 minutes). Turn off heat.

4 Add the remaining filling ingredients, mix well, and set aside. (This filling can be made up to 2 days in advance and kept refrigerated until you are ready to make the pastries.)

5 Knead the dough again for a minute, and divide into 2 equal portions. Using your hands, roll each into a ½ in/1 cm thick rope, and cut into 8 equal parts. Roll the small pieces into smooth balls.

6 Working with one at a time, place a ball on your workboard, dust it lightly with flour, and roll it into a 6 in/15 cm circle. Cut the circle in half. Each semicircle will make a *samosa*.

7 Place a small bowl of water next to the workboard. Form a cone: Moisten half of the semicircle's straight edge with water, and bring the other half of the straight edge over it, so that the dry side overlaps the moistened portion by ¼ in/5 mm. Press the overlapped edges securely together to seal.

8 Place a scant tablespoon of filling in the cone. Moisten the open end of the cone, and quickly pinch the open end shut in a straight line, closing the cone into a triangular shape. Press tightly to seal. (Moistening is essential to ensure a good seal; otherwise, during frying, oil will seep into both pastry and filling, making it taste greasy, heavy, and rich.) Continue with the rest of the dough and filling the same way. (The *samosa* can be rolled and shaped a few hours ahead of time and kept loosely covered with a piece of paper. Do not worry if they dry out slightly. In fact, for best results they *should* be left out to dry for ½ hour. This makes the crust more crunchy and flaky.)

9 When ready to fry the pastries, heat the oil in a *kadhai*, or large pan. When the oil is hot (350°F/175°C), drop in about 8-10 pastries. The temperature of the oil will drop automatically to around 300°F/150°C. Maintain the temperature at this low point by regulating the heat between medium-high and medium-low. This low-temperature cooking is essential for *samosa*, because it enables the pastry dough to brown evenly and become flaky. Fry, stirring and turning the pastries until they are light brown (about 12 minutes). Take them out with a slotted spoon or tongs, and drain on paper towels. Continue with the remaining pastries the same way. Serve hot or warm, accompanied by either Sweet and Sour Tamarind Relish (p. 315), or Fresh Mint Relish (p. 309).

NOTE The pastries can be made several hours ahead, and reheated just before serving by frying them briefly (1½ minutes) in very hot oil (375°F/190°C), provided the pastries were left a little underdone and pale. This last frying will thus both warm and brown them. The pastries can also be reheated, uncovered, in a preheated 375°F/190°C/Gas 5 oven for 8-10 minutes.

These savouries may be followed by any dish that does not contain an excessive amount of potatoes. I like to serve grilled or roast meat or chicken to make the meal meaty and simple. Examples include Royal Roast Leg of Lamb with Saffron Raisin Sauce (p. 141), or Tandoori Chicken (p. 168). These pastries also are ideal for high tea.

SAVOURY MEAT PASTRIES

KEEMA SAMOSA

◆

MAKES 32 PASTRIES

◆

1 recipe pastry dough (p. 105)
1 recipe Dry-cooked Spicy Minced Meat (Sookha Keema, p. 124)
Peanut or corn oil, enough to fill a kadhai or large casserole to a depth of 3 in/ 7.5 cm

To make meat pastries, follow the instructions given in the preceding recipe for Savoury Pastries with Spicy Potato Filling, but substitute meat filling for potato filling. Serve these savoury pastries hot or warm, accompanied by Fresh Mint Relish (p. 309) or Mint Coriander Dip (p. 310).

Follow the menu suggestions given for Savoury Pastries with Spicy Potato Filling, but avoid main dishes that contain minced meat. I find these quite filling, so I often serve them with a vegetarian main dish, such as Green Peas and Indian Cheese in Fragrant Tomato Sauce (p. 196). They may also be served with high tea.

SAVOURY BISCUITS

MATTHI

◆

These beautiful, light, golden wafer-thin biscuits, studded with tiny bubbles, are an absolute delight. They are generally flavoured with carom seeds. Traditionally *matthi* are made with a large proportion of fat, which produces biscuits that taste like savoury short bread. I prefer a less rich taste; therefore I use less fat in the dough.

MAKES ABOUT 4 DOZEN BISCUITS

◆

10 oz/300 g plain flour
3 tablespoons warm melted vegetable shortening, plus 1 teaspoon shortening for kneading
¾ teaspoon carom seeds, crushed
2 teaspoons salt
⅛ teaspoon baking soda
2 tablespoons plain yogurt
10 tablespoons warm water
5-6 tablespoons flour for dusting
Peanut or corn oil, enough to fill a kadhai or any large frying pan to a depth of 1½ in/4 cm

1 Rub the 3 tablespoons of shortening into the flour with your fingers until the mixture is crumbly. Stir in carom seeds, salt, and baking soda. Blend the yogurt with the water and pour over the flour in a thin stream, until the dough can be gathered into a mass and kneaded.

2 Place the dough on a marble or floured wooden board. Coat your fingers and palms with the remaining teaspoon of shortening (to keep the dough from sticking) and knead the dough for 10 minutes. This will be a firm but pliable dough. Place the dough in a greased bowl, cover with a towel or plastic film, and let the dough rest for at least ½ hour at room temperature. (The dough can be made a day in advance and kept refrigerated, tightly sealed in plastic film. Remove about 30 minutes before you are ready to roll it out.)

TO MAKE THE DOUGH USING A FOOD PROCESSOR Mix yogurt and water together. Put flour and three tablespoons of shortening into the workbowl of the processor, with the steel cutting blade attached. Process, turning the machine on and off, until the fat is well distributed. Add the carom seeds, salt, and baking soda, and process for a few seconds to mix all the ingredients. Continue processing, adding yogurt and water mixture in a thin stream through the feedtube, until a ball of dough forms on blades (about 15 seconds). Take out the dough, and gather it into a smooth round ball. Coat the ball with the remaining teaspoon of shortening, and place it in a greased bowl. Cover with a moist towel or plastic film, and let it rest for at least ½ hour at room temperature. The ½ hour resting relaxes and softens the dough, thus making it easier to roll.

3 Knead the dough again for a minute. Divide into 8 equal portions, and shape them into balls.

4 Place one ball at a time on the work board. (Keep the remaining balls covered with a plastic film to prevent a crust from forming.) Dust generously with flour and roll into a 10 in/25 cm circle. Cut round biscuits with a plain 2 in/5 cm round cutter (Reserve the scraps.) With a sharp knife make four to six ¼ in/5 mm slashes in the centre of the biscuits to prevent their puffing up during frying. Continue the same way with the rest of the balls. The reserved scraps may be pressed into different patterns and fried, a few pieces at a time. (These biscuits may be rolled an hour ahead of time, as long as they are kept loosely covered with plastic to keep them from drying out.)

5 When ready to fry the biscuits, heat the oil in a *kadhai* or frying pan until moderately hot (325°F/165°C).

6 Drop 6 to 8 biscuits at a time into the oil. The biscuits will first sink to the bottom of the pan and then rise sizzling, to the surface (about ½ minute). Fry, turning often, until they are cooked through and barely pink (about 3 minutes). Do not let them colour too much. They should remain as pale as possible.

7 Take the biscuits out with a slotted spoon, and place them on a baking sheet lined with several layers of paper towels, to drain. Continue with the rest of the biscuits the same way. When cool, store them in airtight containers. These biscuits keep for 8-10 weeks.

Matthi make perfect appetizers when a heavy meal is to follow. They are also a good choice when the rest of the meal takes a little time to prepare.

INDIAN FENUGREEK BISCUITS

KASOORI MATHARI

◆

Because of their fragrance and slightly bitterish taste, fenugreek (*methi*) leaves are often used to flavour lentils, vegetables, and breads. They are considered a delicacy in the Northern States of India. These biscuits can either be deep fried as Savoury Biscuits (p. 109) or baked by the conventional oven method described in this recipe, which is more popular in India today.

MAKES 6-7 DOZEN BISCUITS

◆

½ oz/ 15 g dry fenugreek leaves (kasoori methi)
10 oz/ 300 g plain flour
2 teaspoons coarse salt
4 tablespoons chilled sweet butter, cut into tiny cubes
4 tablespoons chilled vegetable shortening
4 fl oz/ 12.5 cl cold water
5-6 tablespoons flour for dusting

1 In a large bowl, crumble the fenugreek leaves to a rough powder with your fingertips. Add flour and salt, and mix to distribute the herb evenly. Add butter and shortening, and mix with your fingertips, or with a pastry blender, until they are evenly distributed in the flour, with no lumps of butter to be seen.
2 Pour the cold water, about 1 tablespoon at a time, over the flour until it can be gathered into a mass. Place the dough on a marble or floured wooden board, and knead briefly (about 1 minute) to make a soft, smooth ball. (Do not overknead or dough will become rubbery and difficult to roll.)

(The dough can be made ahead of time and kept refrigerated for up to 6 hours. Remove from the refrigerator 15 minutes before you are ready to roll it out. If however, you want to roll the dough within an hour of refrigeration, you do not need to take it out ahead of time.)

TO MAKE THE DOUGH USING A FOOD PROCESSOR Put the fenugreek leaves into the workbowl and, using the steel cutting blade, process, turning the machine on and off until the leaves are reduced to a coarse powder (about 10 seconds). Add flour and salt and process briefly to distribute the herb. Add butter and shortening, and process, turning the machine on and off, until the butter is cut into very small granules – about the size of rice grains (about 10 seconds). Continue processing, adding cold water through the feed tube, until a ball of dough forms on the blades. Take out the dough and gather it into a smooth round ball.

3 Preheat the oven to 375°F/190°C/Gas 5. Line two 12 × 15½ in/30 × 38 cm baking sheets with foil.

4 Divide the dough into 4 equal portions, and shape each into a round ball. Place one ball at a time on the work board. (Keep the remaining balls covered with the plastic film or a moist towel to prevent a crust from forming.) Dust lightly with flour, and roll into a 10 in/25 cm circle. Cut biscuits with a 1½ in/4 cm cutter. With a fork or a thin skewer, prick the biscuits all over to prevent them from puffing up during baking. Reserve the scraps. Continue with the rest of the balls the same way. Finally, gather the scraps, press them into a ball, roll, and cut them into biscuits until no more scraps remain.

5 Place the biscuits ½ in/1 cm apart on baking sheets. Bake them for 10 minutes, or until a few light brown spots appear on the underside. Gently, using a metal spatula, turn the biscuits, and continue baking for an additional 5 minutes or until they are lightly browned on the edges.

6 Transfer the biscuits to racks, and cook thoroughly before storing in airtight containers. These biscuits should rest for 2-3 days before being served, for the full-bodied aroma of fenugreek to penetrate.

SOUPS

SHORVA

◆

MYSORE SPICY LENTIL BROTH

MYSORE RASAM

◆

Rasam, a highly seasoned lentil broth, is a Southern delicacy. It is either mixed with rice and eaten, or drunk in cups as a soup. It is the most popular soup in India today. There are innumerable variations, but this version from the State of Mysore is the finest by far.

Tamarind is essential on the authentic *Mysore Rasam* flavour. But tomatoes are often substituted and produce an equally delicious soup, although not the classic one.

FOR 8 PERSONS

◆

6 oz/175 g yellow lentils (Toovar dal), *or yellow split peas* (channa dal)
1 teaspoon turmeric
1¼ lb/625 g chopped fresh ripe tomatoes (or 1 lb/500 g chopped canned tomatoes)
2 teaspoons finely chopped garlic
2 oz/60 g tamarind pulp
1 tablespoon ground coriander
1 teaspoon ground cumin
¼ teaspoon each red and black pepper
1 teaspoon treacle or sugar
1 tablespoon coarse salt
2 tablespoons usli ghee *(p. 52), or light vegetable oil*
¾ teaspoon black mustard seeds
⅛ teaspoon ground asafetida
2 tablespoons finely chopped coriander leaves

1 Pick over, clean, and wash lentils following instructions on page 235.

2 Put the lentils in a deep saucepan with the turmeric and 1½ pints/1 litre cold water. Bring to the boil over medium-high heat. Reduce heat and simmer at a gentle bubble, partially covered, until the lentils are tender (about 35 minutes), stirring occasionally to prevent sticking. Set aside.

3 While lentils are cooking, purée tomatoes and garlic with 4 fl oz/12.5 cl cold water in an electric blender or food processor, and set aside.

4 Put the tamarind pulp in a small bowl, add 4 tablespoons boiling water, and let mixture soak for 15 minutes. Then mash the pulp with the back of a spoon, or use your fingers. Pour the liquid through a strainer into a small bowl, being sure to squeeze as much juice out of the tamarind pulp as possible (discard the stringy fibre).

5 Purée the lentils in an electric blender, food processor, or food mill, and return to the pan. Blend in 1¼ pints/70 cl hot water with a wire whisk, and mix thoroughly. Let lentils rest, undisturbed, for 15 minutes. Pour the lentil broth that has accumulated at the top into another bowl. (There should be about 1½ pints/1 litre of broth. If not, add enough water to bring it up to that quantity.) Transfer the thick lentil purée left at the bottom of the pan into a small bowl. (This can be saved and used for making lentil stews [*Sambaar*, p. 204], or enriched with Spice-Perfumed Butter [*Tadka*, p. 68] and served as a side dish.)

6 Return the lentil broth to the pan, and add the tomato purée, tamarind juice, coriander, cumin, red and black pepper, treacle or sugar, and salt. Bring the broth to the boil over medium-high heat. Reduce heat to low and simmer, partially covered, for 15 minutes. Turn off heat. (The lentil broth may be made ahead up to this stage and set aside, covered, for up to 4 hours, refrigerated for up to 4 days, or frozen. Defrost and heat thoroughly before proceeding with the recipe.)

7 Heat the *ghee* over high heat in a small frying pan. When it is very hot, carefully add the mustard seeds. Keep a pot lid or spatter screen handy, since the seeds may sputter when added. When the sputtering stops and the seeds turn grey (about 5 seconds), add the asafetida. Then immediately turn off the heat, and pour the spiced butter over the lentil broth. Stir to mix. Cover the pan, and let the broth rest briefly (about 5 minutes). When ready to serve, simmer until heated through. Check for salt, and stir in the coriander leaves. Serve piping hot.

NOTE This soup should definitely be classified as a clear soup or, even better, as an Indian consommé. Sometimes, however, a little lentil purée or tomato pulp escapes into the clear broth, and this is quite acceptable. The residue usually sinks to the bottom of the pan, so always stir the soup thoroughly before serving, to distribute it evenly. Because of its brothlike consistency, this soup is always served in a cup – not in a soup bowl – with a saucer, and a teaspoon to stir the soup frequently. It is meant to be sipped.

To maintain a southern mood, follow this soup with other southern delicacies, such as Spicy Brussels Sprouts, Green Beans, and Lentil Stew (p. 204), or Goanese Hot and Pungent Curry (p. 150). Or if you wish to serve a simple light lunch, omit the main dish and serve a pilaf, such as Mint Pilaf (p. 270) or Vegetable and Rice Casserole with Herbs (p. 272), accompanied by a cool yogurt salad (*raita*).

MULLIGATAWNY SOUP
MULLAGATANNI
◆

The exact origin of this soup is somewhat sketchy, but one thing is certain: it was created two centuries ago by local cooks in the south of India for their English masters. It is believed that the cooks originally served the South Indian soup *rasam*, made with black pepper known as *Mullaga Rasam*, also known as *Mullagatanni* (*mullaga* means pepper, and *tanni* means water or broth). With time, however, the ingredients in the soup changed so completely that the present version bears no resemblance whatever to the traditional *rasam*. Today the soup essentially consists of a rich broth flavoured with onions and spices (turmeric for colour, coriander for piquancy, and red pepper for a hot taste) and finished with coconut milk, almond milk, peanut butter, or sweet cream. Because of its unorthodox origin, Indian cooks have had a field day exercising their creative genius with it. As a result, there are innumerable variations of this soup around the world today.

FOR 8 PERSONS

◆

1 lb/500 g chopped vegetables (mixture of onions, carrots, celery, parsnips, mushrooms)
2½ pints/1½ litres homemade meat broth (p. 47), or vegetable broth (p. 48), or canned chicken broth
1 teaspoon finely chopped garlic
1 sprig coriander leaves
¼ teaspoon black pepper
2 tablespoons usli ghee (p. 52), or light vegetable oil
1 medium-sized onion, finely chopped
4 teaspoons curry powder
3 tablespoons plain flour
4 fl oz/12.5 cl double cream
Coarse salt
2 tablespoons finely minced coriander leaves

1 Put the vegetables in a deep heavy-bottomed saucepan with the broth, garlic, sprig of coriander, and black pepper. Bring to the boil over medium-high heat. Reduce heat and simmer, covered, for 45 minutes or until vegetables are soft. Turn off the heat.

2 When the vegetables in broth are slightly cool, purée the mixture in an electric blender or food processor. Then pass the soup through a fine sieve. Return the soup to the pan and bring it to a gentle simmer.

3 While the soup is simmering, put the *ghee* and onion in a small frying pan over medium heat. Fry onion until it turns caramel brown (about 10 minutes), stirring constantly to prevent burning. Add curry powder and flour, and cook the mixture for 1 minute, stirring rapidly. Turn off heat, and whisk this mixture into the gently simmering soup, stirring constantly to prevent lumping. Simmer until the soup is thickened (about 2 minutes). Turn off heat. (The soup may be made up to this point and set aside, covered, for several hours, or refrigerated for up to 3 days, or frozen. Defrost, and heat thoroughly before proceeding with the recipe.)

4 TO SERVE Stir in cream, salt to taste, and coriander leaves. Simmer over low heat until warmed through. Serve hot.

This soup goes well with just about any main dish. To provide contrast in flavour and colour I like to serve cream- and yogurt-based dishes, such as Lamb Fillets Braised in Yogurt Cardamom Sauce (p. 131), or Royal Braised Vegetables in Cardamom Nut Sauce (p. 198).

CREAM OF SPINACH SOUP

PALAK SHORVA

◆

This refreshing soup with its appealing green colour is ideal for the summer months. All you need is some precooked spinach, cooked rice, and a lot of rich chicken broth. This soup has an interesting texture because of the cooked rice. You may also try using rice flour (about 2-3 tablespoons) instead of cooked rice; it needs to simmer in the soup for 5 minutes to cook fully.

FOR 8 PERSONS

◆

4 *tablespoons* usli ghee *(p. 52), or light vegetable oil*
12 oz/375 g thinly sliced onions
1 teaspoon finely chopped garlic
1 teaspoon ground cumin
¼ teaspoon each ground cloves, nutmeg, and black pepper
1½ pints/1 litre homemade meat broth (p. 47), or vegetable broth (p. 48), or canned chicken broth
2½ oz/75 g tightly packed cooked rice
½ recipe cooked spinach (p. 229)
8 fl oz/25 cl milk
Coarse salt
4 tablespoons double cream
Juice of ½ lemon
½ lemon, thinly sliced

1 Heat the *ghee* in a small frying pan, and add the onions and garlic. Over medium-high heat, sauté until the onions turn golden yellow (about 5 minutes), stirring constantly to prevent burning. Do not let the onions brown, or they will impart a bitter flavour to the soup. Add cumin, stir rapidly for 15 seconds, and add cloves, nutmeg, and black pepper. Turn off heat.

2 Put 8 fl oz/2.5 dl of broth along with the rice in the container of an electric blender, or food processor, and purée until smooth. Add the onion mixture and spinach, and continue processing until the vegetables are reduced to a fine smooth purée, using more broth as needed.
3 Pour the vegetable purée into a pan and stir in the remaining broth, milk, and salt to taste. (The soup may be made up to this stage several hours ahead, set aside, covered, or refrigerated for a day, or frozen. Defrost thoroughly before proceeding with the recipe.)
4 When ready to serve the soup, add cream and heat it until warmed through. Check for salt, and serve in soup bowls, sprinkled with lemon juice, garnished with lemon slices and, if desired, a little black pepper.

NOTE The consistency of this soup should be thick. If you prefer a thinner soup, add a little broth or water, but do not thin it too much or the spinach and rice will separate.

This hearty soup is filling, and therefore needs to be followed by a light main dish. Examples include Fried Fillet of Sole Laced with Carom (p. 184), and Chick-pea Batter Fish (p. 185).

CUCUMBER AND MUNG BEAN SOUP

KHEERA DAL SHORVA

◆

Made with shreds of young cucumber, potatoes, and onions, all bound together in a thick bean purée, this thick hearty soup is particularly good on a cold winter day. Interestingly, the combination of cucumber and onions gives the soup a delicate taste much like a cream of fish soup. If you don't like that taste, substitute potatoes for the onions. If you make the soup with pink lentils (*masar dal*) instead of mung beans, you will produce a much heartier soup.

▷◁▽◁▽◁▽◁▽◁▽◁▽◁▽◁▽◁▽◁▽◁▽◁▽◁▽◁▽◁▽◁▽◁▷

FOR 8 PERSONS

◆

5 oz/ 150 g yellow split mung beans (moong dal)
⅛ teaspoon turmeric
6 oz/ 175 g grated potatoes
4 oz/ 125 g thinly sliced onions
2 large cucumbers, grated
1½ teaspoons coarse salt
4 tablespoons usli ghee *(p. 52), or light vegetable oil*
¾ teaspoon cumin seeds
¼ teaspoon black pepper
Juice of ½ lemon
2 tablespoons finely minced fresh coriander leaves

1 Pick over, clean, and wash mung beans following the instructions on p. 235.
2 Put the beans in a pan with the turmeric and 1 pint/60 cl cold water. Bring to the boil over medium-high heat. Reduce heat and simmer, partially covered, until the beans are tender and cooked through (about 30 minutes). Stir from time to time to keep them from burning. Turn off heat.
3 Beat the cooked beans with an electric beater or wire whisk for a minute, to make a coarse purée. Add enough hot water to make 2 pints/1 litre.
4 Add potatoes, onions, cucumbers, and salt to the purée, and bring to the boil, stirring, over medium heat. Reduce heat and simmer, uncovered, until the vegetables are cooked but still firm (about 5 minutes). (This soup may be made up to this point and set aside, covered, for up to 4 hours, or refrigerated for a day. Reheat the soup until it comes to a gentle simmer.)
5 While the soup is simmering, heat the *ghee* over high heat in a small frying pan. When it is very hot, add the cumin and black pepper and fry until the cumin turns dark brown (about 5 seconds). Remove from heat and pour this perfumed butter with the spices over the soup. Add lemon juice and chopped coriander, and mix thoroughly. Check for salt and serve hot, sprinkled with a few more coriander leaves.

NOTE The consistency of this soup should be thick. If you prefer a thinner soup add broth or water to thin to the desired consistency. Be careful not to overthin, or the bean purée and vegetables will separate and begin to float.

This soup is good enough to be eaten as a main dish. It is so substantial, all you need is a simple light meal consisting of pilaf and yogurt salads.

MAIN DISHES

MEAT

GOSHT

◆

The most commonly eaten red meat throughout India is the meat of goat, a cousin of the sheep, except that it is a much smaller and thinner animal. Goat's meat in India is known as *Bakara* (goat) *ka gosht* (meat) or just *gosht*. In Kashmir, however, where the weather is cool, sheep are raised and so lamb is the traditional meat. The meat of the sheep, or lamb, is known as *Katch* (sheep's) *maanz/gosht* (meat), or simply as *maanz/gosht*. The Anglicized name for both these meats in India is 'mutton', which has caused tremendous confusion, because outside of India 'mutton' refers to a completely different meat. Consequently, Indians on visits here or recently immigrating go through much grief before they discover the difference. They ask the butcher for mutton, expecting mild and lean goat's meat; instead they are given the aged meat of old sheep, which has a strong and gamey flavour.

HOW TO BUY LAMB FOR COOKING

The lamb that comes closest to the Indian variety, is the meat of the young sheep (between five months and one year), known as yearling or spring lamb. It has pinkish-red flesh, a sweet fragrance, and a mild subtle flavour when cooked. Goat's meat is still in the exotic meats category and therefore it is difficult to find. You may find it in Middle Eastern, Indian, Italian, and Greek neighbourhoods or ask your butcher if he will order it for you.

Mutton is the meat of a mature sheep (between two and three years old). Its flesh is deep red, and it has a strong flavour. Mutton became very popular in the last century, particularly when there were no facilities for preserving and storing tender juicy young meats. Because mutton is a much drier meat with a tight texture and less prone to spoilage, it became the common meat.

Almost any cut of lamb can be used in Indian cooking. Meat from the leg and loin are almost free of fat and gristle and are good for roasting, grilling and in fried meat preparations and certain pilafs. The shoulder, breast, and neck are particularly good choices for braising. The muscle and corrective tissue are broken down in the long moist cooking, making the meat tender.

Unless otherwise indicated, in most recipes beef or lamb can be used interchangeably with total success. There is no change in cooking technique, or time, or preparation, provided that equivalent cuts of beef are used. But whatever the meat, it must be trimmed of all visible fat before being cubed or ground as the recipe requires.

There is one point of caution. Lamb or goat's meat, after trimming, is essentially lean, whereas even average quality beef is marbled with a certain amount of almost invisible fat that cannot be trimmed away. Therefore, the finished beef dishes very often have a layer of fat, mostly released by the beef, floating on the surface. In the Indian subcontinent, Middle Eastern countries, and the countries of Southeast Asia, excess fat in food has never posed a problem. In fact, it has traditionally been considered an important source of good nutrition and energy. Its lavish use in food symbolizes one's affluence and high status in society. Often during banquets and wedding receptions, extra fat is folded into a dish for enrichment to pamper the guests and exhibit one's wealth and fortune. Therefore, degreasing a dish before serving is totally unthinkable in India. We have an opposite outlook here: Fat floating on the surface of a dish is considered aesthetically unappealing and is often frowned upon as unnecessary calories. I therefore suggest that you degrease the dish by scooping out the excess fat with a spoon, leaving just enough to coat and glaze the dish.

In Indian cooking, meat is cooked until very tender. This is essential, as food is traditionally eaten with the fingers and should pull apart at a touch.

Most meat dishes can be stretched to increase the number of servings by adding potatoes while the dish is cooking. Or you can keep the specified number of servings and substitute potatoes for part of the meat. Peel the potatoes, cut them to about the same size as the meat pieces, and add them during the last 30 to 50 minutes of cooking. The potatoes will absorb the wonderful sauce and end up tasting much like meat. In Indian homes this is done very commonly, not just to stretch the dish but because Indians love potatoes braised or stewed in meaty gravies.

A FINAL WORD OF CAUTION Do not reduce or omit the fat suggested in the recipe on the assumption that if you start off with less, or no fat at all, then there will be no extra fat to degrease. The suggested amount of butter fat or oil is the bare minimum essential for browning and frying all the ingredients properly. Also, for the authentic classic Indian flavouring, the meat must be cooked in *ghee* or oil, not in suet or lard.

DRY-COOKED SPICY MINCED MEAT

SOOKHA KEEMA

◆

Keema means minced meat. Any dish made with minced meat is also referred to as a *keema*.

This refreshing, coriander-scented dish has as many uses in Indian cooking as the ingenious cook can come up with. It can be served as a main dish in its own right, or it can be folded into cooked rice and become a *keema pullao*. It is the basic stuffing for a variety of breads, vegetables, and *samosas*. It is used in Savoury Meat Pastries (p. 108) and Meat-Stuffed Cabbage Rolls with Ginger Lemon Sauce (p. 148).

FOR 4-6 PERSONS

◆

2 tablespoons light vegetable oil
1 medium-sized onion, finely chopped
4 teaspoons finely chopped garlic
1½ teaspoons finely chopped fresh ginger root
2 green chilies, seeded and minced
1 lb/500 g lean lamb or beef
¼ teaspoon turmeric
1½ teaspoons coarse salt
2 teaspoons garam masala (p. 42)
2 teaspoons lemon juice
2 tablespoons chopped coriander leaves

1 Heat the oil in a skillet or large frying pan and add the onions. Fry the onions over medium-high heat until they turn caramel brown (about 10 minutes), stirring constantly to ensure even browning.

2 Add garlic, ginger, and green chilies, and cook for an additional 2 minutes. Add lamb or beef, and cook until the meat loses its pink colour and begins to brown. Sprinkle turmeric and salt over the meat, stir for a moment or two, and then add 4 tablespoons hot water. Reduce heat, cover, and let the meat cook thoroughly for about 25 minutes, stirring the mixture often to prevent burning. (The moisture should be totally absorbed; if it is not, uncover the pan, increase the heat, and cook until all the moisture has evaporated.) Turn off heat and stir in *garam masala*, lemon juice, and chopped coriander. Serve, if desired, enclosed in a ring of Roasted Onions (p. 227) or Crisp Fried Okra (p. 225).

This *keema* is traditionally cooked very dry – a texture greatly relished by Indians. It is perfectly acceptable, however, if you prefer to leave it slightly wet (cooking it only 15–20 minutes), especially when serving it straight as a main dish. When using it as a stuffing, you *must* cook it dry, as suggested in the recipe, or it will be difficult to fill and seal *samosa* or cutlets.

NOTE The cooked *keema* is usually lumpy and coarse and not very pleasing to the eye. I like to mash it with a potato masher or the back of a measuring cup for a minute to break up the lumps of meat into tiny springy granules. This gives the *keema* a fine silky texture. This final mashing is essential when the *keema* is used as stuffing for Savoury Meat Pastries (*Keema Samosa*, p. 108).

Sookha Keema should be served with bread, such as *Chapati* (p. 279), *Phulka* (p. 282), or *Poori* (p. 293). Since both the main dish and the bread are on the dry side, the meal should feature a moist vegetable, such as Buttered Smothered Cabbage (p. 215) or Smoked Aubergine with Fresh Herbs (p. 220). You may also want to add a *dal*: Spice- and Herb-Laced Split Peas (p. 237) or Buttered Black Beans (p. 242) are good choices. For a cool touch add a yogurt salad, such as Spinach and Yogurt Salad (p. 247). Perfect accompaniments to this meal are Sweet Lemon Pickle with Cumin (p. 318), and Onion Vegetable Relish (*Kachoomar*, p. 304).

MINCED MEAT IN CASHEW NUT SAUCE WITH CHICK-PEAS

KEEMA MATAR

◆

This dish is made with beef or lamb and green peas (*matar*). I prefer a more robust pea and therefore use chick-peas. In the traditional recipe the *keema* is either left unthickened, causing the meat and the sauce to separate, or thickeners like flour or cornflour are used, which give the *keema* a pasty look. I have experimented with this recipe and found that nut butter, especially cashew butter, functions as a natural thickening agent and imparts a nutty flavour to the dish.

NOTE Nut butters are available in health food stores. Or you can make your own in the blender or food processor; see the instructions at the end of this recipe.

FOR 8 PERSONS

◆

4 tablespoons light vegetable oil
12 oz/375 g finely chopped onions
2 teaspoons finely chopped garlic
1 tablespoon finely chopped fresh ginger root
1 teaspoon ground cumin
2 teaspoons ground coriander
1 teaspoon turmeric
½ teaspoon red pepper or more, to taste
2 bay leaves
2 lb/1 kg lean minced beef or lamb
1½ teaspoons coarse salt
1¼ lb/625 g fresh, or 1 lb/500 g canned, chopped tomatoes
3 tablespoons cashew nut butter, or 4 tablespoons ground roasted cashew nuts
1¼ lb/625 g can chick-peas with liquid, or 1 lb/500 g cooked chick-peas with 4 fl oz/12.5 cl liquid
2 teaspoons garam masala (p. 42) or ground roasted cumin seeds (p. 62)
THE GARNISH
1 medium-sized onion, peeled and thinly sliced
1 green chili, shredded
1 medium-sized tomato, cut into ½ in/1 cm wedges

1 Heat the oil in a large pan and add onions. Over medium-high heat, cook onions until they turn a caramel brown (about 25 minutes), stirring constantly so that they do not burn. (See directions for Brown-frying Onions, p. 66).

2 Add garlic and ginger, and cook for an additional 2 minutes. Add cumin, coriander, turmeric, red pepper, and bay leaves. Stir for a moment or two. Add the meat, breaking it up with a fork or wooden spoon, and cook until it loses its pink colour. Add salt, chopped tomatoes, nut butter, and chick-peas with their liquid.

3 Add 4 fl oz/12.5 cl hot water, and bring the contents to boil. Reduce heat and simmer, covered, for about 45 minutes or until the meat is cooked through and the sauce thickened. Check and stir often to keep the sauce from sticking and burning. Turn off heat, and stir in *garam masala*. Check for salt, and serve in a heated serving bowl. If desired, garnish the dish with onion and chili shreds and tomato wedges.

NOTE This dish can be made ahead and kept refrigerated for up to 2 days, or frozen. Defrost thoroughly before reheating. To reheat, gently simmer the *keema* over low heat until warmed through. Refrigeration, and particularly freezing, subdues the fragrance of *garam masala* and of the salt. Therefore, taste the dish, and add a little *garam masala* and salt as needed before serving.

NUT BUTTER

To make 8 oz/250 g of nut butter, place 8 oz/250 g unsalted roasted nuts in the container of a food processor or electric blender and blend for 1 minute, turning the machine off every 10 seconds. The nuts will reduce to a fine powder but will have the texture of coarse meal because of the natural oil still being released. Continue processing, turning machine off every 30 seconds and scraping down the sides of the container, until the coarse powder becomes a thick fudgelike paste (about 3 minutes in the food processor; 5 minutes in the blender). Add 1½ tablespoons of walnut or other vegetable oil and run the machine for an additional 30 seconds, or until the oil is thoroughly blended in.

Keema matar is best accompanied by a fried bread, such as *Poori* (p. 293). To balance the spicy flavour of *keema* and soothe the palate serve a yogurt salad, such as Cucumber and Yogurt Salad (p. 246), and a soothing Onion Vegetable Relish (p. 304).

LAMB BRAISED IN AROMATIC CREAM SAUCE

ROGANI GOSHT

◆

This dish represents the subtle flavouring that is the hallmark of Moghul cooking. Tender chunks of lamb and cubes of potatoes are slowly braised in a cream and yogurt sauce until the meat becomes very tender and the sauce is glazed with a satiny sheen. The best thing about this dish is that it's extremely simple to prepare and can be made quickly. All you need to do is mix the ingredients in a pot and cook them until they are done – no initial frying and no garnishing to worry about.

Since this dish requires expensive ingredients such as double cream and almonds, in India it is generally reserved for banquets.

◆◇◆

FOR 6-8 PERSONS

◆

8 oz/250 g plain yogurt
2 medium-sized onions, peeled and quartered
1½ tablespoons chopped fresh ginger root
2 tablespoons slivered blanched almonds
2 tablespoons ground coriander
2½ teaspoons ground cardamom
1 teaspoon black pepper
1 tablespoon coarse salt
8 fl oz/25 cl double cream
2 lb/1 kg boneless lean lamb or beef, cut into 1½ in/4 cm pieces
1 lb/500 g medium-sized potatoes, peeled and quartered
4-5 tablespoons milk (if needed)

1 Put yogurt, onions, ginger, and almonds in the container of an electric blender or food processor, and run the machine until the ingredients are reduced to a fine purée (use a few tablespoons of cream from the 8 fl oz/25 cl in the recipe if necessary).

2 Put the puréed mixture along with the coriander, cardamom, black pepper, salt, cream, and the meat in a large heavy-bottomed pan (preferably one with a non-stick surface). Place the pan over medium-high heat and bring to the boil. Reduce to a simmer, and cook, covered, for 1¾ hours. Add potatoes, and continue simmering until the potatoes are done and the meat is very tender (about 40 minutes). Check and stir often during cooking to keep the sauce from sticking and burning. When stirring, be careful not to break the fragile meat and potato pieces.

3 Degrease the dish, if necessary, as suggested in the introduction to the meat recipes. Check for salt, and serve.

NOTE For the best flavour, make the dish several hours before it is to be served and leave it at room temperature. It may be kept in the refrigerator for up to 2 days, or frozen. Defrost thoroughly before reheating.

Cream sauce dishes are traditionally eaten with a pilaf. This lovely dish should be accompanied by one that does not interfere with or mask the subtle flavour of the dish. A superb choice would be Saffron Pilaf with Peaches (p. 266). For a side dish, serve a vegetable, such as Broccoli Smothered in Garlic Oil (p. 214) or Smoked Aubergine with Fresh Herbs (p. 220). For a more elaborate meal include a *dal*, such as Buttered Black Beans (p. 242).

MEAT SMOTHERED WITH ONIONS

GOSHT DO-PIAZA

◆

Gosht Do-piaza, literally translated, means meat in twice as many onions, and that's exactly what the dish is supposed to be. But most Indian cooks, including myself, add only half the prescribed amount; otherwise the entire dish tastes of nothing but onions.

This recipe, a speciality of my mother-in-law, is a far more subtle dish than the common, more popular version consisting of fried onions and several different spices. Here the spicing is kept to a bare minimum; turmeric is used to perfume the meat with its woody scent. Also, to keep the overall flavour mellow and delicate, *raw* (not fried) onions are folded into the meat after it is cooked. The onions lose their raw sharp taste and become sweet and glazed, without losing their crispness, by steaming in the vapours of the meat.

FOR 6 PERSONS

◆

4 fl oz/ 12.5 cl light vegetable oil
2 tablespoons minced garlic
3 tablespoons ground, grated, or crushed fresh ginger root
2 teaspoons turmeric
1 teaspoon red pepper, or to taste
2 lb/ 1 kg lean boneless lamb, cut into 1 in/ 2.5 cm cubes
2½ teaspoons coarse salt
2 large Spanish onions, peeled and sliced into ¼ in/ 5 mm slices

1 Heat oil in a large heavy-bottomed pan and add garlic and ginger. Over medium heat, fry until they turn light golden (about 5 minutes), stirring constantly to ensure even browning. Add turmeric and red pepper, and, stirring rapidly, fry for an additional 10 seconds.

2 Add meat, and mix thoroughly. Reduce heat to low, cover the pot tightly, and let the meat cook in its juices for 15 minutes (at the end of cooking, the moisture should be totally absorbed by the meat, leaving behind the oil; the contents of the pan will look quite dry). Check and stir often during this period to ensure the meat is not sticking to the pan and burning.

3 Add salt, along with ¾ pint/45 cl boiling water. Stir well, and simmer, covered, until the meat is very tender and the liquid has turned into a thick sauce (about 1-1¼ hours).

(The meat may be prepared up to this stage and set aside, covered, for several hours, or refrigerated for up to 2 days, or frozen. Defrost thoroughly before reheating and proceeding with the recipe. To reheat, bring the sauce to a gentle simmer over low heat, until thoroughly warmed.)

4 Add onion slices, mix thoroughly to distribute them evenly with meat and sauce, and replace the cover. Increase heat to high for exactly 15 seconds (to build up steam), and turn off heat. Let the onions steam, undisturbed, for 5 minutes. Under no circumstances should the pan be opened during this time, because that would cause the steam to escape, thus leaving the onions raw and hot. Check for salt, and serve.

This *Do-piaza* must be served with a bread such as *Chapati* (p. 279) or *Phulka* (p. 282). Since the dish contains a lot of onions, you don't need to serve any extra vegetables, but if you want, Smoked Aubergine with Fresh Herbs (p. 220) is an excellent choice.

LAMB FILLETS BRAISED
IN YOGURT CARDAMOM SAUCE

KHARA PASANDA

◆

This is another exquisite example of classic Moghul cooking: lamb fillets (*pasanda*) gently braised in a cumin- and green cardamom-laced yogurt sauce.

FOR 4-6 PERSONS

◆

8 tablespoons light vegetable oil
12 oz/375 g finely chopped onions
4 teaspoons finely chopped garlic
1½ tablespoons finely chopped fresh ginger root
2 oz/60 g slivered blanched almonds
1 teaspoon black cumin seeds (optional)
¾ teaspoon ground cardamom
1 teaspoon black pepper
8 fl oz/25 cl plain yogurt
2 teaspoons coarse salt
2 lb/1 kg boneless lean lamb, or beef, cut into ¼ in/5 mm thick, 2½ in/6 cm long, and 1 in/2.5 cm wide strips
4-5 tablespoons double cream

1 Heat 4 tablespoons of the oil in a heavy-bottomed pan (preferably one with a non-stick surface), and add onions. Over medium-high heat, fry the onions until they turn light brown (about 15 minutes), stirring constantly to prevent their burning. (See directions for Brown-frying Onions, p. 66.)

2 Add garlic, ginger, and almonds, and fry until the almonds are lightly coloured (about 5 minutes). Add cumin, if you are using it, cardamom, and black pepper, and fry briefly to release their fragrance (about 1-2 minutes).

3 Put the entire contents of the pan into the container of an electric blender or food processor. Add yogurt, salt, and 8 fl oz/25 cl hot water, and finely purée the mixture. Set aside.

4 Add the remaining 4 tablespoons of oil to the pan, and turn the heat high. Pat dry the meat pieces on paper towels (or they will not brown), and add when the oil is very hot. Brown them quickly and evenly on all sides (about 3-5 minutes). The pan should not be overcrowded with too many pieces of meat, as crowding will cool the pan and the meat will steam instead of being seared. Therefore, the browning should be done in batches. As each batch is browned, transfer it with a slotted spoon to a bowl. When all the pieces are browned, return them to the pan. Add the puréed mixture and bring to the boil. Reduce heat and cook, covered, until the meat is very tender (about 1¼-1½ hours). Check every 15 minutes to make sure the sauce is not sticking to the bottom of the pan and burning. The sauce should be fairly thick; if it is not, uncover, increase heat, and boil rapidly until it reduces to a thick creamy consistency. Also, if there is excessive fat floating on the surface (particularly if you are using beef), carefully scoop it out. Do not take out all the fat, as there should be a thin film of it left to coat the sauce and meat pieces.

5 Stir in the cream, check for salt, simmer until heated through, and serve.

NOTE The flavour of this dish improves noticeably with keeping, so make it at least a couple of hours before you are ready to serve the dish, or a day before and refrigerate. It can also be frozen successfully. Defrost the dish thoroughly before reheating.

Accompany this noble dish with a pilaf that is fragrant with Moghul spices, such as The Emperor's Pilaf with Black Mushrooms (p. 268) or for a sweeter taste, Sweet Saffron Pilaf (p. 264). For a side dish, serve Spicy Baby Aubergine (p. 219), or Turmeric Potatoes with Green Peppers (p. 228).

For an elaborate meal, serve a *dal* such as Lucknow Sour Lentils (p. 241), and a yogurt salad such as Dumplings in Fragrant Yogurt (p. 250). Hot Hyderabad Tomato Relish (p. 314) goes extremely well with this meal.

BEEF IN SPICY TOMATO GRAVY

MASALA GOSHT

◆

Masala Gosht is a popular meat dish in North India. The beef is braised in a turmeric-laced fried onion sauce enriched with puréed tomatoes and yogurt.

FOR 6 PERSONS

◆

2 medium-sized ripe fresh tomatoes
4 large cloves garlic
1½ tablespoons chopped fresh ginger root
5 tablespoons plain yogurt
6 tablespoons light vegetable oil
2 lb/ 1 kg lean beef, cut into 1½ in/ 4 cm cubes
3 meaty beef bones (optional)
12 oz/ 375 g finely chopped onions
4 black (or 8 green) cardamom pods
8 whole cloves
2 teaspoons turmeric
½ teaspoon red pepper, or to taste
2 teaspoons coarse salt
1½ teaspoons ground roasted cumin seeds (p. 62)
2 tablespoons chopped coriander leaves

1 Preheat the oven to 325°F/165°C/Gas 3.

2 Put tomatoes, garlic, chopped ginger, and yogurt in the container of an electric blender or food processor, and run the machine until the ingredients are reduced to a fine smooth purée. Set aside.

3 Heat 2 tablespoons of the oil in a large frying pan over high heat until very hot. Pat dry the meat pieces and bones (if you are using them) on paper towels (otherwise the meat will not brown, but steam instead), and add to the pan. Brown them, turning and tossing the pieces, for 3-5 minutes. (The frying pan should be large enough to accommodate the pieces in one layer without overlapping. The best way to brown them is in batches.) Transfer the meat to a heavy-bottomed casserole.

4 Add the remaining 4 tablespoons of oil to the frying pan, along with the onions. Reduce heat to medium-high, and fry until the onions turn caramel brown (about 20 minutes), stirring frequently to prevent burning. (See directions for Brown-frying Onions, p. 66).

Add cardamom, cloves, turmeric, red pepper, and salt, and fry for an additional minute. Add the tomato yogurt purée, and continue frying the mixture until it reduces to a thick paste and the oil begins to separate from the paste (about 5 minutes). Turn off heat.

5 Add this paste to the meat in the casserole. Add 1¼ pints/75 cl of hot water to the frying pan. Scrape the sides and bottom of the pan to release the pieces clinging to it, and pour into the casserole. Stir the meat to distribute the spices and liquid evenly. Place the casserole over medium-high heat and bring the contents to the boil. Place a sheet of foil over the top of the casserole, and cover tightly with the lid.

6 Bake for 2 hours. Check and stir meat every 30 minutes to ensure it won't burn. Turn off the oven. Let the casserole remain in the oven for 15 minutes longer.

7 Take the casserole out of the oven, uncover, and discard the bones. Check for salt, and serve sprinkled with roasted cumin seeds and finely chopped coriander leaves.

NOTE This is one of those dishes that taste best when allowed to rest for a couple of hours at room temperature or refrigerated for a day or two before serving. It also freezes extremely well; but defrost thoroughly before reheating.

This gorgeous curry with its garnet-coloured sauce should be served with a plain cooked rice (p. 256), or a simple baked bread. You can serve any of the vegetable side dishes. For an additional side dish, serve Lentils with Garlic Butter (p. 238) if you are serving a staple of rice; try Buttered Black Beans (p. 242) if you are serving bread.

ROYAL BRAISED LAMB WITH SPICES

SHAHI KORMA

◆

Korma, or braising, is the classic technique used to prepare lamb in Moghul cooking (see description on p. 70). There are several basic recipes, varying in the spicing, but all *korma* dishes are essentially butter- or cream-braised meat dishes perfumed with Moghul spices. I like to accentuate the flavour of mace in this recipe because it imparts a lovely sweet fragrance well-suited to this lordly dish (*Shahi* means Royal).

Korma may be served by itself as a main dish or used for making another classic – Emperor's Layered Meat and Fragrant Rice Casserole (p. 146).

FOR 8 PERSONS

◆

4 oz/ 125 g usli ghee, (p. 52) or light vegetable oil
8 oz/ 250 g thinly sliced onions
1 tablespoon finely chopped garlic
1½ tablespoons finely chopped fresh ginger root
2 teaspoons black cumin seeds, or 1½ teaspoons ground cumin
1½ teaspoons ground mace
⅓ teaspoon ground cinnamon
1 teaspoon Mughal garam masala *(p. 41)*
½ teaspoon red pepper, or to taste
1 teaspoon paprika
3 lb/ 1.5 kg lean boneless lamb, cut into 1½ in/ 4 cm cubes
8 fl oz/ 25 cl plain yogurt
8 fl oz/ 25 cl sour cream or double cream
1 tablespoon coarse salt
Milk (if needed)

1 Heat the *ghee* in a large heavy-bottomed pan, preferably a non-stick type, and add onions. Over medium-high heat, fry the onions until they turn caramel brown (about 15 minutes), stirring constantly to prevent burning. (See directions for Brown-frying Onions p. 66.)

2 Add garlic and ginger, and cook for an additional 2 minutes. Add cumin, mace, cinnamon, *Mughal garam masala*, red pepper, and paprika, and stir rapidly for a moment or two to distribute the spices into the fried onions.

3 Dry meat pieces thoroughly on paper towels. Increase heat to high, add meat pieces, and brown them on all sides evenly, turning and tossing them rapidly (about 5 minutes). Add the salt and ½ of the amount of both yogurt and sour cream or double cream. Bring the mixture to the boil, reduce heat, and simmer the meat, covered, until very tender (about 2 hours). The meat should be checked and stirred frequently during cooking to keep the sauce from sticking and burning. If the sauce evaporates too fast while cooking, add a little milk. When the *korma* is fully cooked, it should look quite dry, with just enough gravy to coat the meat pieces. Stir in the remaining yogurt and cream, and turn off heat.

NOTE Because the *korma* is practically sauceless, a considerable amount of fat usually separates and floats on the surface. This is characteristic of *korma* dishes. The dishes are traditionally served with the fat. For various reasons, however, I prefer to degrease the dish slightly, leaving just enough fat to coat and glaze the gravy and meat pieces.

This dish may be made ahead and refrigerated for up to 3 days. Since it is practically dry, with thick scanty gravy, it does not take well to freezing.

This *korma* perfumed with butter and spices must be matched with an equally fragrant pilaf such as Sweet Saffron Pilaf (p. 264). Any vegetable may be served.

LAMB IN GARLIC CREAM SAUCE

ROGAN JOSH

◆

This is truly the finest example of the superb flavouring of Moghul cooking. Although there are several versions of *Rogan Josh,* no variation equals this one from Kashmir, the northernmost state of India.

Traditionally, the meat is first marinated for several hours in a yogurt-spice mixture before being cooked in the marinade. This process tenderizes the meat. But the lamb in Britain is so tender and of such good quality that I cut short this step. Instead, I let the cooked meat sit in its sauce for a short time before serving it. This allows the flavours of the sauce to permeate the meat.

FOR 8 PERSONS

◆

3 lb/1.5 kg lean boneless lamb, cut into 1½ in/4 cm cubes
4 tablespoons usli ghee, *or 2 tablespoons unsalted butter mixed with 2 tablespoons light vegetable oil*
1 tablespoon minced garlic
1 tablespoon black cumin seeds, crushed, or 2 teaspoons ground cumin
2 teaspoons ground cardamom
1 teaspoon Mughal garam masala *(p. 41)*
8 fl oz/25 cl double cream
Milk or water if needed
THE MARINADE
4 medium-sized onions, peeled and quartered
2 tablespoons finely chopped fresh ginger root
2 tablespoons ground coriander
¾ teaspoon red pepper, or to taste
1 pint/60 cl plain yogurt
4 fl oz/12.5 cl sour cream
1 tablespoon coarse salt
4 oz/125 g melted usli ghee *(p. 52)*
melted unsalted butter

1 Put all the ingredients of the marinade except *ghee* into the container of an electric blender or food processor, and run the machine until the ingredients are finely puréed.

2 Place the lamb in a large bowl, and pour the marinade and melted *ghee* over it. Mix thoroughly to coat the meat pieces with the marinade. Cover, and let the meat marinate for at least ½ hour at room temperature, or 2 hours in the refrigerator. (Remove from the refrigerator about 30 minutes before you are ready to cook the meat.)

3 Transfer the meat, along with the marinade, to a heavy-bottomed pan (preferably one with a non-stick surface). Place the pan over medium-low heat, and gently bring the contents to the boil. Reduce heat, and simmer, covered, until the lamb is very tender. The lamb is done when a fork or a thin skewer pierces it without any resistance (about 2-2½ hours depending upon the heat, pan used, and above all, the quality of the meat). Stir frequently to prevent the sauce sticking to the bottom of the pan and burning.

4 Heat the 4 tablespoons *usli ghee* in a small frying pan over high heat. When it is very hot, add garlic, and stirring rapidly, fry for 15 seconds. Immediately add cumin, cardamom, and *Mughal garam masala*. As soon as the spices begin to sizzle and release their fragrance (about 3-5 seconds), turn off heat and pour the perfumed butter, along with the spices, over the meat. Add cream, and stir to distribute the ingredients. Let the meat rest at room temperature for 2 hours.

5 When ready to serve, check for salt, then reheat the meat until piping hot.

NOTE Sometimes too much moisture evaporates during cooking, causing the *ghee* to separate from the sauce. If that happens, add a little milk or water, a tablespoon at a time, until the fat is incorporated back into the sauce. Do not degrease, as the fragrant *ghee* is one of the primary flavouring ingredients in this dish.

Rogan Josh definitely improves in flavour with keeping. Therefore I would advise you to make it the day before you are planning to serve it. It keeps well in the refrigerator for up to 3 days, and also freezes well. Defrost thoroughly before reheating.

BEEF IN FRAGRANT SPINACH SAUCE

SAAG GOSHT

◆

This beautiful dish – another variation of the Moghul rulers' fine cooking – is based on the use of different greens. You can substitute kale, sorrel or Swiss chard leaves, or combine any of these with the spinach.

FOR 8 PERSONS

◆

3 lb/1.5 kg spinach, cooked
6 tablespoons light vegetable oil
3 lb/1.5 kg lean boneless beef or lamb, cut into 1½ in/4 cm cubes
1 lb/500 g thinly sliced onions
1½ tablespoons finely chopped garlic
3 tablespoons finely chopped fresh ginger root
1 tablespoon ground cumin
2 tablespoons ground coriander
1 teaspoon turmeric
1 medium-sized ripe tomato, finely chopped
3 green chilies, seeded and minced, or 1 teaspoon red pepper
3 tablespoons plain yogurt or sour cream
1 cinnamon stick, 3 in/7.5 cm long, broken into small pieces
6 black (or 12 green) cardamom pods
9 whole cloves
3 bay leaves, crumbled
1 tablespoon coarse salt
4 teaspoons garam masala (p. 42), or ground roasted cumin seeds (p. 62)
2-4 tablespoons light vegetable oil (if needed)

1 Finely purée the spinach, using a food processor or electric blender, or mince it with a knife on a chopping board. Set aside.

2 Preheat the oven to 325°F/165°C/Gas 3.

3 Heat 2 tablespoons of the oil in a large frying pan over high heat until very hot. Pat the meat dry on paper towels (or it will not brown), and add. Brown the meat, turning and tossing the pieces, until nicely seared on all sides. (This is best done in batches so that the frying pan is not overcrowded. As each batch is browned, transfer to a heavy-bottomed casserole.)

4 Add the remaining 4 tablespoons oil to the frying pan, and add onions. Reduce heat to medium-high, and fry until they turn caramel brown (about 25 minutes), stirring constantly to prevent burning. (See directions for Brown-frying Onions, p. 66). Add garlic and ginger, and fry for an additional 2 minutes. Add cumin, coriander, and turmeric, and stir rapidly for 15 seconds. Add tomatoes and chilies, and continue frying until the tomato is cooked and the entire mixture is turned into a thick pulpy paste (about 3 minutes). Add yogurt or sour cream, and immediately turn off heat. When slightly cool, purée the mixture in an electric blender or food processor, and add to the meat in the casserole.

5   Place a double layer of muslin about 6 in/15 cm square, on the work surface. Put cinnamon, cardamom, cloves, bay leaves in the centre, bring up the four corners of the muslin to wrap the spices, and tie them to form a bag. Crush the bag slightly with a wooden mallet or any heavy tool to break up the spices. Add the spice bag to the casserole.

6   Add 1½ pints/1 litre boiling water along with the salt, and stir to distribute the meat into the sauce. Place a piece of foil on top of the casserole, and cover tightly with the lid. Bring the contents to the boil on top of the stove.

7   Place the casserole in the oven for 2½ hours. Or alternatively, it may be cooked on top of the stove over low heat for 2-2½ hours, or until the meat is fork tender.

8   Remove the casserole from the oven and take off the lid. Remove the spice bag, and squeeze hard to extract as much juice as possible. Discard the bag. Add the cooked spinach and *garam masala*, and blend well, being careful not to break the fragile meat pieces. Cover the pot, return it to the oven or stove, and cook for 5 minutes more. Turn off the oven, and let the pot remain undisturbed for an additional 10 minutes. Check for salt, and if the sauce lacks adequate glaze, stir in a few tablespoons of oil. Serve.

NOTE This dish, like any other braised dish, tastes better with keeping, so make it a few hours in advance, and leave to rest at room temperature before being reheated and served. It keeps well in the refrigerator for up to 2 days, and also freezes well. Defrost thoroughly before reheating.

You can serve this dish with Fragrant Pilaf Banaras Style (p. 263). Even simple plain cooked rice goes well (p. 256). For a bread, try *Paratha* (p. 285), Chick-pea Flour Bread (p. 283), or *Poori* (p. 293). For a side dish, serve a yogurt salad like Dumplings in Fragrant Yogurt (p. 250).

ROYAL ROAST LEG OF LAMB
WITH SAFFRON RAISIN SAUCE

SHAHI RAAN

◆

This slightly sweet pot roast of lamb laced with saffron and *Mughal garam masala* is probably the most beautifully flavoured and stunning presentation in all of Moghul cooking. Traditionally, the roast is broken into chunks and served on a large platter over a bed of rice, with the sauce poured over it, but I think that serving the roast separately with the sauce on the side is much more suitable to modern ways of eating.

Leftover *Shahi Raan* can be turned into a pilaf or rolled sandwich-style between two layers of Indian bread (*roti*) with slices of raw tomato and onions, or sliced in strips and eaten as an appetizer (*kati kabab*).

FOR 10-12 PERSONS

◆

1 leg of lamb, about 7½-9 lb/ 3¾-4½ kg, boned, rolled and tied
THE MARINADE
1 tablespoon chopped garlic
2 tablespoons chopped fresh ginger root
1 teaspoon black cumin seeds or white cumin
1 teaspoon red pepper, or to taste
1½ teaspoons Mughal garam masala *(p. 41)*
4 teaspoons coarse salt
4 oz/ 125 g seedless raisins
3 oz/ 90 g raw pistachio nuts, or walnuts
4 tablespoons lemon juice
1½ oz/ 45 g light brown sugar
6 oz/ 175 g plain yogurt
4 tablespoons sour cream
2 teaspoons saffron threads
2 tablespoons plain flour or cornflour, dissolved in 3 tablespoons cold water

1 Prick the top of the lamb with a fork or thin skewer, and place it in a large flameproof nonmetal casserole that can hold the lamb snugly. Set aside.

2 Put all the ingredients of the marinade into the container of a food processor or electric blender, and process until the ingredients are reduced to a fine thick paste. If the machine begins to clog, add 2-3 tablespoons water.

3 Pour the marinade all over the lamb and spread to coat it thoroughly. Cover, and let it marinate in the refrigerator for 3 days. Take the casserole from the refrigerator about one hour before cooking (or 4 hours before serving), and let it come to room temperature.

4 Preheat the oven to 350°F/175°C/Gas 4.

5 Put the saffron threads in a small bowl or saucer and, using your fingers, powder it as fine as possible. Add 2 tablespoons hot water, and let soak for 15 minutes. Sprinkle the saffron water over the lamb.

6 Place the casserole on the stove at medium-heat and bring the contents to the boil. Pour 8 fl oz/25 cl of boiling water down the sides of the casserole. Place a piece of foil on top of the casserole and cover tightly with the lid.

7 Roast the lamb for 1½ hours. Lower heat to 225°F/105°C/Gas ¼ and continue roasting for an additional 45 minutes. Turn off heat and let the casserole remain in the oven, with the door shut, for another 45 minutes. The cooking process is now completed, but keep the casserole in the oven until you are ready to serve the lamb. The roast will remain warm for about 45 minutes in the oven.

8 To serve, take the casserole from the oven, and place the lamb on a carving board. Discard the trussing strings. Heat the contents of the casserole to a gentle simmer over low heat on top of the stove, skimming off the fat floating on the surface. Add the flour-water mixture and cook, stirring rapidly, until the sauce is thickened (1-2 minutes). Check for salt. Slice the meat in very thin slices and arrange them on a warm serving platter. Spoon some sauce over the slices and serve the rest of it in a heated bowl or gravy boat.

NOTE You can make ½ recipe of *Shahi Raan* by using ½ leg, weighing about 1 lb/1.5-2 kg, and reducing all the other ingredients by half. To cook the lamb, use a small casserole and pour only 4 fl oz/12.5 cl of boiling water down the sides of the casserole. Roast the lamb at 350°F/175°C/Gas 4 for 45 minutes, lower heat to 225°F/105°C/Gas ½ and continue roasting for 20 minutes. Turn off heat and let the casserole remain in the oven for 15 minutes before serving. This will serve 4-6 persons.

For a perfect meal, precede this dish with an elegant appetizer or first course. My choice would be Crab Malabar (p. 87), Cauliflower Fritters (p. 97), or Mulligatawny Soup (p. 115). This roast should be accompanied by a plain fragrant pilaf, so that the sweet flavours of saffron and lamb may emerge and be enjoyed to the fullest. I always serve either Broccoli Smothered in Garlic Oil (p. 214) or Glazed Cauliflower with Ginger (p. 216) with this meal.

LAMB PILAF

MUGHALAI PULLAO

◆

A pilaf made with lamb is one of the most festive and comforting of all dishes. Pilaf is generally made with the best of ingredients, the tenderest chunks of meat, the finest *Basmati* rice, the freshest spices, because there is no sauce or gravy to shield the inadequacies of any ingredient.

FOR 8-10 PERSONS

◆

3 lb/1.5 kg loin lamb chops (about 8-12 chops)
12 oz/375 g basmati rice
14 tablespoons light vegetable oil
1½ lb/750 g finely chopped onions
2 tablespoons coarse salt
3 tablespoons finely chopped garlic
4 tablespoons finely chopped fresh ginger root
THE SPICE BAG
4 black and 6 green cardamom pods, or 14 green cardamom pods
1 stick cinnamon, 3 in/7.5 cm long, broken into 2-3 pieces
½ teaspoon black peppercorns
10 whole cloves
1½ teaspoons each cumin and coriander seeds
3 bay leaves, crumbled

1 Trim every trace of fat off the chops. The meat should be as lean as possible.
2 Place all the spices for the spice bag on a double layer of muslin, about 6 in/15 cm square, and tie the corners to form a bag. Hit lightly with a wooden mallet, rolling pin, or any heavy tool to crush the spices slightly, and set aside.

3 Pick over, clean, wash, and soak rice, following instructions given under Preparing Basmati Rice for Cooking on p. 255.

4 Bring 5 pints/3 litres water to the boil in a deep pot. Add the soaked rice, and stir immediately for ½ minute (this keeps the rice from settling), being careful not to break the fragile rice grains. Bring the water to a second boil (it will take about 3 minutes) and cook the rice for 2 minutes. Pour the entire contents of the pot into a large sieve held over the kitchen sink. Hold the sieve under the tap, and let cold water run through the rice and sieve at medium speed for 3-5 seconds. Shake sieve to drain the rice thoroughly. Return the rice to the pot, add a little oil (about 1 teaspoon), and mix gently but thoroughly to coat the rice grains evenly. Cover and set aside until needed.

5 Heat 6 tablespoons of the oil in a large heavy-bottomed ovenproof casserole, and add onions. Over medium-high heat, fry the onions until they turn caramel brown (about 30 minutes), stirring constantly to prevent burning. (See directions for Brown-frying Onions, p. 66.) Put the fried onions, along with 5 tablespoons warm water and 1 tablespoon salt, into the container of an electric blender or food processor, and blend until finely puréed. Set aside.

6 Add the remaining 8 tablespoons of oil to the casserole, and heat. Add garlic and ginger, and cook over medium heat until they turn light brown (about 5 minutes). Add lamb chops in one layer, and cook, turning frequently until the meat loses its pink colour (about 4 minutes). The chops at this point will begin to give out their juices and to steam. Let the meat steam undisturbed, uncovered, until most of the moisture evaporates (about 5 minutes). Watch the chops carefully during this period, because as soon as the moisture evaporates, the browning begins almost instantly, and unless the meat is stirred immediately it will burn.

7 Add 1½ pints/1 litre boiling water along with the remaining tablespoon of salt and the spice bag. Reduce heat and simmer, covered, for 45 minutes, or until the meat is cooked through. Increase heat to medium and continue cooking, uncovered, until most of the moisture is absorbed and the meat is melting tender (about 30 minutes).

8 Preheat the oven to 300°F/150°C/Gas 2. Remove spice bag from the meat, squeeze hard to extract as much juice as possible, and discard. Add reserved onion purée, and cook for 2 minutes, stirring constantly to mix in the ingredients and flavours. (The meat, rice, and onion purée may all be prepared ahead and set aside, covered, for several hours, or refrigerated for up to 3 days. The meat and onions may be frozen, but not the rice. Defrost and bring to room temperature before proceeding with the recipe.)

9 Using a flat spatula, fold the cooked rice into the meat mixture. Place foil on top of the casserole and cover tightly with the lid. Bake the pilaf for 30 minutes. Turn off the oven, and leave the casserole inside for an additional 10 minutes. The pilaf, left in the oven, will remain warm for an additional 30 minutes.

NOTE The classic way of making pilaf is with meat on the bone, as described above. If, however, you prefer a boneless meat pilaf, do not use boneless chops for much of the flavour of the pilaf comes from the bones. Instead, remove the bones carefully from the meat when you remove the spice bag.

A freshly made and assembled pilaf will keep in the refrigerator for up to 5 days. In fact, the flavour mellows and improves with each day of keeping. To reheat, place the casserole, tightly covered with foil and lid, in the middle level of a preheated 300°F/150°C/Gas 2 oven for 20-25 minutes.

This pilaf requires no special side dishes or staple. For a light meal, serve it with Onion and Roasted Tomato Relish (p. 306). If you want to expand the meal, serve any stir-fried vegetable or *dal*.

EMPEROR'S LAYERED MEAT AND FRAGRANT RICE CASSEROLE

SHAH JAHANI BIRIYANI

◆

Biriyani, an elaborate pilaf with breathtaking garnishes and decorations, is another Moghul creation. It takes a little extra time and trouble to prepare, but once you make it, you will agree that the results are well worth the effort. *Biriyani* is prepared by layering partially cooked rice and partially or fully cooked meat in a casserole and adding different flavourings, such as saffron, *kewra* essence, and mint. The entire dish is then steamed by the *dum* process (see p. 70). Then the pilaf is arranged decoratively on a platter and garnished with fried onions and sautéed nuts. It is traditionally decorated with silver foil (*vark*). This particular *biriyani* is named after the Moghul emperor Shah Jahan, who built the Taj Mahal. The dish, like that architectural marvel, is stunning.

FOR 8-10 PERSONS

◆

*All the ingredients for making Rice Cooked in Meat Broth (*Yakhni Chawal, p. 259)
*All the ingredients for making Royal Braised Lamb with Spices (*Shahi Korma, p. 134)
8 tablespoons light vegetable oil
2 oz/60 g each slivered blanched almonds, raw cashew nuts, and seedless raisins
12 oz/375 g thinly sliced or shredded onions
1 oz/30 g mint leaves
2 green chilies, seeded and minced
4 fl oz/12.5 cl milk
2 teaspoons saffron threads
4 tablespoons usli ghee *(p. 52)*
2-3 teaspoons screw-pine essence (Ruh Kewra — *optional*)
2 × 3 in/7.5 cm square pieces silver foil (vark — *optional*)

1 Prepare *Yakhni Chawal* following instructions on p. 259.
2 Prepare *Shahi Korma* following instructions on p. 134.

3 Heat 2 tablespoons of the oil in a frying pan or *kadhai* over medium heat. Add almonds, and fry until they are light brown (about 2 minutes). Take them out with a slotted spoon, and drain on paper towels. Add cashew nuts to the oil, and brown and drain them similarly. Finally, add the raisins and fry them, turning and tossing rapidly, until they puff up (about 30 seconds). Drain them also on paper towels. Set nuts and raisins aside for garnish.

4 Add the remaining 6 tablespoons of oil to the pan along with the onions. Increase heat to high, and fry them until they turn dark brown (about 12 minutes), stirring constantly to prevent burning. Drain onions on paper towels, and set aside for garnish.

5 Mix mint and green chilies with half the milk in a small bowl. In another bowl put the saffron, and powder it with your fingers. Scald the remaining milk, add to the saffron, and let soak for at least 15 minutes. (All this can be prepared several hours ahead and set aside until you are ready to serve. About an hour before you are going to serve, begin assembling the *biriyani*.)

6 Preheat the oven to 300°F/150°C/Gas 2.

7 Place a heavy-bottomed casserole on the work surface. Arrange all other ingredients for assembling the *biriyani* next to it. Pour 2 tablespoons of *ghee* into the casserole. Tilt the casserole gently, or use a pastry brush, to coat the bottom and sides thoroughly. Add ¼ of the rice to the casserole, and even it with a spatula. Sprinkle ½ the mint mixture evenly over the rice. Add ½ the lamb, making sure the meat pieces are in one layer. Add another ¼ of the rice, spreading it out evenly. Sprinkle the remaining mint mixture over it, and add the rest of the lamb in one layer. Cover the lamb with the remaining ½ of the rice. Press it gently to compact it slightly. Dribble the saffron and the remaining 2 tablespoons of *ghee* on top. Lastly, sprinkle the *Kewra* essence over it. Place foil on top of the casserole and cover tightly with the lid.

8 Bake the *biriyani* for 30 minutes. Turn off the oven and leave the casserole inside for an additional 10 minutes.

9 Take the casserole from the oven and place it on the work surface. Gently scoop out as much of the top layer of rice as is possible without disturbing the lamb mixture, and put it in another bowl. Carefully mix the meat and rice that remains in the casserole. Mound the lamb-rice mixture on a large heated serving platter, and cover it with reserved rice, enclosing the meat completely. Garnish with the toasted nuts, raisins, fried onion shreds, and silver foil (*vark*). Serve immediately.

MEAT-STUFFED CABBAGE ROLLS WITH GINGER LEMON SAUCE

KEEMA BHARE BANDH GOBHI

◆

This is an ideal dish to serve when you have a mixed group of vegetarians and meat-eaters. You can serve its vegetable counter-part, Spicy Potato-Stuffed Cabbage Rolls with Ginger Lemon Sauce (p. 195), to the vegetarians.

The wonderful thing about this dish is that it freezes superbly. I always make a batch and keep it ready in the freezer for those occasions when I am running short of time.

Stuffing vegetables with *keema* is a popular technique in North Indian cooking. It not only creates interesting flavours but stretches the meat to serve more people. Although just about any vegetable can be stuffed with *keema*, the most popular are cabbage, aubergine, and green pepper.

FOR 4-6 PERSONS

◆

All the ingredients for making Dry-cooked Spicy Minced Meat (Sookha Keema, p. 124)
1 small cabbage
3 tablespoons light vegetable oil
8 oz/250 g thinly sliced onions
10 oz/300 g chopped fresh ripe tomatoes, or 8 oz/250 g canned tomatoes with their juices, chopped
1 tablespoon shredded fresh ginger root
1 lemon, peeled, seeded and thinly sliced
2½ teaspoons coarse salt
¼ teaspoon black pepper

1 Prepare *Sookha Keema* following instructions on p. 124.

2 Insert a sharp-pointed knife into the cabbage where the leaves join the stem. Slowly run the knife around the stem, in a conical circle, to disjoin it from the cabbage leaves. Discard the stem and the attached hard core.

3 Rinse the cabbage thoroughly, place it in a deep pot, and add enough cold water to cover the cabbage by at least 1 in/2.5 cm. Bring to the boil, add 1 tablespoon of salt, and cook for 5 minutes. Let the cabbage drain thoroughly in a colander placed in the kitchen sink. When cool enough to handle, separate the leaves of the cabbage carefully, so as not to tear them. (If some should tear a little, don't worry – they can be sealed when you are rolling them.) Save 15-16 leaves, and finely shred the remainder. Set aside.

4 Heat the oil in a medium-sized saucepan, and add onions. Over medium heat, sauté the onions until they are wilted and begin to colour (about 5 minutes). Add shredded cabbage, tomatoes, ginger, lemon slices, salt, pepper, and ½ pint/30 cl of water, and bring the contents to the boil. Reduce heat and simmer, uncovered, for 2 minutes. Turn off heat, and set sauce aside. The cabbage and the sauce can be prepared a day ahead and refrigerated until you are ready to assemble the dish.

5 About 1¼ hours before you are ready to serve, begin assembling. Preheat the oven to 375°F/190°C/Gas 5.

6 Place one large cabbage leaf at a time on the workboard. If there is a large rip in a leaf, cover it with another small piece of cabbage leaf. Put about 2½ tablespoons of the filling in the centre of the leaf, and fold the cabbage leaf over, and roll it up, tucking in the ends as you roll. There should be 12 cabbage rolls in all.

7 Put ⅓ of the pulpy tomato sauce in the bottom of a baking dish just large enough to hold all the cabbage rolls snugly in one layer. Pour the remaining sauce over the rolls, distributing the shredded cabbage evenly. Cover and seal the dish tightly with a piece of foil.

8 Bake for 50 minutes. Uncover the pan and continue baking for an additional 10 minutes. Serve immediately.

NOTE This dish may be prepared a day ahead and refrigerated or frozen. Defrost thoroughly before reheating. To reheat, place the covered dish in an oven preheated to 350°F/175°C/Gas 4 for 50 minutes.

These cabbage rolls are so subtly flavoured that anything more than plain cooked rice (p. 256) would probably detract from the full enjoyment of them. A good vegetable choice is Turmeric Potatoes with Green Peppers (p. 228). Ideal *dals* are Lentils with Garlic Butter (p. 238) or Mung Beans Laced with Black Mustard Seeds (p. 240). To add to the meal, serve Spinach and Mung Bean Dumplings (p. 101).

GOANESE HOT AND PUNGENT CURRY

VENDALOO

◆

Vendaloo is the famous fiery-hot, mustard-laced dish from Goa, a state on the southwest coast of India. Traditionally, *vendaloo* is made with pork but there are many variations prepared with beef, chicken, lamb, and even duck. Pork is rarely eaten in India, except by the Portuguese Christians in Goa. Even though some religious sects permit the eating of pork, it is not as highly prized a meat in India as lamb or chicken.

Vendaloo is made by first marinating the pork in a mixture of spices and seasonings. It is then cooked in the marinade along with such additional flavourings as fried onions and tamarind juice. The ingredient that imparts the authentic *vendaloo* flavour is mustard oil. Mustard oil in its raw form has a very strong smell that many people find unpleasant. Before Indians use it in cooking, it is put through a mellowing process. This is done by heating the oil to a very high temperature (the smoking point), which releases the pungent smell and vaporizes the oil. When cool, the mustard oil is ready for use.

FOR 4 PERSONS

◆

6 pork chops
THE MARINADE
1 teaspoon cumin seeds
1 teaspoon black mustard seeds
1 medium-sized onion, peeled and quartered
4 medium-sized cloves garlic
1 tablespoon chopped fresh ginger root
2 tablespoons cider vinegar
2 tablespoons light vegetable oil
½ teaspoon ground cinnamon
¼ teaspoon ground cloves

FOR COOKING

2 oz/60 g tamarind pulp
4 fl oz/12.5 cl mustard oil, or light vegetable oil
8 oz/250 g thinly sliced onions
1½ teaspoons turmeric
1½ teaspoons red pepper
1½ teaspoons paprika
2 teaspoons coarse salt

1 Using a sharp boning knife, cut the meat off the bone. Reserve the bones. Trim all traces of fat from the meat and bones, and discard. Cut the meat into ¾ in/2 cm cubes, and set aside.

2 Heat a small frying pan over medium heat, and add cumin and mustard seeds. Roast the seeds, stirring constantly, until the cumin seeds turn dark and the mustard seeds grey (about 3 minutes). Transfer to a small bowl and let cool briefly. Then grind to a fine powder. Set aside.

3 Put onion, garlic, ginger, vinegar, and oil into the container of an electric blender or food processor, and run the machine until the contents have formed a fine purée.

4 Place the pork, along with the bones, in a nonmetallic bowl. Add ground cumin and mustard seeds, puréed mixture, cinnamon, and clove. Mix thoroughly to distribute the spice paste over the meat pieces. Cover and marinate for 8 hours, or refrigerate for 48 hours.

5 Put the tamarind pulp in a bowl, add ½ pint/30 cl boiling water, and let it soak for 15 minutes. Mash the pulp with the back of a spoon, or use your fingers. Strain the liquid, squeezing the pulp as much as possible, into another small bowl, and set aside. Discard the stringy fibre.

6 When ready to cook the meat, heat the mustard oil over high heat in a large enamel-coated pan. When the oil begins to smoke, turn off the heat, and let it cool completely. (Skip this step if you are using a vegetable oil rather than mustard oil.)

7 Heat the oil again over medium-high heat, and add onions. Fry them until they turn caramel brown (about 12 minutes), stirring constantly to prevent burning. Reduce heat to medium, add turmeric, red pepper, and paprika. When the spices begin to sizzle and turn dark (about 15 seconds), add the meat and bones (reserve any marinade left in the bowl), and fry until the meat pieces are slightly seared and the oil begins to separate from the gravy (about 10 minutes). Add tamarind juice, salt, and any remaining marinade, and bring it to the boil. Lower heat and cook, partially covered, until meat is thoroughly done and very tender (about 30 minutes). Carefully pick out the bones, and discard. Check for salt, and serve.

NOTE This dish improves with keeping. It may be made ahead and refrigerated for up to 4 days, or frozen. Defrost thoroughly before reheating.

Vendaloo is traditionally eaten with rice, but I also like to serve it with bread. For a vegetable, serve Green Beans with Coconut and Black Mustard Seeds (p. 223) or Cauliflower and Spring Onions with Black Mustard Seeds (p. 218). It is a good idea to serve a yogurt salad with this dish because it will offset the hot taste nicely and is the classic accompaniment to most southern Indian dishes. Good choices are Tomato and Yogurt Salad (p. 248) or Okra and Yogurt Salad (p. 249).

POULTRY AND EGGS

MURGHI AU ANDA

◆

In North India when a marriage is arranged between families, one of the things the bride's father says to the bridegroom's father is *'Khoob Badhia murghi khilayenge'*, meaning plenty of chicken will be served at the wedding reception. This line never fails to please the bridegroom's father and his family. If all other aspects of the arrangement are found satisfactory, the marriage contract is considered concluded.

Chicken is still a very expensive meat in India and is therefore highly regarded. Another reason for this special attachment to chicken is that it is generally believed that while Moslems in India excel at lamb preparations, Hindus have mastery of the art of cooking chicken. And among Hindus, it is the Punjabis who have always preferred chicken to any other meat. They are famous for their delicately flavoured, exquisite chicken preparations.

PREPARING CHICKEN FOR COOKING Except when it is roasted, the chicken in Indian cooking is cut into small serving pieces. The wing tips and neck bone are often removed and saved for the stockpot. In Indian cooking the chicken is always – and I mean always – skinned before being cooked. This is because, first, Indians believe the skin to be unclean and, along with feathers, beak, and other inedible parts, not to be eaten. Second – a more valid reason – the skin prevents the seasonings and flavourings from penetrating the meat, an essential process in Indian cooking.

Skinning a chicken is very simple. The only difficulty is that both the skin and the flesh are slippery, so that getting a good grip can be a problem. This can be solved by using a kitchen towel. To skin, hold the chicken firmly with one hand and, with the other, grip the skin near the neck with the towel and pull away to release the skin from the flesh. Slash and tear the skin with a sharp boning knife as you go along. Skinning, of course, is much easier if the chicken is cut up into pieces.

TIPS ON COOKING CHICKEN Chicken is done two ways in Indian cooking: either in a sauce (braised or stewed) or dry (fried, roasted, or grilled). Indians do not like their chicken to be slightly pink near the bone with the juices still running; by Indian standards, such chicken is still raw. The Indian way, therefore, is to cook the chicken until the juices have stopped running and the meat is moist and tender, with solid firm flesh.

Since the fried, roasted, and grilled preparations take only a few minutes to cook, the chicken is usually marinated in a spice-laced yogurt marinade which, in addition to flavouring the chicken, tenderizes it. In the braised and stewed preparations, the chicken is usually browned separately before being added to other ingredients and cooked.

A few precautions are necessary while browning chicken. The chicken pieces should be thoroughly patted dry with a kitchen or paper towel before being cooked, or they will not brown. And a lid should be kept handy because the chicken blood and other moisture is sometimes released from the joints and bones during frying. When this moisture comes in contact with the hot fat, it may explode in all directions.

NOTE ON PREPARING IN ADVANCE AND FREEZING For best results, the following chicken recipes can be prepared at least a couple of hours before serving, or a day or two in advance. This allows the flavours and sauce to penetrate the chicken. The chicken recipes that are best suited to freezing are those with an abundant amount of sauce. The Moghul Braised Chicken (p. 155), Chicken Smothered in Aromatic Herbs and Almonds (p. 165), and Chicken Pilaf (p. 172), are fairly dry preparations and do not freeze well. Defrost any frozen dish thoroughly in the refrigerator, overnight, before reheating. If a dish is reheated or frozen, reheat gently over a low heat or in a warm oven. Retaste for seasonings and add any garnish just before serving.

MOGHUL BRAISED CHICKEN

MUGHALAI KORMA

◆

This delectable *korma* of chicken takes no time at all to prepare. Once you have sautéed the seasonings, spices, and yogurt, simply braise the chicken in the mixture. I prefer to use whole rather than powdered spices, so the beautiful creamy colour of the dish isn't destroyed.

This particular *korma* is delicious by itself, but it is often mixed with cooked rice to create the classic Chicken Pilaf (p. 172).

FOR 4 PERSONS

◆

1½ lb/750 g skinned boneless chicken breast meat
6 fl oz/20 cl light vegetable oil
8 oz/250 g finely chopped onions
1 tablespoon finely chopped garlic
1½ tablespoons finely chopped fresh ginger root
12 green cardamom pods, slightly crushed
24 whole cloves
4 bay leaves
2 teaspoons ground coriander
¼-½ teaspoon red pepper
8 oz/250 g plain yogurt
2 teaspoons coarse salt
4 fl oz/12.5 cl double cream

1 Place the chicken breasts on a cutting board, and, using a sharp knife, slice them thinly into ¼ in/5 mm thick medallions. Cut the medallions into 2½ × 1½ in/6 × 4 cm pieces, and set aside.

2 Heat the oil in a wide heavy-bottomed pan, preferably one with a non-stick surface, and add onions, garlic, and ginger. Over medium-high heat, cook them until they turn pale and begin to brown (about 10 minutes), stirring constantly to prevent burning. Add cardamom, cloves, and bay leaves, and cook, stirring rapidly, until cardamom pods and cloves are fried and puffed and the bay leaves turn brown (about 5 minutes). The onions should by now be light golden brown. Add coriander and red pepper, stir for 10-15 seconds, and add 2 tablespoons of the yogurt. Continue frying the mixture until the moisture from the yogurt evaporates. Then add two more tablespoons of yogurt, and fry. Keep adding yogurt and frying until all the yogurt is used up (about 5 minutes).

3 Add the chicken pieces, and sauté, turning and tossing until the meat loses its pink colour (about 3-5 minutes). Add 4 fl oz/12.5 cl boiling water with the salt, and mix. Reduce heat to medium-low and simmer, covered, until the fillets are cooked and tender (about 25 minutes). The oil will begin to separate from the gravy, which should be fairly thick by now, and to coat the chicken pieces. Stir in the cream, and turn off heat. Let the *korma* rest, covered, for an hour before serving. When ready to serve, heat thoroughly, check for salt, and then serve.

NOTE *Mughalai Korma* may be prepared ahead and refrigerated for up to 2 days.

Either plain cooked rice (p. 256) or Saffron Pilaf with Peaches (p. 266) should accompany this *korma*. *Paratha* (p. 285) or *Phulka* (p. 282) are equally good. Appropriate side dishes are Lucknow Sour Lentils (p.241) or Lentils with Garlic Butter (p. 238). You can serve any appetizer except kebabs and dumplings. Fresh Mint Relish (p. 309) goes extremely well with this meal.

CHICKEN IN ONION TOMATO GRAVY

MURGH MASALA

◆

This is a classic dish from Punjab, a state in the North of India. Traditionally, the chicken is cut into small pieces and stewed in a tomato and fried-onion gravy. Chopped fresh coriander is folded in immediately before serving to lend herbal fragrance and to provide a nice colour contrast to the reddish brown gravy. The whole spices (cinnamon and cardamom) in this dish are not eaten, but no harm will come to you if you bite into them.

FOR 8 PERSONS

◆

2 × 3 lb/1.5 kg chickens cut into 8-10 pieces each (or use cut-up legs and breasts in any combination)
10 tablespoons light vegetable oil
2 lb/1 kg thinly sliced onions
2 tablespoons finely chopped garlic
3 tablespoons finely chopped fresh ginger root
2 cinnamon sticks, 3 in/7.5 cm long
4 black (or 8 green) cardamom pods
1 tablespoon turmeric
1 teaspoon red pepper
1¼ lb/625 g fresh ripe tomatoes, puréed or finely chopped
1 tablespoon coarse salt
¾ pint/45 cl boiling water
1 tablespoon ground roasted cumin seeds (p. 62)
3-4 tablespoons chopped fresh coriander leaves

1 Cut off the wing tips, and pull the skin away from the chicken pieces, using a kitchen towel to get a better grip. (Reserve the wing tips and skin for the stockpot.)
2 Heat 2 tablespoons of the oil in a large heavy-bottomed pan, preferably one with a non-stick surface, over high heat. When the oil is very hot, add the chicken pieces, a few at a time, and sear them until they lose their pink colour and get nicely browned on all sides (about 3-4 minutes). Remove them with a

slotted spoon and reserve them in a bowl. Continue with the rest of the chicken pieces until all of them are seared.

3 Add the remaining 8 tablespoons of oil to the pan, along with the onions. Reduce heat to medium-high, and fry the onions until they turn light brown (about 30 minutes), stirring constantly to prevent burning. (See directions for Brown-frying Onions, p. 66.) Add garlic and ginger, and fry for an additional 5 minutes. Add cinnamon and cardamom, and continue frying until the spices are slightly puffed and begin to brown (about 2 minutes). Add turmeric and red pepper, and stir rapidly for 10-15 seconds. Add puréed or chopped tomatoes, along with the chicken, salt, and ¾ pint/45 cl of boiling water. Stir to mix, reduce heat and simmer, covered, until chicken is cooked and very tender and the gravy has thickened (about 45 minutes). If the gravy has not thickened adequately, increase heat and boil rapidly, uncovered, until it thickens to the consistency of a beef stew. If, on the other hand, the evaporation is too fast, add a little water. The finished dish should have plenty of thick pulpy gravy. Turn off heat, and let the dish rest, covered, for at least 1 hour, preferably 2, before serving. When ready to serve, heat thoroughly, fold in roasted cumin and chopped coriander, check for salt, and serve.

I like to serve this dish with a bread. You may also serve it with a plain cooked rice for a simple meal; or with a pilaf for more substantial fare. For a vegetable, serve Turmeric Potatoes with Green Peppers (p. 228). A *raita*, such as Dumplings in Fragrant Yogurt (p. 250), may be included if you want another side dish. Serve an onion relish on the side.

YOGURT-BRAISED CHICKEN

DAHI MURGHI

◆

This is a simple everyday method of preparing chicken that is utterly delicious. The chicken pieces are called yogurt-braised, even though only a small amount of yogurt is used. The fragrance and flavour of yogurt is distinct, because only certain spices are added, and in very moderate amounts.

FOR 4-6 PERSONS

◆

3 lb/1.5 kg chicken cut into 8-10 pieces (or use cut-up legs and breasts in any combination)
4 tablespoons light vegetable oil
1 lb/500 g thinly sliced onions
1 tablespoon finely chopped garlic
1 tablespoon ground coriander
½ teaspoon red pepper, or to taste
1½ teaspoons garam masala (p. 42)
1 teaspoon ground roasted Indian poppy seeds (p. 62)
8 fl oz/25 cl plain yogurt
4 tablespoons sour cream
4 tablespoons usli ghee (p. 52), or light vegetable oil
1 tablespoon coarse salt

1 Cut off the wing tips, and pull the skin from the chicken pieces, using a kitchen towel to get a good grip. Set aside. (Reserve the wing tips and skin for the stockpot.)

2 Heat the oil in a large heavy-bottomed pan, and add onions. Over medium-high heat, fry the onions until they turn limp and pale golden and begin to brown (about 10 minutes), stirring constantly to ensure even browning. Add garlic, and cook for an additional 2 minutes. Add coriander, red pepper, *garam masala*, and poppy seeds, and stir rapidly for 1 minute. Add yogurt, sour cream, and 5 tablespoons water, and bring to the boil. Reduce heat and simmer the mixture, covered, for 5 minutes. Turn off heat, and let the mixture cool slightly. Finely purée it in either an electric blender or a food processor. Set aside until needed.

3 Put the *ghee* into the pan, and place it over medium heat. When the *ghee* is very hot, add chicken pieces and sauté, turning and tossing, until they lose their pink colour (about 4 minutes). Add the puréed mixture and salt, and bring to the boil. Reduce heat and cook the chicken, covered, until very tender but not falling apart (about 45 minutes). Check often during cooking to ensure the sauce is not sticking to the bottom of the pan and burning. By this time the gravy should have thickened to a smooth white sauce, and a glaze will be coating the chicken pieces.

It is absolutely essential that the sauce be of the right consistency in this dish. If the sauce has not thickened enough, it will be thin and runny with no shine. To remedy, simply increase heat and boil rapidly, uncovered, to evaporate excess moisture, until the sauce reduces to the desired consistency and glaze. On the other hand, the sauce may be too thick and pasty, in which case a considerable amount of fat will separate and float on the surface. In this instance, add some water or milk, little by little, until the sauce is thinned to the desired consistency and the fat has been incorporated back into the sauce. Turn off heat and let the dish rest, covered, at least 1 hour before serving. When ready to serve, heat thoroughly, check for salt, and serve.

This dish can be accompanied by a simple pilaf, such as Fragrant Pilaf Banaras Style (p. 263) or Indian Fried Rice (p. 261). Any baked bread may also be served. For a side dish, serve Smoked Aubergine with Fresh Herbs (p. 220) if you are having bread; and Cauliflower and Spring Onions with Black Mustard Seeds (p. 218) if you are serving rice. A good hot relish to spice this meal is Hot Hyderabad Tomato Relish (p. 314).

CHICKEN IN CREAMED COCONUT SAUCE

MALAI MURGH

◆

In India it is commonly believed that if a dish contains coconut it must be from southern India. This dish proves otherwise. Even though the use of coconut is limited in the North, the dishes created with it are very special indeed. Coconut cream is called *malai* in the North. In this recipe the chicken is simmered in rich coconut milk and a blend of Moghul spices to produce a marvellously flavoured and very satisfying dish.

The cardamom, cloves, and cinnamon in this dish are not meant to be eaten, but no harm will come to you if by chance you swallow a clove or bite into the cinnamon stick.

FOR 4-6 PERSONS

◆

2½ lb/ 1.25 kg chicken breasts on the bone
4 fl oz/ 12.5 cl light vegetable oil
3 oz/ 90 g finely chopped onions
4 teaspoons finely chopped garlic
4 teaspoons finely chopped fresh ginger root
8 green cardamom pods
12 whole cloves
1 cinnamon stick, 3 in/ 7.5 cm long
2 tablespoons ground blanched almonds
½ pint/ 30 cl fresh coconut milk (p. 50)
¼ teaspoon turmeric
½ teaspoon red pepper, or more, to taste
2 teaspoons coarse salt
4 tablespoons double cream
2 tablespoons finely chopped coriander leaves

1 Pull the skin off the chicken breasts and cut into pieces. You should have a total of 8 pieces of skinned chicken breasts with bone.
2 Heat the oil in a large heavy-bottomed pan, and add onions, garlic, and ginger. Over medium-high heat, cook them until onions are pale and limp

(about 5 minutes). Add cardamom, cloves, and cinnamon, and cook until the spices are slightly puffed and begin to brown (about 5 minutes). Add almond powder and cook, stirring rapidly, for an additional 2 minutes. Reduce heat to medium, and add chicken pieces in one layer. Let cook undisturbed for 1 minute. Turn the chicken pieces and continue cooking just until they lose their pink colour (about 2 minutes altogether). The chicken should remain as white as possible.

3 Add coconut milk, turmeric, red pepper, and salt, and bring to the boil. Reduce heat and simmer, covered, until the chicken pieces are thoroughly cooked and melting tender (about 30 minutes). Check often to ensure the sauce is not evaporating too fast and burning. Stir in the cream, and turn off heat. Let the dish rest, covered, for at least 1 hour before serving. When ready to serve, heat thoroughly, check for salt, and serve sprinkled with finely chopped coriander leaves.

NOTE This dish definitely tastes better if made several hours ahead. It can be kept in the refrigerator for up to 2 days, or frozen.

Follow the menu suggestions given for Yogurt-Braised Chicken on page 159.

ROYAL CHICKEN IN SILKY WHITE ALMOND SAUCE

SHAHI MURGH BADAAMI

◆

Almonds (*Badaam*) were a great favourite of the Moghuls; they used them as an occasion to create many sensational dishes. Of all the *Badaami* (meaning 'in almond sauce') dishes, this is by far the most delicious. This recipe produces a very subtly flavoured dish. If you want a hotter taste, add all eight pepper pods as suggested. In this recipe the word 'silky' refers to the appearance of the sauce, not to its texture, which is indeed grainy.

FOR 6 PERSONS

◆

8-10 chicken pieces
10 tablespoons light vegetable oil
1½ lb/750 g onions, thinly sliced
6 tablespoons slivered blanched almonds
4 tablespoons coriander seeds
4 teaspoons green cardamom pods (about 50 pods)
4-8 hot red pepper pods, or 1-2 teaspoons red pepper
¾ pt/45 cl plain yogurt
2½ teaspoons coarse salt

1 Cut off the wing tips, and pull the skin away from all the chicken pieces, using a paper towel to get a better grip. (Reserve the wing tips and skin for the stockpot.)

2 Heat 2 tablespoons of the oil over medium heat in a wide, heavy-bottomed pan. When the oil is hot, add chicken pieces, a few at a time, and cook, turning constantly, until they lose their pink colour and begin to sear. Do not allow them to brown or the sauce will turn dark. Take them out with a slotted spoon and reserve them in a bowl. Continue with the rest of the chicken pieces until they are seared. Set aside.

3 Add the remaining 8 tablespoons of oil to the pan, along with the onions. Fry the onions until they are wilted and pale golden (about 10 minutes), stirring constantly to keep them from colouring unevenly. Do not let the onions overbrown or the sauce will be dark. Add almonds, coriander, cardamom, and red pepper pods (if you are using red pepper powder, do not add it at this stage), and cook for an additional 3-5 minutes or until the almonds are lightly coloured and the cardamom pods are puffed up. If you are using red pepper powder, add it now, and stir. Turn off the heat.

4 Put the entire mixture, along with 8 fl oz/25 cl water, into the container of an electric blender or food processor, and run the machine until the mixture is reduced to a fine smooth purée.

5 Return the purée to the pan, along with the chicken pieces, yogurt, and salt, and bring to the boil. Reduce heat and simmer, covered, until the chicken is tender and the sauce has thickened nicely (about 45 minutes). At this point, the oil will begin to separate from the sauce, and a thin glaze will form over both sauce and chicken. Turn off the heat and let the dish rest, covered, for ½ hour before serving. When ready to serve, reheat the dish until piping hot, check for salt, and serve.

NOTE This dish tastes absolutely divine if made a day ahead and refrigerated. This prolonged resting allows the flavours to penetrate the meat of the chicken, and makes it taste even better. This dish may be kept in the refrigerator for up to 2 days, or it can be frozen. Defrost thoroughly before reheating. To reheat, simmer gently until warmed through.

Present a fragrant pilaf with this elegant dish. Serve Sweet Saffron Pilaf (p. 264) to introduce a subtle contrast of colours. Equally good is Fragrant Pilaf Banaras Style (p. 263). All baked breads go well with this dish. Good vegetable choices are Green Beans with Coconut and Black Mustard Seeds (p. 223), and Broccoli Smothered in Garlic Oil (p. 214).

CHICKEN SMOTHERED
IN AROMATIC HERBS AND ALMONDS

BADAAMI MURGH

◆

This is a classic North Indian dish. It is traditionally reserved for entertaining and special festive occasions. The beautifully rich, thick, garnet-coloured sauce that coats the chicken pieces is created from a blend of tomatoes, fried onions with spices, and almond butter.

The whole spices – cinnamon, cardamom, and clove – are not meant to be eaten. If you do bite into them, however, no harm will come to you.

FOR 4-6 PERSONS

◆

1 × 3½ lb/1.75 kg chicken cut in 8-10 pieces (or use cut-up legs and breasts in any combination)
1½ teaspoons lemon juice
2 teaspoons coarse salt
6 tablespoons light vegetable oil
3 tablespoons sliced or slivered blanched almonds
12 oz/375 g finely chopped onions
1 tablespoon finely chopped garlic
1 tablespoon finely chopped fresh ginger root
1 stick cinnamon, 3 in/7.5 cm long
4 black (or 8 green) cardamom pods
4 whole cloves
1 teaspoon ground cumin
1 teaspoon ground coriander
½ teaspoon turmeric
½ teaspoon red pepper, or to taste
8 oz/250 g finely chopped or puréed fresh ripe tomatoes (or 4 oz/125 g drained canned tomatoes, chopped)
2-3 tablespoons almond butter (see p. 127), or 4 tablespoons ground blanched almonds
1-2 tablespoons finely chopped coriander leaves

1 Cut off the wing tips and pull the skin off all the chicken pieces, using a kitchen towel to get a better grip. (Reserve the wing tips and skin for the stockpot.) Prick the chicken pieces all over with a fork or a thin skewer. Place them in a bowl and rub lemon juice and salt over them.

2 Cover and marinate for ½ hour, or refrigerate overnight. (If you are rushed, skip the marinating and simply proceed to the next step.)

3 Heat 1 tablespoon of the oil in a large heavy-bottomed pan, preferably with a non-stick surface. Add sliced or slivered almonds, and sauté over medium-low heat, turning and tossing until they turn light brown (about 3 minutes). Take them out immediately and drain on paper towels. Set them aside until needed for garnish.

4 Put the remaining 5 tablespoons of oil in the pan, and add onions. Over medium-high heat, fry the onions until they turn light brown (about 15 minutes), stirring constantly to prevent burning. Add garlic and ginger, and cook for an additional 2 minutes. Add cinnamon, cardamom, and cloves, and cook until the spices are slightly puffed and begin to brown (about 2 minutes).

5 Reduce heat to medium, add chicken pieces, and cook, turning and tossing until they lose their pink colour and are lightly seared (about 5-7 minutes). Add cumin, coriander, turmeric, and red pepper. Stir rapidly for a couple of minutes to distribute the ground spices, and add tomatoes, almond butter or powder, along with 4 fl oz/12.5 cl of hot water. Bring to the boil. Reduce heat, and simmer the chicken, covered, for 50 minutes or until the chicken is fork-tender. Stir frequently during cooking to keep the sauce from sticking and burning. If the evaporation is too fast, add a few tablespoons of water. Turn off heat, and let the dish rest, covered, for at least 1 hour. When ready to serve, heat thoroughly, check for salt, and transfer to a warm serving platter. Serve sprinkled with chopped coriander and toasted almonds.

For a simple meal, serve this dish with plain cooked rice (p. 256) or *Poori* (p. 293). For a fancier meal, serve the Emperor's Pilaf with Black Mushrooms (p. 268) and a yogurt salad, such as Dumplings in Fragrant Yogurt (p. 250). Sweet Lemon Pickle with Cumin (p. 318) is a good accompaniment.

CHICKEN KABULI

MURGH KABULI

◆

The almond-coloured sauce swathing the chunks of creamy-white chicken, with specks of cracked pepper and deep green coriander for contrast, looks absolutely breathtaking.

FOR 8 PERSONS

◆

4 large cloves garlic, peeled
3 tablespoons chopped fresh ginger root
3 medium-sized ripe tomatoes (about 12 oz/375 g)
8 fl oz/25 cl plain yogurt
6 fl oz/20 cl light vegetable oil
3 lb/1.5 kg skinned boneless chicken-breast meat cut into 1½ in/4 cm cubes
½ teaspoon mace
1 teaspoon nutmeg
2 tablespoons ground blanched almonds
1 teaspoon ground cardamom
1 teaspoon ground cumin
1 teaspoon ground coriander
½ teaspoon fennel seeds, ground
1 tablespoon coarse salt
4 fl oz/12.5 cl double cream
2-3 teaspoons black peppercorns, coarsely ground
4-5 tablespoons finely chopped fresh coriander leaves

1 Put garlic, ginger, tomatoes, and yogurt into the container of an electric blender or food processor, and run the machine until the ingredients are reduced to a fine smooth purée.

2 Put oil and the puréed mixture in a large heavy-bottomed pan, preferably one with a non-stick surface. Place the pan over medium-high heat, and cook the purée until it reduces to a thick sauce and the fat begins to separate from it (about 15 minutes) stirring constantly to prevent the purée sticking to the pan and burning. During the last few minutes of cooking, the sauce begins to spatter a little, so keep a lid or spatter screen handy.

3 Add chicken pieces and cook, stirring rapidly, until they lose their pink colour and begin to sear slightly (about 5 minutes), but do not let them brown. Add mace, nutmeg, almond powder, cardamom, cumin, coriander, fennel, and salt, and mix well. Reduce heat, cover the pot, and let the chicken cook in its own juices for 15 minutes. Uncover, and continue cooking until the chicken is fully cooked and fork-tender and the sauce has almost dried (about 15 minutes). Stir in cream, black pepper, and coriander leaves, and turn off heat. Let the dish rest, covered, for at least 1 hour. When ready to serve, reheat thoroughly, check for salt, and serve.

NOTE For best results, make this dish at least 4 hours, preferably a day, before you are going to serve it to allow the flavours to blend.

You can serve this dish with any fried bread, or with a simple pilaf, and include a vegetable like Broccoli Smothered in Garlic Oil (p. 214). Or instead, combine the staple and side dish, and serve either a stuffed bread, such as Cauliflower-Stuffed Bread (p. 287) or Spinach Bread (p. 291), or a vegetable pilaf, such as Mint Pilaf (p. 270). Raw Onion Relish (p. 304) and Sweet Lemon Pickle with Cumin (p. 318) are wonderful accompaniments.

TANDOORI (INDIAN BARBECUED) CHICKEN

TANDOORI MURGHI

◆

Of all the food cooked in a *tandoor*, the most popular and best-tasting is chicken. The distinctive flavour, texture, and colour of this dish are achieved by a particular yogurt marinade, by the use of tenderizers, a special *tandoori* colouring, and finally, by being cooked in the Indian clay oven. The recipe given here is designed for the conventional oven and charcoal grill.

FOR 6 PERSONS

◆

3 very young chickens (about 2 lb/ 1 kg each)
2½ teaspoons unseasoned natural meat tenderizer
5 tablespoons lemon juice

THE MARINADE
2 large cloves garlic
1 tablespoon chopped fresh ginger root
1 teaspoon ground roasted cumin seeds
½ teaspoon ground cardamom
½ teaspoon red pepper
1 teaspoon tandoori colouring, or 1 tablespoon paprika
5 tablespoons plain yogurt
Usli ghee (p. 52), Indian vegetable shortening, or light vegetable oil for basting

1 Cut the wings off the chickens. Remove the neckbone carefully. Place the chickens on a cutting board and quarter them neatly. Then pull away the skin, using kitchen towels for a better grip if necessary. (Reserve the wings, neck, and skin for the stockpot.) Prick the chicken all over with a fork or thin skewer. Make diagonal slashes, ½ in/1 cm deep, 1 in/2.5 cm apart on the meat. Put the meat in a large bowl.

2 Add meat tenderizer and lemon juice to the chicken, and rub them into the slashes and all over for 2 minutes. Cover and marinate for ½ hour.

3 Put all the ingredients of the marinade into the container of an electric blender or food processor, and blend until reduced to a smooth sauce. (Alternatively, garlic and ginger may be crushed to a paste and blended with the remaining ingredients.)

4 Pour this marinade over the chicken pieces and mix, turning and tossing, to coat all the pieces well. (A *note of caution*: Since certain brands of *tandoori* colouring tend to stain the fingers, it is advisable either to use a fork to turn the chicken pieces in the marinade or use a pastry brush to spread it over the chicken.) Cover and marinate for 4 hours at room temperature, or refrigerate overnight, turning several times. Chicken should not remain in the marinade for more than 2 days, because the marinade contains a meat tenderizer which, with prolonged marinating, alters the texture of the chicken meat to very soft and doughy.

5 Take the chicken from the refrigerator at least 1 hour before cooking to bring to room temperature. The chicken is now ready to be either roasted in the oven or grilled on an electric or charcoal grill.

TO ROAST IN THE OVEN Start heating the oven to 500°F/260°C/Gas 9. Take the chicken pieces out of the marinade. Brush them with *ghee*, and place on an extra-large shallow roasting pan, preferably on a wire rack. Set the pan in the oven, and roast for 25-30 minutes, or until the meat is cooked through. There is no need to baste while the chicken pieces are roasting, because the enclosed environment keeps the chickens from drying excessively.

TO GRILL INDOORS Preheat the grill. Brush the grill with a little oil to prevent the meat sticking. Place the chicken pieces, slashed side up, on the grill, and brush the slashed side with *ghee*. Cook 2-3 in/5-7.5 cm away from the heat for 20 minutes. Turn and cook the other side for another 10 minutes, or until the chicken pieces are cooked through. Brush the chicken often with *ghee* during cooking.

TO GRILL OUTDOORS Fire the coal well in advance (about 1½ hours before you are ready to begin cooking), so that a white ash forms over the surface of the coal. This is when the coal is at its hottest. Place the grill at least 5 in/12.5 cm away from the heat, and rub generously with oil. Place the chicken pieces, slashed side up, over the grill and brush them with *ghee*. Let them cook without turning for 10 minutes. Turn, baste the other side, and cook for 10 minutes. Continue to cook, turning and basting the chicken every 10 minutes, until it is done. The time depends upon the intensity of the heat and its distance from the chicken. The point to remember is that the chicken pieces have been marinating in a very strong tenderizing solution for two days and therefore will cook much faster than standard barbecued chicken.

Serve the chicken immediately, lightly brushed with *ghee* or oil and accompanied by Roasted Onions (*Bhone Piaz*, p. 227).

Both Sweet Saffron Pilaf (p. 264), and Saffron Pilaf with Peaches (p. 266) are excellent served with *tandoori* chicken. If you want to expand the meal, serve Buttered Black Beans (p. 242), and a *raita* such as Sweet Banana and Yogurt Salad (p. 251).

VELVET BUTTER CHICKEN

MAKHANI MURGH

◆

This chicken preparation is a classic example of the true flair and skill of Indian cooks. In this dish, *Makhani* (meaning 'buttered', or 'in butter') and *Murgh* (meaning chicken, and referring in this context to the leftover day-old *tandoori* chicken pieces) are combined. They are simmered in cumin-scented butter and a creamy rich tomato sauce and become a delicacy craved far more than *tandoori* chicken. An important element in the special flavour of this dish is the chopped coriander leaves that are folded in prior to serving.

CRCK

FOR 8 PERSONS

◆

²⁄₃ recipe Tandoori Chicken from preceding recipe (8 legs and breasts of chicken in any combination), or 2 tandoori chickens (about 2 lb/1 kg each) cooked by any recipe
1½ lb/750 g canned tomatoes in purée, measured with purée (or 2 lb/1 kg chopped fresh ripe tomatoes)
4 green chilies, seeded (or substitute ½ teaspoon red pepper, or to taste)
2 tablespoons chopped fresh ginger root
10 tablespoons sweet butter
4 teaspoons ground cumin
1 tablespoon paprika
2 teaspoons coarse salt
½ pint/30 cl double cream
2 teaspoons garam masala (p. 42)
2 teaspoons ground roasted cumin seeds (p. 62, optional)
4 tablespoons minced coriander leaves

1 Cut the chicken pieces neatly into halves, so that you have 16 pieces of chicken.

2 Put tomatoes, green chilies, and ginger in the container of an electric blender or food processor, and blend to a fine purée.

3 Place 8 tablespoons of butter in large heavy-bottomed pan, preferably one with a non-stick surface, over medium heat. As the butter melts, tilt the pan in all directions to coat the bottom. When the foam begins to subside, add chicken pieces a few at a time, and brown until they are nicely seared all over (about 2-3 minutes per batch). Remove them with a slotted spoon into a reserved bowl. Continue with the rest of the chicken pieces until all are browned.

4 Add cumin and paprika to the butter in the pan, and cook, stirring rapidly, for 10-15 seconds. Add tomato purée and cook, uncovered, until the sauce is thickened (about 5-8 minutes), stirring constantly to prevent sticking.

5 Add salt, cream, and chicken pieces (with any juices that may have accumulated in the bowl). Gently stir the chicken to coat the pieces evenly and thoroughly with the sauce. Be careful not to break the fragile chicken pieces. Reduce heat to medium-low, and simmer, uncovered, until the fat begins to separate from the sauce and a thin glaze appears on the surface (about 10 minutes). Check and stir often (but only one or two stirs at a time) to ensure that the sauce is not burning. Stir in the remaining 2 tablespoons of butter, *garam masala*, and roasted cumin if you are using it. Turn off heat, and let the dish stand, covered, for ½ hour before serving. When ready to serve, heat thoroughly, check for salt, and fold in chopped coriander leaves.

NOTE This dish may be prepared and refrigerated for up to 2 days, or frozen. Defrost thoroughly before reheating.

You can serve this either with a pilaf, such as Fragrant Pilaf Banaras Style (p. 263), or a fried bread. Buttered Smothered Cabbage (p. 215) or Buttered Greens (p. 231) are good choices for vegetables.

CHICKEN PILAF

MURGH BIRIYANI

◆

Chicken pilaf is truly the most authentic of all North Indian pilafs – a speciality of Hindus and Sikhs. Chicken pilaf is generally made in one of two ways: either all the ingredients are mixed and cooked together, or the chicken and rice are cooked separately and mixed just before serving. I prefer the latter procedure, because there is no danger of the chicken remaining undercooked or the rice becoming overcooked, or of the rice grains falling apart with numerous stirrings. This pilaf, made with a *korma* of chicken and cooked rice, takes no time at all to prepare. It can be made with all parts of the chicken.

NOTE Do not overfry the onions or the sauce will become too dark. Also, it is good to use a tart yogurt here; otherwise the pilaf will taste slightly bland.

FOR 6 PERSONS

◆

All the ingredients for making Moghul Braised Chicken (Mughalai Korma, *p. 155*)
12 oz/375 g basmati *rice*
1 lb/500 g seedless grapes (optional)
1 tablespoon minced coriander leaves (optional)

1 Prepare *Mughalai Korma* following instructions on page 155.

2 Pick over, clean, wash, and soak rice, following instructions given under Preparing Basmati Rice for Cooking on page 255.

3 Preheat oven to 300°F/150°C/Gas 2.

4 Bring 5 pints/3 litres of water to the boil in a deep pot. Add the soaked rice and stir immediately for half a minute (this prevents the rice from settling) being careful not to break the fragile grains. Bring the water to a second boil (it will take about 3 minutes) and cook the rice for 2 minutes. Pour the entire contents of the pot into a large sieve held over a kitchen sink. Hold the sieve under the tap and let the cold water run through the rice at medium speed for 3-5 seconds. Shake sieve to drain the rice thoroughly, and let it cool briefly.

5 Put the chicken with its gravy in a heavy oven-proof casserole with a tight-fitting lid. Add rice, and fold it in carefully. Place aluminium foil on top of the casserole and cover tightly with the lid.

6 Bake for 30 minutes. Turn off the oven, leaving the casserole inside for an additional 10 minutes. The pilaf, left in the oven, will remain warm for an additional 30 minutes. Transfer the pilaf to a heated serving platter, and if desired, surround it with a ring of grapes and sprinkle with finely chopped coriander leaves.

This pilaf is a complete meal in itself, but if you want additional side dishes, include a *raita*, such as Cucumber and Yogurt Salad (p. 246) or Sweet Banana and Yogurt Salad (p. 251).

SCRAMBLED EGGS WITH CUMIN AND FRAGRANT HERBS

ANDE KI BHORJI

◆

Bhorji means scramble. Indians scramble eggs in much the same way they cook meat and chicken, so that the eggs look and feel more like stir-fried vegetables that can be picked up with a piece of bread. Indians also add a lot of onions – enough to equal the quantity of the eggs. Since no Indian dish is complete without the addition of spices and herbs, cumin, green chilies, and fresh chopped coriander leaves are added at the end of the cooking to flavour the eggs properly.

FOR 4-6 PERSONS

◆

6 large eggs
½ teaspoon salt
2 tablespoons Indian vegetable shortening, or light vegetable oil
2 medium-sized onions, peeled and cut into ¾ in/2 cm pieces
½ teaspoon ground roasted cumin seeds (p. 62)
1 tablespoon finely chopped coriander leaves
1-2 green chilies, seeded and sliced (optional)

1 Break the eggs into a small bowl, add salt, and beat slightly to mix. Do not overbeat, as eggs should not be foamy or frothy.
2 Heat the shortening or oil in a frying pan (9-10 in/23-25 cm in diameter), and add onions. Over medium-low heat, sauté onions until they are translucent but still firm and crisp (about 3-4 minutes).
3 Reduce heat to low, and add the beaten eggs. Let the eggs settle in the pan for 5 seconds. Then, using a fork, begin pushing the egg towards the centre of the pan so that it cooks like a thick cake. When most of the egg has coagulated, turn it gently and cook the other side. (Do not worry if it breaks, as the finished dish will, in fact, look like little cakes of scrambled egg studded with onions.) Continue stirring and turning until the eggs are fully cooked (about 3 minutes). Do not let them brown. Turn off heat, and transfer to a warm serving platter.

Serve sprinkled with roasted cumin, chopped coriander leaves, and sliced green chilies.

This flavourful *Bhorji* is traditionally eaten with *Paratha* (p. 285), a classic northern breakfast combination usually accompanied by a pickle. A good choice is Sweet Lemon Pickle with Cumin (p. 318).

WHOLE EGGS IN SPICY TOMATO SAUCE

ANDE KI KARI

◆

Of all Indian egg preparations, *Ande ki Kari* is by far the most popular, especially with vegetarians who include eggs in their diet. This dish is made in two steps: First, the tomato and onion sauce is prepared. When the sauce is fully cooked, hard-boiled egg halves are carefully added. The contrast of the yellow-and-white of the eggs against the glazed reddish tomato sauce is handsome indeed.

TWO IMPORTANT POINTS TO KEEP IN MIND The eggs should be as fresh as possible and boiled at the time you make the entire dish. (With keeping, the yolks begin to turn grey around the edges.) Secondly, after the egg halves have been added, the dish must be stirred with utmost caution or, if possible, not stirred at all, because the yolks have a tendency to slip out of the whites, scatter into the sauce, and look unappetizing.

NOTE The cinnamon and cardamom in this dish are not meant to be eaten. But no harm will come to you if you bite into them.

FOR 8 PERSONS

◆

8 large eggs
10 tablespoons Indian vegetable shortening, or light vegetable oil
12 oz/375 g finely chopped onions
4 teaspoons finely chopped garlic
2 tablespoons finely chopped fresh ginger root
1 stick cinnamon, 3 in/7.5 cm long
4 black (or 8 green) cardamom pods
2 teaspoons ground coriander
1 teaspoon turmeric
¼ teaspoon each red and black pepper
1 lb/500 g finely chopped or puréed fresh ripe tomatoes
2 teaspoons coarse salt
2 teaspoons garam masala (p. 42)
3 tablespoons finely chopped fresh coriander leaves

1 Hard-boil the eggs, peel them, and put them in a bowl of cold water. Set aside until needed.

2 Heat the shortening in a large heavy-bottomed pan, preferably one with a non-stick surface, and add onions. Over medium-high heat, fry the onions until they turn caramel brown (about 20 minutes), stirring constantly to ensure even browning. (See directions for Brown-frying Onions, p. 66.) Add garlic and ginger, and fry for an additional 2 minutes. Add cinnamon and cardamom, and fry until the spices are puffed and begin to brown (about 1 minute). Add coriander, turmeric, red and black pepper. Stir rapidly for a moment or two, and immediately add tomatoes. Cook, uncovered, until the mixture turns into a thick pulpy sauce and the fat begins to separate from the gravy (about 10 minutes). Stir frequently to keep the sauce from sticking and burning. Add salt and 1 pint/60 cl boiling water, and stir to mix. Reduce heat to medium, and simmer the sauce, covered, for 20-25 minutes. At the end of the simmering, the sauce should be fairly thick, and a satiny glaze should develop to coat it. If it is too thin, uncover and boil briskly until the sauce reduces to the right consistency.

Turn off heat, and let the sauce rest, covered, for at least ½ hour before serving. (The sauce may be prepared several hours ahead and kept, covered, at room temperature, or refrigerated for up to 4 days, or frozen. Defrost thoroughly before proceeding with the recipe.)

3 When ready to serve, drain the eggs and pat them dry on paper towels. Cut them neatly into halves lengthwise.

4 Simmer the sauce gently over low heat until piping hot, stir in *garam masala*, and check for salt. Carefully slip in the egg halves, and continue simmering until the eggs are heated through. Serve sprinkled with finely chopped coriander leaves.

SHELLFISH AND FISH

MACHI

◆

Looking at the menu in an Indian restaurant, one is often struck by the fact that there are hardly any seafood or fish selections offered. One may immediately conclude that either Indians are not fish eaters, probably because of limited varieties of fish available in India, or that their repertoire in the field of fish and shellfish cooking is simply too insignificant to be mentioned. All this is a gross misconception, for India has a coastline of over three thousand miles and the land itself is sculptured with rivers, streams, and lakes. These bodies of water support a variety of marine life so large that it would take an entire volume to enumerate all the dishes native to the various regions. For the people living along these waters, fish and seafood have always been part of their daily diet.

Then why is there so little mention of the fish and the shellfish cooking of India? The reasons are twofold.

First, Indian restaurants have traditionally served North Indian food (often known by the classic name, 'Moghul' food). This style of cooking is noted for its meat and poultry preparations. Its repertoire has always been restricted, due to the limited availability – or in many cases, outright lack – of fish and shellfish. Therefore, the few seafood preparations served in these restaurants originated in Bengal (specially East Bengal), where fish and seafood are plentiful. Since the Moghul influence was strong in this region, the dishes had the familiar flavours and appearance. Most other seafood dishes are adaptations to seafood cooking of popular North Indian meat-cooking techniques.

Second, the fish found in Indian waters are very different from those found in other parts of the world. The sweet and succulent giant prawns (*bagda jheengari*), each weighing as much as 1½ lb/750 g, are unique to India, as is the fatty fish *eleesh*, found in the Hoogli river, whose flesh is so delicate and aromatic that it is often simply steamed, smothered with mustard paste, in a dish called *bhapa eleesh* or baked with cinnamon and clove in *dum eleesh*. Other fish particular to India include *vekti, topshe*, or *roi*, sold in *Bag Bazaar*, the famous marketplace in Calcutta. One of the most divine-tasting fish in the world is *pomfret*, found along the Bombay coast. Its size and bone structure is similar to Dover sole.

All the regions along the Indian coast, particularly Bengal in the East and Malabar and Goa to the West, are known for their wonderful fish and seafood preparations. Many of their cooking techniques have been developed around a particular variety of fish or shellfish, to complement and further enhance the flavour. Thus a prerequisite for reproducing many such preparations is the right kind of fish. Equally important is its freshness. Keeping that in mind, I have particularly chosen a few recipes which are easily adaptable.

PRAWNS WITH MILD SPICES

MASALA JHEENGARI

◆

Originally prepared by the Moslems in Bengal, this dish today is as common and popular throughout North India as *Murgh Masala* (p. 157), or *Masala Gosht* (p. 133). Large prawns are folded into a luscious brownish maroon sauce of fried onions and spices, which is then finished with cream. An interesting ingredient here is poppy seeds, which are roasted and ground before being added to the sauce. The poppy seeds, besides thickening and enriching the sauce, give it a special nutty aroma.

FOR 6 PERSONS

◆

2 lb/ 1 kg prawns
½ teaspoon turmeric
4 fl oz/ 12.5 cl light vegetable oil, or a mixture of oil and usli ghee (p. 52)
8 oz/ 250 g finely chopped onions
2 teaspoons finely chopped garlic
1½ teaspoons ground roasted white poppy seeds (p. 62)
1 teaspoon ground cumin
2 teaspoons ground coriander
1½ teaspoons paprika
4 tablespoons plain yogurt
1½ teaspoons coarse salt
2 green chilies, seeded and minced (or substitute ½ teaspoon red pepper)
4-5 tablespoons double cream
2 tablespoons finely chopped coriander leaves

1 Shell and devein prawns and wash them thoroughly.

2 Bring 1½ pints/1 litre of water to the boil on high heat. Add turmeric and shrimps, and cook for about 4 minutes. Drain the prawns, reserving the water, and set aside.

3 Heat oil in a large heavy-bottomed pan, preferably one with a non-stick surface, and add onions. Over high heat, fry the onions until they turn golden brown (about 8 minutes), stirring constantly to prevent burning. Add garlic, and cook for an additional ½ minute. Reduce heat, and add ground poppy seeds, cumin, coriander, and paprika. Stir rapidly for 5 seconds, and add half the reserved liquid. Increase heat to high and boil rapidly, uncovered, for 10 minutes. Add the remaining liquid, and continue boiling, uncovered, until the sauce reduces to a thick pulpy gravy (about 20 minutes). Stir occasionally to ensure that the sauce does not stick to the pan. Add yogurt, salt, and chilies or red pepper, and continue cooking for an additional 2-3 minutes, stirring constantly. Add cooked prawns, and stir to mix. Reduce heat and gently simmer, covered, for a couple of minutes, or until the prawns are heated through and absorb some of the gravy. Turn off the heat, and stir in cream. Let the dish rest at least 1 hour. When ready to serve, gently simmer until heated through. Check for salt, stir in the chopped coriander leaves, and serve sprinkled with a few more chopped leaves.

NOTE This dish improves with keeping. For best results, prepare it the day before you are going to serve it, and refrigerate. It also freezes well. Defrost thoroughly before reheating.

Serve *masala* prawns with The Emperor's Pilaf with Black Mushrooms (p. 268), or Mint Pilaf (p. 270). A vegetable side dish goes best with this. Good choices are: Glazed Cauliflower with Ginger (p. 216), or Broccoli Smothered in Garlic Oil (p. 214). For an additional side dish choose a *dal* such as Buttered Black Beans (*Kali Dal*, p. 242).

PRAWNS POACHED IN COCONUT MILK WITH FRESH HERBS

YERRA MOOLEE

◆

In this dish from Kerala, a state on the southwestern coast of India, fresh juicy prawns are gently poached in herb-laced coconut milk. The spicing here is intentionally kept very subtle, so that the natural flavours of the prawns and the coconut milk can be relished to their fullest. *Yerra Moolee*, with its shimmering ivory-white sauce, can be made to taste much hotter than this recipe by increasing the quantity of green chilies.

FOR 6 PERSONS

◆

2 lb/1 kg prawns
7 tablespoons light vegetable oil
12 oz/375 g finely chopped onions
2 teaspoons minced garlic
1½ tablespoons ground or crushed fresh ginger root
2 green chilies, or more, to taste, seeded and minced
¼ teaspoon turmeric
2 tablespoons ground coriander
1¼ pints/75 cl coconut milk (see p. 50)
1½ teaspoons coarse salt
2 tablespoons minced coriander leaves

1 Shell and devein prawns. Wash them thoroughly, and set aside.
2 Heat the oil in a large heavy-bottomed pan, and add onions. Over high heat, fry the onions until they turn golden brown (about 10 minutes), stirring constantly to prevent burning. Reduce heat to medium, add garlic, ginger, and chilies, and fry for an additional 2 minutes. Add turmeric and coriander, stir rapidly for 15 seconds, and add coconut milk and salt. Cook the sauce, uncovered, until it thickens (about 10 minutes). Stir frequently to ensure that the sauce does not stick and burn.
3 Add prawns, mix, reduce heat to medium-low, and simmer, covered, for 5-7 minutes, or until the prawns are cooked through. Do not overcook or they will become tough and chewy. Check for salt, stir in coriander leaves, and serve.

NOTE This dish may be prepared a day ahead, refrigerated, and reheated just before serving. It does not freeze well.

This dish has a lot of gravy and must be served with rice. Best, of course, is plain cooked rice (p. 256). Green Beans with Coconut and Black Mustard Seeds (p. 223), Cauliflower and Spring Onions with Black Mustard Seeds (p. 218) are excellent vegetable choices. Accompany with Shredded Carrot and Mustard Seed Relish (p. 308), Puffy Lentil Wafers (p. 301), and if you like, Quick Mango and Shredded Ginger Pickle (p. 320).

CREAMED PRAWNS

JHEENGA MALAI KHASA

◆

Malai means cream – not only milk cream but also coconut cream. This dish, a popular preparation from Bengal, is also made with coconut. The flavour, colour, and texture of the dish, however, are distinctly different from the coconut prawns of Kerala because in this recipe, dry coconut, known as *khopra*, is used. It is roasted and ground and added to the sauce to lend it a spicy, nutty flavour. The whole spices in this dish – cinnamon, cloves, and cardamom – are not meant to be eaten, but if you bite into one, no harm will come to you.

FOR 6 PERSONS

◆

3 oz/90 g dry flaked unsweetened coconut
6 fl oz/20 cl plain yogurt
2 teaspoons finely chopped garlic
1 tablespoon finely chopped fresh ginger root
2 green chilies, seeded
2 lb/1 kg prawns
4 fl oz/12.5 cl light vegetable oil

1 stick cinnamon, 3 in/7.5 cm long
8 whole cloves
8 green cardamom pods
1 medium onion, finely chopped
3 tablespoons ground blanched almonds
1½ teaspoons coarse salt
2 tablespoons finely chopped coriander leaves

1 Place a frying pan over medium heat. When it is hot, add flaked coconut, and toast, stirring and tossing, until it turns dark caramel brown (about 5-8 minutes). Transfer the toasted coconut to the container of an electric blender or food processor. Add yogurt, garlic, ginger, and green chilies, and run the machine until the mixture is finely puréed. Set aside.

2 Shell and devein prawns. Wash them thoroughly, and set aside.

3 Heat the oil in a shallow non-stick pan over medium heat. When the oil is hot, add cinnamon, cloves, and cardamom. When the spices get slightly puffed and begin to brown (about ½ minute), add onions. Increase the heat to high, and fry onions until they turn caramel brown (about 10 minutes), stirring constantly to prevent burning. (See directions for Brown-frying Onions, p. 66.) Add ground almonds, stir rapidly for ½ minute, and add coconut purée. Cook the mixture, uncovered, until the oil begins to separate from the sauce (about 3 minutes).

4 Add ½ pint/30 cl boiling water and salt. Reduce heat and simmer, covered, for 5 minutes. Add prawns, and stir well to distribute them evenly into the sauce. Continue cooking, covered, for an additional 5-7 minutes, or until they are cooked through but still tender. Check for salt, and serve sprinkled with chopped coriander leaves.

NOTE This dish may be prepared ahead, refrigerated for up to 2 days, and reheated just before serving.

Serve the prawns with a saffron pilaf and Smoked Aubergine with Fresh Herbs (p. 220), Buttered Smothered Cabbage (p. 215), or Turmeric Potatoes with Green Peppers (p. 228). Sweet Lemon Pickle with Cumin (p. 318) goes particularly well with this meal.

FRIED FILLET OF SOLE LACED WITH CAROM

BHONI MACHI

◆

Breading fish fillets and shallow-frying them is a relatively new technique in Indian cooking. Since it is Western, it is more popular with urban Indians and in restaurants.

The fish fillets are first marinated in lemon juice, which has an effect not unlike pickling. Consequently, when they are fried they cook in no time at all; they also stay creamy and tender, insulated by the crisp cooking. The delicate fragrance of the fried fish is lent by the garlic and carom seeds in the lemon juice marinade. The taste of this marinade is so wonderful, I have often simply grilled the marinated fish and served it.

FOR 6 PERSONS

◆

6 skinned sole fillets, about 6-8 oz/175-250 g each
THE MARINADE
1 teaspoon coarse salt
2 tablespoons lemon juice
1 tablespoon minced garlic
½ teaspoon carom seeds, crushed
THE SPICY CRUMB COATING
4 tablespoons plain flour
2 large eggs
6 oz/175 g dry breadcrumbs
½ teaspoon salt
½ teaspoon black pepper
Peanut or corn oil, enough to fill a frying pan to a depth of ¾ in/2 cm

1 Rinse fish fillets in cold water, and pat them dry on paper towels.
2 Put the fish in a large shallow bowl. Add all the ingredients for the marinade, and rub it over the fillets, turning and tossing them. Cover and marinate in the refrigerator for 24 hours (the fish may be in the marinade for up to 48 hours).

3 When ready to serve the fillets, place three shallow bowls on the work board. Add flour to one bowl, beat the 2 eggs slightly in the second, and into the third bowl put the bread crumbs, salt, and pepper, and mix well.

4 Take the fish fillets from the refrigerator. One at a time, roll fillets in the flour, then in the beaten egg, and finally in breadcrumbs (make sure the fillets are thoroughly breaded), and place them on greaseproof paper. Continue till all fillets are coated.

5 Heat the oil in a frying pan until very hot (350°-375°F/175°-190°C), and slip 2-3 fillets in the oil. (Do not overcrowd the pan, or the oil will cool causing the fillets to brown unevenly.) Fry the fillets on one side for 3 minutes, then carefully flip them over with a wide spatula, and continue frying until they are light golden on both sides. Drain them briefly on paper towels, and place them on a serving dish in a low oven to keep warm while you cook the remaining fillets. Serve hot.

Serve this delicious fish with a Sweet Tomato Relish (p. 313). For a vegetable, you may serve Turmeric Potatoes with Green Peppers (p. 228). Or omit the vegetable and serve a vegetable rice dish, such as Indian Fried Rice (p. 261) or Vegetable and Rice Casserole with Herbs (p. 272).

CHICK-PEA BATTER FISH

TALI MACHI

◆

Tali means deep-fried. In this dish the fish fillets are coated with a spicy batter and deep-fried. They come out golden and spongy and delicious. The flavour comes from a batter made with chick-pea flour and cumin. The same fish, cut into thin strips and fried in the same batter, is called a fish fritter and is popular as an appetizer or a snack.

NOTE For a crispier coating, eliminate the baking powder from the batter. For variation in the flavour, substitute ⅓ teaspoon carom seeds for the cumin.

The batter left over after coating the fish fillets may be used to make vegetable fritters, especially potato and onion fritters. Simply dip thin slices of onion and potato in the batter, and deep fry. They are excellent with the fried fish.

FOR 6 PERSONS

◆

THE BATTER
6 oz/175 g unsifted chick-pea flour (besan)
2 teaspoons garlic, ground to a paste
2 tablespoons light vegetable oil
½ pint/30 cl warm water
2 teaspoons ground cumin
½ teaspoon black pepper
½ teaspoon turmeric
¾ teaspoon baking powder (optional)
1½ teaspoons coarse salt
6 firm-fleshed fish fillets, skinned, about 6-8 oz/175-250 g each
Peanut or corn oil, enough to fill a kadhai or deep pan to a depth of 3 in/7.5 cm

1 Put all the ingredients for the batter in a bowl, and beat with a beater, wire whisk, or fork until thoroughly blended and free of lumps. (Alternatively, the batter may be mixed in an electric blender or food processor.) Cover, and let the batter rest for ½ hour.

2 Rinse the fillets under running cold water, and pat them dry with paper towels. Cut each fillet in half lengthwise along the central line.

3 When ready to fry the fish, heat the oil in a *kadhai* or any deep pan until very hot (375°F/190°C). Dip a fillet into the batter to coat it. Hold the fillet briefly over the bowl to let excess batter drip off, and then drop it into the hot oil. Fry only 3-4 fillets at a time, so that there is ample room for them to float easily in the oil. Fry the fillets for 3 minutes. Then flip them over with a slotted spoon, and continue frying until they are light golden on both sides. Drain on paper towels, put the fillets on a serving dish, and keep them warm in a low oven. Serve hot, accompanied by either Sweet Tomato Relish (p. 313), or Fresh Mint Relish (p. 309).

FISH IN VELVET YOGURT SAUCE

DAHI MACHI

◆

This Bengali preparation of fish fillets poached in a mild onion-rich yogurt sauce is eaten every day by the local people.

FOR 4 PERSONS

◆

1 lb/500 g haddock fillets, skinned
8 tablespoons light vegetable oil
4 tablespoons plain flour
12 oz/375 g finely chopped onions
1½ tablespoons finely chopped fresh ginger root
⅛ teaspoon turmeric
¾ teaspoon coarse salt
Small pinch each ground cinnamon and cloves
6 fl oz/20 cl plain yogurt
2 tablespoons finely chopped coriander leaves
2-4 green chilies, seeded and minced

1 Rinse the fillets in cold water, pat dry with paper towels, and cut them neatly into 1 × 2 in/2.5 × 5 cm pieces. Set aside.

2 Heat 3 or 4 tablespoons of the oil in a large shallow non-stick pan over medium-high heat. Dust the fish fillets lightly with flour, and add them to the pan in one layer. (Add no more pieces than may be accommodated comfortably without overlapping.) Fry until they are lightly browned (about 1 minute). Flip them with a spatula, and continue frying for another ½ minute or until they are seared on both sides. As each batch is seared, remove the pieces to a platter, and continue with the remainder the same way, adding more oil to the pan as necessary. Set aside.

3 Add the remaining oil to the pan along with the onions. Fry the onions until they turn butterscotch brown (about 15 minutes), stirring constantly so they do not burn. Add ginger, and continue frying for an additional minute. Add turmeric, salt, cinnamon, and clove, stir rapidly for 15 seconds, and add yogurt.

4 Pour the onion mixture into the container of an electric blender or food processor, and blend until you have a smooth sauce. Return sauce to the pan.

Over low heat, simmer gently until hot and bubbling. Slip the fried pieces of fish carefully into the sauce, along with any oil and juices that may have collected in the platter. Make sure the fish pieces are evenly distributed in the sauce. Simmer covered, until the fish is cooked through (not more than 3-4 minutes). Check for salt, and serve sprinkled with chopped coriander leaves and chopped green chilies.

To enjoy the mellow flavour of this dish to the fullest, serve a plain cooked rice (p. 256). Green Beans with Coconut and Black Mustard Seeds (p. 223) or Spicy Baby Aubergine (p. 219) are good vegetable choices. For accompaniments, serve Lentil Wafers (p. 300) and Hot Lemon Pickle (p. 319).

VEGETABLES AND CHEESE

SABZI AUR PANEER

◆

CAULIFLOWER, GREEN PEAS, AND POTATOES IN SPICY HERB SAUCE

GOBHI MATAR RASEDAR

◆

This dish, with its bright contrasting colours and lovely bouquet of fresh herbs, is spectacular. For the cauliflower, peas, and potatoes, you may substitute green peppers, green beans, courgettes, and/or mushrooms. The consistency of the dish should be like thin vegetable soup, with the vegetables cooked until soft. Stir carefully so that the pieces of vegetable do not break.

NOTE A speciality of the Brahmins of Kanuj, a city in the state of Uttar Pradesh, this preparation is a typical example of their onion- and garlic-free cooking. It is traditionally served at wedding banquets accompanied by special stuffed bread, *Kachauri* (p. 295).

FOR 6-8 PERSONS

◆

1 small head cauliflower
2 medium-sized potatoes
4 oz/125 g usli ghee *(p. 52), or light vegetable oil*
2 teaspoons cumin seeds
1 teaspoon ground cumin
2 tablespoons ground coriander
1 teaspoon turmeric
½-1 teaspoon red pepper
10 oz/300 g shelled peas, or frozen peas, defrosted
12 oz/375 g puréed or finely chopped fresh ripe tomatoes
4 teaspoons coarse salt
3 tablespoons finely chopped coriander leaves

1 Wash cauliflower in running cold water. Break or cut it into about 1½ in/4 cm florets. Peel the central stem, and cut into thin slices.
2 Peel the potatoes, and cut each into 6 pieces.
3 Measure out all spices and place them, and all the vegetables, right next to the stove.
4 Heat the *ghee* over medium-high heat in a deep heavy-bottomed pan. When the fat is hot, add cumin seeds, and fry until they turn dark brown (about 20 seconds). Add cumin powder, coriander, turmeric, and red pepper, all at once, stir for a moment, and immediately add cauliflower, potatoes, and fresh peas (if you are using frozen peas, do not add them yet). Fry, stirring constantly, until the vegetables begin to sear a bit (about 5 minutes). Add tomatoes, and continue frying until the mixture thickens and the fat begins to separate from the sauce (about 3 minutes). Add 1 pint/60 cl boiling water along with the salt. Reduce heat and simmer the vegetables, covered, until they are tender and cooked through (about 15 minutes). If you are using frozen peas, add them now, and continue cooking for 5 minutes. Turn off heat. Check for salt, and serve sprinkled with chopped coriander leaves.

NOTE This dish must be served in small bowls, such as *katoori*, since its consistency is much like a minestrone with the vegetables cut into large chunks. Traditionally, a little vegetable shortening or *ghee* (about 2-3 tablespoons) is poured over the dish before sprinkling coriander leaves. This, in addition to enhancing and enriching the flavours, makes the dish taste mellow and subtle. It may be prepared ahead and refrigerated for up to 4 days. It also freezes well. Defrost thoroughly before reheating.

Traditionally, this dish should be accompanied by *Kachauri* (p. 295), but *Phulka* (p. 282) and *Poori* (p. 293) are equally good. For a side dish, good choices are Spice- and Herb-Laced Split Peas (p. 237) or Mung Beans Laced with Black Mustard Seeds (p. 240), or try a cool yogurt salad. A vegetarian meal should traditionally be accompanied by relishes and pickles. Fresh Mint Relish (p. 309) and Sweet Lemon Pickle with Cumin (p. 318) are good choices.

WHOLE POTATOES IN SPICY YOGURT GRAVY

DUM ALOO

◆

Indians love potatoes because they have a mellow, almost neutral taste that allows them to absorb the flavours of spices. Here, whole potatoes are first peeled and pricked (so that the seasonings will penetrate fully), sautéed, and then simmered in spiced yogurt sauce. *Dum Aloo*, a popular dish throughout North India, is cooked by the *dum* process (see page 70).

FOR 6-8 PERSONS

◆

2 lb/1 kg small even-sized boiling potatoes
7 tablespoons Indian vegetable shortening, or light vegetable oil
8 oz/250 g finely chopped onions
1 tablespoon finely chopped fresh ginger root
2 teaspoons ground cumin
4 teaspoons ground coriander
1 teaspoon turmeric
½-1 teaspoon red pepper
1 teaspoon Mughal garam masala *(p. 41)*
1 lb/500 g chopped or puréed fresh tomatoes, or 8 oz/ 250 g canned tomato sauce
6 fl oz/20 cl plain yogurt
4 teaspoons coarse salt
5 tablespoons double cream

1 Peel potatoes, and prick them with a thin skewer or knife in 4 or 5 places. Put in a bowl of cold water until you are ready to cook them.

2 Heat 5 tablespoons of the shortening in a large non-stick pan that can hold all the potatoes in one layer over medium-high heat. When the shortening is very hot, drain the potatoes, pat them dry on paper towels, and add. Fry them until they acquire several tiny browned spots and a crust (about 8-10 minutes), turning and tossing them to ensure even browning. (This is an essential step, as the browning prevents the potatoes falling apart during prolonged cooking.) With a slotted spoon, transfer them to a bowl.

3 Add the rest of the shortening to the pan along with the onions. Fry until the onions turn caramel brown (about 15 minutes), stirring constantly so that they do not burn. Add ginger, and fry for an additional ½ minute. Add cumin, coriander, turmeric, red pepper, and *Mughal garam masala* all at once, and stir rapidly for 15 seconds. Add tomatoes, yogurt, salt, and the fried potatoes (in one layer), and bring to the boil. Reduce heat and simmer very gently, covered, for 35 minutes or until the potatoes are fully cooked. Check during cooking to make sure the gravy is not sticking and burning. The gravy should be thick enough to coat the potatoes. If it looks thin and runny, increase heat and boil rapidly, uncovered, until it reduces to the desired consistency. If, on the other hand, the gravy is too thick, add a few tablespoons of water.
4 Add cream, stir, and simmer until heated through. If you want the dish to taste milder and subtler, stir in a little more shortening or oil (about 2 tablespoons). Check for salt, and serve.

NOTE This dish improves with keeping. For best results make at least a few hours before you are going to serve it. It can be refrigerated for up to 4 days without loss of flavour.

This dish is traditionally served with either staple. I prefer a rice pilaf and a *dal* side dish. If you want to serve a vegetable instead, try Buttered Smothered Cabbage (p. 215) or Stir-fried Okra (p. 224).

POTATOES IN FRAGRANT GRAVY

TARI ALOO

◆

Like most southern Indian dishes, this one begins with sizzling black mustard seeds. The onions are used as a vegetable rather than as a seasoning. Traditionally it is served with *poori* for a Sunday brunch, accompanied by tea in North India and coffee in the South, but it is perfectly suitable as a light luncheon dish. The lack of garlic makes this dish a truly Indian vegetarian dish.

FOR 8 PERSONS

◆

4 fl oz/12.5 cl light vegetable oil
1 teaspoon black mustard seeds
2 teaspoons yellow split peas (channa dal – optional)
2 tablespoons fresh ginger root, chopped into tiny cubes
1-2 green chilies, seeded and sliced, or ¼ to ½ teaspoon red pepper
1 tablespoon ground coriander
1 teaspoon turmeric
½ teaspoon paprika
6 medium-sized potatoes
4 medium-sized onions, roughly chopped
3½ teaspoons coarse salt
2 teaspoons lemon juice
3-4 tablespoons chopped coriander leaves

1 Boil potatoes in their jackets, in water to cover, until fully cooked (a skewer or cake tester will pierce right through the potato without resistance). Drain, plunge them in cold water, peel, and cut into roughly ½-in/1 cm pieces.
2 Measure out all the spices and place with the vegetables ready to hand.
3 Heat the oil over high heat in a deep saucepan. When the oil is very hot, carefully add the mustard seeds. Keep a saucepan lid handy, since the seeds may sputter when added.
4 When the mustard seeds start to turn grey and sputtering begins to subside, add yellow split peas, if you are using them. Fry until the peas turn light brown

(about ½ to 1 minute), stirring constantly to ensure even browning, and lifting the pan away from the heat if it is too hot.

5 Reduce heat to medium, add ginger and chilies, and cook for 2 minutes or until they begin to brown (if you are using red pepper, add it with the dry spices). Add coriander powder, turmeric, and paprika, stir for a moment, and add potatoes and onions. Sauté the vegetables for 10 minutes or until they are lightly browned, stirring frequently.

6 Add 1½ pints/1 litre hot water along with the salt, and bring to the boil. Reduce heat and simmer, covered, for 15 minutes or until the potatoes are very tender. With the back of the spoon, mash a few pieces of potato; this will thicken the gravy to a nice consistency. Serve piping hot in individual bowls or a tureen, sprinkled with the lemon juice, chopped coriander, and if desired, a little paprika or red pepper.

NOTE This dish may be prepared ahead and kept refrigerated for up to 2 days, or frozen. Defrost thoroughly before reheating. The potatoes in *Tari Aloo* are usually very soft and broken up, and the gravy is more like a broth used for dipping bread. The dish thickens with keeping, as the starch from the mashed pieces of potato mixes with the gravy. If the gravy thickens too much, simply add a little water to thin it.

Serve *Tari Aloo* with *Poori* (p. 293). The classic combination of this dish with bread is called *Aloo-Poori*. It could be served for a brunch, accompanied by Spiced Tea (p. 346), or Cardamom Tea (p. 347). Also, Sweet Lemon Pickle with Cumin (p. 318) goes beautifully with *Tari Aloo*.

SPICY POTATO-STUFFED CABBAGE ROLLS WITH GINGER LEMON SAUCE

ALOO BHARE BANDH GOBHI

◆

These cabbage rolls are a speciality of Uttar Pradesh. The rolls can have a variety of stuffings ranging from mixed vegetables to *paneer* or mashed cooked lentils. The potato-stuffed version is by far the most popular.

FOR 4-6 PERSONS

◆

1 small cabbage
3 tablespoons light vegetable oil
8 oz/250 g thinly sliced onions
12 oz/375 g chopped fresh ripe tomatoes, or 8 oz/250 g canned tomatoes with their juices, chopped
1 tablespoon shredded fresh ginger root
1 lemon, peeled, seeded, and thinly sliced
2½ teaspoons coarse salt
¼ teaspoon black pepper
1 recipe Spicy Potato Filling (p. 105)
2 tablespoons chopped coriander leaves
2 green chilies, seeded and sliced
½ teaspoon paprika

Follow the directions given for Meat-stuffed Cabbage Rolls with Ginger Lemon Sauce (*Keema Bhare Bandh Gobhi*, p. 148) substituting potato filling for meat filling. Also, before serving, sprinkle with chopped coriander leaves, green chilies, and paprika.

When serving the cabbage rolls, follow the menu suggestions given on page 149.

GREEN PEAS AND INDIAN CHEESE IN FRAGRANT TOMATO SAUCE

MATAR PANEER

◆

Indian cheese, known as *paneer* or *chenna*, is a delicacy that all Indians – particularly northerners – love. Its use in the preparation of savoury dishes is limited, but the few dishes created with it are absolute masterpieces. The most popular, without doubt, is *Matar Paneer* – moist pieces of sautéed cheese with sweet green peas in a red sauce bursting with the fragrance of spices and fresh coriander leaves. *Matar Paneer*, a classic North Indian dish, is popular with vegetarians and nonvegetarians alike.

The flavour and texture of the *paneer* are of prime importance here. The cheese should be sweet and fresh-smelling; it should feel firm to the touch but not hard; it should be moist but not wet; and finally, its texture should be close and compact, not porous. (If the *paneer* is dry and too solid, the cheese pieces will taste hard and rubbery, and the sauce will not penetrate the *paneer*, leaving it with a bland taste. If the *paneer* is too wet and loose-textured, it will not hold its shape, but will fall apart while it is being fried.)

FOR 6 PERSONS

◆

Indian cheese (paneer) *made with 3pints/2 litres milk (p. 53) and cut into ½ × ½ × 1½ in/1 × 1 × 4 cm pieces*
12 tablespoons usli ghee *(p. 52), or Indian vegetable shortening, or light vegetable oil*
12 oz/375 g finely chopped onions
1 teaspoon finely chopped garlic
2 tablespoons finely chopped fresh ginger root
2 teaspoons ground coriander
1 teaspoon turmeric
¼-½ teaspoon each red and black pepper
1 teaspoon paprika
1 lb/500 g finely chopped or puréed fresh ripe tomatoes, or 12 oz/375 g canned tomatoes with their juice, chopped
10 oz/300 g shelled fresh green peas, or frozen peas, defrosted

2 *teaspoons coarse salt*
2 *teaspoons* garam masala *(p. 42)*
4 *tablespoons finely chopped coriander leaves*

1 Spread the *paneer* pieces on a piece of greaseproof paper and leave them to dry slightly for ½ hour.

2 Heat 3 tablespoons of the *ghee* over medium heat in a large heavy-bottomed pan, preferably one with a non-stick interior. When the *ghee* is hot, add cheese pieces. Keep a saucepan lid or spatter screen handy, since the moisture from the cheese may be released explosively, causing tiny particles of cheese to fly all over. Dusting the *paneer* pieces with a little flour prevents spattering. Fry the cheese, turning and tossing often to prevent sticking and burning, until lightly seared (about 5 minutes). Transfer the pieces to a bowl. (The *paneer* should be fried in batches so that there is ample room in the pan for turning them without fear of their breaking.)

3 Add the remaining *ghee* to the pan, and increase the heat to high. Add onions, and fry until they turn light brown (about 5 minutes), stirring constantly so that they do not burn. Add garlic and ginger, and fry for an additional 2 minutes. Add coriander, turmeric, red and black pepper, and paprika, all at once. Stir rapidly for a moment, and immediately add tomatoes. Cook until the mixture thickens to a pulpy sauce and the fat begins to separate (about 10 minutes), stirring often.

4 Add ½ pint/30 cl hot water, and bring the sauce to the boil. Reduce heat to medium, and cook the sauce, covered, for 20 minutes. Cool the sauce briefly. Then purée it in an electric blender or food processor, leaving the sauce a little coarse so that it has a certain texture.

5 Return the sauce to the pan. Add peas, salt, and the fried cheese, along with 4 fl oz/12.5 cl hot water, and bring the sauce to the boil. Reduce heat to medium and simmer, covered, until the peas are cooked through (about 15 minutes for fresh peas and 5 for frozen). Turn off heat and let the dish rest, covered, for an hour before serving. When ready to serve, heat thoroughly. Fold in *garam masala* and chopped coriander leaves. Check for salt, and serve.

NOTE This dish tastes best if made a couple of hours before serving. The resting allows the flavours of the different ingredients to blend and mellow. It may be refrigerated for up to 3 days without loss of flavour.

Serve with a fragrant pilaf such as Fragrant Pilaf Banaras Style (p. 263). It goes beautifully with all plain baked or fried breads. For a side dish, serve Smoked Aubergine with Fresh Herbs (p. 220) or a *dal* or a cool *raita*.

ROYAL BRAISED VEGETABLES IN CARDAMOM NUT SAUCE

SHAHI SABZ KORMA

◆

This ivory-white dish with its shimmering glaze is indeed, as the name suggests, royal. Except for carrots, only light-coloured vegetables are chosen, to blend harmoniously with the almond-yogurt sauce. The vegetables are carefully cut to a uniform size to make them look attractive. If you are running short of time, you may substitute for the *paneer* 1 additional medium sized potato, cut like the others. The *korma* can also be folded into plain cooked rice and transformed into a complete meal.

FOR 6-8 PERSONS

◆

2 medium-sized potatoes
2 medium-sized turnips
1 large carrot
12 tablespoons Indian vegetable shortening or light vegetable oil
Indian cheese (paneer) made with 1½ pints/1 litre (p. 53) and cut into ½ × ½ × 1½ in/1 × 1 × 4 cm pieces
12 oz/375 g finely chopped onions
1 tablespoon finely chopped garlic
1½ tablespoons finely chopped fresh ginger root
2 green chilies, seeded and minced
12 green cardamom pods
1 stick cinnamon, 3 in/7.5 cm long
24 whole cloves
5 tablespoons ground blanched almonds
8 fl oz/25 cl plain yogurt
4 tablespoons shelled fresh green peas, or frozen peas, defrosted
1 tablespoon coarse salt
4 tablespoons double cream

1 Peel potatoes, turnips, and carrot, and cut them into uniform pieces the same size as the *paneer*. Put them in a bowl of cold water to prevent discolouring, and set aside.

2 Heat 3 tablespoons of the shortening over medium heat in a large heavy-bottomed pan, preferably one with a non-stick interior. When the fat is hot, add the cheese pieces very carefully. Keep a saucepan lid handy, since the moisture in the cheese may be released and cause tiny particles of cheese to fly all over. Dusting the *paneer* pieces with a little flour will prevent sputtering. Fry the cheese until lightly coloured on both sides (about 5 minutes), turning and tossing often to prevent sticking and burning. Transfer it to a bowl.

3 Add the remaining shortening to the pan along with the onions, garlic, ginger, and chilies. Increase heat to high, and fry the seasonings until they turn light brown (about 10 minutes), stirring constantly to prevent uneven browning or burning. Add cardamom, cinnamon, and cloves, and continue frying for an additional 5 minutes. Add almond powder, stirring rapidly, and fry for 2 more minutes.

4 Add 2 tablespoons of the yogurt and fry the mixture. When the moisture from the yogurt evaporates, add 2 more tablespoons of yogurt. Continue adding yogurt and frying until all the yogurt is used up (about 5 minutes). Stir constantly while frying, making sure that the sauce does not stick to the bottom of the pan and burn.

5 Drain and add the vegetables. Add the fresh green peas (if you are using frozen peas do not add them now), salt, and ½ pint/30 cl hot water to the sauce. Bring to the boil, reduce heat to medium-low, and cook the vegetables, covered, until tender but still firm (about 30 minutes). Add fried cheese pieces, cream, and frozen peas (if you are using them). Cook, uncovered, for 10 minutes. The sauce should be thick in this *korma*. If the sauce is not thick enough, increase heat to medium and simmer until the sauce thickens to the desired consistency. If, on the other hand, the sauce is too thick, add a few tablespoons of milk or water. Check for salt, and serve.

NOTE This dish definitely tastes better if prepared a day ahead, refrigerated, and reheated before serving. It keeps in the refrigerator for up to 3 days. It also freezes well. Defrost thoroughly before reheating. The freezing process sometimes produces a thick and grainy texture. If this happens, add enough milk or water to bind the sauce while it is simmering. Taste, and if necessary add salt. To perk up flavours add ½ teaspoon *Mughal garam masala*.

The *korma* may be served with either bread or rice. A side dish of Buttered Black Beans (p. 242) goes perfectly with this meal and serve a relish too: Fresh Mint Relish (p. 309) and Onion Vegetable Relish (p. 304) all go well.

PULSES

DAL

◆

CHICK-PEAS IN TANGY TAMARIND SAUCE

KHATTE CHANNE

◆

Channa, or chick-peas, can be a true delicacy, a gourmet's delight, if they are properly cooked and appropriately flavoured. No one knows this art better than the people of Punjab and particularly the Sikhs. The three most popular dishes are *Khatte Channe*, in which the peas are cooked in a tamarind or pomegranate sauce; *Safaid Channe*, peas cooked in a light ginger sauce; and *Kale Channe*, peas cooked with *garam masala* and mango powder. Often, brown fried onions and colouring are added to darken the sauce

The consistency of the dish ranges anywhere from that of a very thick pea soup to very dry. The following recipe produces a fairly thick souplike dish with the whole chick-peas intact.

FOR 6-8 PERSONS

◆

2 × 20 oz/ 600 g cans chick-peas, or 1 lb/ 500 g cooked chick-peas with 8 fl oz/ 25 cl liquid
2 oz/ 60 g tamarind pulp
4 fl oz/ 12.5 cl light vegetable oil
8 oz/ 250 g thinly sliced onions
2 teaspoons minced garlic
½ teaspoon turmeric
½ teaspoon red pepper
8 oz/ 250 g fresh or canned chopped tomatoes
1 tablespoon grated fresh ginger root
1¼ teaspoons garam masala (p. 42)
1¼ teaspoons ground roasted cumin seeds (p. 62)

THE GARNISH

1 medium-sized onion, peeled and thinly sliced
1-2 green chilies, seeded and shredded

1 Drain chick-peas, reserving the liquid.

2 Put the tamarind pulp in a small bowl, add ½ pint/30 cl boiling water, and let soak for 15 minutes. Mash the pulp with the back of a spoon, or use your fingers. Strain the liquid into another small bowl, squeezing the pulp as much as possible, and set aside, Discard the fibrous residue.

3 Heat the oil in a large heavy-bottomed pan over medium-high heat. Add onions, and fry until they turn caramel brown (about 20 minutes), stirring constantly so that they do not burn. (See directions for Brown-frying Onions p. 66.) Add garlic, and cook for an additional 2 minutes. Add turmeric and red pepper, stir rapidly for a moment, and add tomato purée along with ginger shreds. Reduce heat to medium, and cook until the fat begins to separate from the gravy (about 5 minutes).

4 Add tamarind juice and the reserved chick-pea liquid. Cover, and simmer the mixture over low heat for 15 minutes.

5 Add drained chick-peas, *garam masala*, and roasted cumin, and continue cooking for an additional 10 minutes. Check for salt, and transfer to a heated serving dish. Serve, garnished with sliced onions and shredded chilies.

NOTE This dish may be prepared ahead and refrigerated for up to 3 days. It also freezes very well. Defrost thoroughly before reheating.

Although *Khatte Channe* is usually served with a *Bhatoora*, it is quite common to serve it with *Poori* (p. 293). *Bhatoora* and *Poori* are both deep-fried. The only difference is that *Bhatoora* is leavened and therefore richer. This combination is perfect for lunch. Generally, vegetables are not served with this meal. The meal may, however, include a yogurt salad.

CHICK-PEAS IN GINGER SAUCE

SAFAID CHANNE

◆

This chick-pea dish has a thinner, lighter, more fragrant sauce than *Khatte Channe*. It is also more mildly flavoured. *Safaid Channe* is traditionally served with *Poori* (p. 293) and plenty of tea.

FOR 6-8 PERSONS

◆

2 × 20 oz/600 g cans chick-peas with their liquid, or 1 lb/500 g cooked chick-peas with 8 fl oz/25 cl liquid
4 fl oz/12.5 cl light vegetable oil
12 oz/375 g finely chopped onions
2 teaspoons finely chopped garlic
2 tablespoons finely shredded fresh ginger root
2 teaspoons ground coriander
⅓ teaspoon ground cardamom
½ teaspoon mango powder, or 1½ teaspoons lemon juice
¼ teaspoon each red and black pepper
1 medium-sized tomato, finely chopped
1 teaspoon coarse salt, or to taste
THE GARNISH
1 medium-sized onion, peeled and thinly sliced
1 green chili, shredded

1 Drain chick-peas, reserving the liquid.
2 Heat the oil in a large pan over medium-high heat. Add onions, and fry for about 5 minutes or until light brown, stirring constantly to prevent burning.
3 Add garlic and ginger, reduce heat to medium, and fry for an additional 2 minutes. Add coriander powder, cardamom, mango powder and red and black pepper. Mix well, and fry for a moment or two. Add the chopped tomato, and cook until the oil begins to separate from the tomato-spice mixture (about 6 minutes).
4 Add the reserved chick-pea liquid, the lemon juice if you are using it, salt, and 4 fl oz/12.5 cl water. Cover and simmer over low heat for 10 minutes or

until the mixture is reduced to a pulpy gravy. Add the drained chick-peas, and continue cooking, covered, for an additional 10 minutes. Turn off heat. Check for salt, and transfer to a serving bowl. Serve garnished with onion slices and shredded chilies.

NOTE This dish may be made ahead and kept refrigerated for up to 3 days, or frozen. Defrost thoroughly before reheating.

In addition to *Poori* serve this dish with a Spinach and Yogurt Salad (p. 247).

SPICY BRUSSELS SPROUTS, GREEN BEANS, AND LENTIL STEW

CHAUNK GOBHI AUR SEM SAMBAAR

◆

An interesting way of making a *dal* is to add many different vegetables and spices. Cooking them in combination gives the vegetables a chance to exchange flavours and enhance the savour of the dish. Mixed vegetable *dal* stews are common throughout India, but it is the people of the South who create the most intriguing flavours and the most popular *dal* stews in all of India. Of the many different varieties, the *sambaar*, or vegetable and yellow lentil stew, is the most widely eaten. *Sambaar* is usually made with a spice blend called *Sambaar podi* (powder). The dish is very spicy, but when mixed with its classic accompaniments, *ghee* and glazed rice, it mellows to become one of the most satisfying of all vegetarian dishes.

FOR 4-6 PERSONS

◆

6 oz/175 g yellow lentils (toovar dal) *or yellow split peas* (channa dal)
⅓ teaspoon turmeric
1 lb/500 g Brussels sprouts
4 oz/125 g fresh green beans, trimmed and cut into 1 in/2.5 cm pieces
2 oz/60 g tamarind pulp (or 1 large tomato plus 1 teaspoon lemon juice)
3 tablespoons light sesame oil or light vegetable oil
¾ teaspoon black mustard seeds
¼ teaspoon fenugreek seeds
2 teaspoons chopped garlic
1 tablespoon sambaar *powder (p. 42)*
2½ teaspoons coarse salt
6-8 kari leaves (fresh or dry), or 2 tablespoons chopped fresh coriander leaves

1 Pick over, clean, and wash lentils following directions for cleaning pulses on page 235.

2 Put the lentils in a deep 5 pint/3 litre pot with turmeric and 1½ pints/1 litre cold water and bring to the boil. Reduce heat to medium-low and cook, partially covered, until the lentils are tender and cooked through (about 30 minutes). Add another ¼ pint/15 cl water, and simmer, covered, over very low heat for an additional 30 minutes or until the lentils are very soft and reduced to a fine purée. Stir often during these 30 minutes to prevent burning. Turn off heat. Beat the purée vigorously, using a wire whisk or a spoon, for 1 minute and set aside.

3 While the lentils are cooking, wash the vegetables in cold water and pat dry on paper towels. Trim off the hard stem of each Brussels sprout, and using a sharp knife, slash the base, making a cross about ¼ in/5 mm deep (this will ensure even cooking of the Brussels sprouts).

4 Put tamarind pulp in a small bowl, add 4 fl oz/12.5 cl boiling water, and let it soak for 15 minutes. Mash the pulp with the back of a spoon, or use your fingers. Strain the liquid into another small bowl, squeezing the pulp as much as possible, and set aside. Discard the fibrous residue. If you are using tomato instead, purée it with its skin or chop it finely, and stir in the lemon juice.

5 Place all the ingredients right next to the stove. Heat the oil over high heat in a deep saucepan. When the oil is very hot, carefully add the mustard seeds. Keep a pot lid handy, since the seeds may splutter when added. When the seeds turn grey (about 15 seconds), add fenugreek seeds. When the fenugreek seeds turn dark, add garlic, and *sambaar* powder. Stir for a moment, and add Brussels sprouts and beans. Fry the vegetables, turning and tossing them, for 2-3 minutes. Add tamarind juice (or tomato purée), salt, and 4 tablespoons of warm water. Reduce heat slightly, and cook the vegetables, covered, for 20 minutes or until they are partially cooked.

6 Add lentil purée, stir to mix, and continue cooking until the vegetables are tender and cooked through (about 10-15 minutes). Turn off heat and stir in kari leaves or chopped coriander leaves. Check for salt, and serve.

NOTE This stew may be made ahead and refrigerated for a day. Reheat thoroughly before serving. The keeping time depends upon the vegetables used in the stew. Some keep longer than others. For example, a stew made with potatoes, onions, and shallots will keep for up to 3 days whereas stews made with courgettes, Brussels sprouts and cabbage are at their best for up to 24 hours after cooking.

This stew is traditionally served with plain cooked rice (p. 256). Accompany it with a bowl of *usli ghee* (p. 52) to be poured, about two or three teaspoons to each serving of *sambaar*, over either the *sambaar*, or the rice, or both. The contents are then mixed together before eating.

For a side dish, serve Cauliflower and Spring Onions with Black Mustard Seeds (p. 218) or Green Beans with Coconut and Black Mustard Seeds (p. 223). Since the *sambaar* is a fairly spicy dish, the meal is always accompanied with plain yogurt but I prefer to serve a yogurt salad, such as Tomato and Yogurt Salad (p. 248), or Okra and Yogurt Salad (p. 249). The accompaniments to this meal may be wafers (especially *Puppadam*, p. 301), Shredded Carrot and Mustard Seed Relish (p. 308), and Hot Lemon Pickle (p. 319) or Quick Mango and Shredded Ginger Pickle (p. 320).

MUNG BEAN AND CAULIFLOWER STEW

GOBHI MOONG

◆

This dish is indeed for mung-bean lovers. The flavourings are kept subtle so that the delicate taste of the cauliflower and mung beans can be enjoyed to their fullest. In place of cauliflower, other vegetables, such as cucumber, broccoli, spinach, or kohlrabi, may be substituted. But remember to adjust the cooking time to suit your choice of vegetable.

FOR 6-8 PERSONS

◆

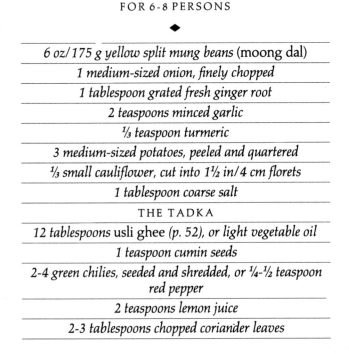

6 oz/175 g yellow split mung beans (moong dal)
1 medium-sized onion, finely chopped
1 tablespoon grated fresh ginger root
2 teaspoons minced garlic
⅓ teaspoon turmeric
3 medium-sized potatoes, peeled and quartered
⅓ small cauliflower, cut into 1½ in/4 cm florets
1 tablespoon coarse salt
THE TADKA
12 tablespoons usli ghee *(p. 52), or light vegetable oil*
1 teaspoon cumin seeds
2-4 green chilies, seeded and shredded, or ¼-½ teaspoon red pepper
2 teaspoons lemon juice
2-3 tablespoons chopped coriander leaves

1 Pick over, clean, and wash mung beans following directions for cleaning *dal* on page 235.

2 Put the mung beans in a deep pot, along with chopped onion, ginger, garlic, and 1¼ pints/75 cl water. Add turmeric, and bring to the boil. Reduce heat and simmer, partially covered, for 15 minutes or until the mung beans are cooked but are still very firm.

3 Add potatoes, cauliflower, salt, and ¾ pint/45 cl of water, and cook for an additional 15 minutes or until the vegetables are tender and the beans are thoroughly cooked. (The dish may be cooked to this point and kept refrigerated for up to 2 days. Reheat thoroughly before proceeding with the recipe. These beans usually thicken with keeping. In addition, the vegetables, especially the potatoes, have a tendency to absorb a great deal of moisture from the stew. Therefore, always check the consistency of the stew before serving. If necessary add water to thin it to the desired consistency.)

4 *To make the* tadka: Heat the *ghee* over high heat in a frying pan. When it is very hot, add cumin seeds, and fry until they turn dark brown (about 15 seconds). Add green chilies or red pepper, stir for a moment, and immediately pour the contents of the frying pan into the stew. Add lemon juice and chopped coriander leaves. Stir well to mix. Check for salt, transfer the stew to a heated serving dish, and serve.

This simple dish should be served with plain cooked rice (p. 256) or a plain bread. For a more substantial meal, include a stir-fried vegetable, such as Spicy Baby Aubergine (p. 219), Stir-fried Okra (p. 224), or Stuffed Okra with Spices (p. 226). Accompany the meal with Lentil Wafers (p. 300), Hot Hyderabad Tomato Relish (p. 314), and Hot Lemon Pickle (p. 319).

MIXED LENTILS AND VEGETABLE STEW

GUJRATI DAL

◆

This stew offers just a glimpse of the wonderful cuisine from the state of Gujrat. The food of the Gujratis, especially the Gujrati Jains, flavoured with a blend of northern and southern spices, reflects a warm merger. The technique for cooking this stew is very similar to making *sambaar*, except that here the *dal* is cooked with several ingredients before being added to the vegetable, instead of being cooked plain. This is the characteristic feature of Gujrati cooking. The stew, flavoured with cumin as well as black mustard seeds, makes a very satisfying dish if simply accompanied by plain cooked rice. Like other Gujrati Jain food, this stew contains no garlic, but I often add a few cloves of it, because I happen to like garlic and because I think it does wonders for the stew.

FOR 4-6 PERSONS

◆

6 oz/175 g dal — use a mixture of yellow lentils (toovar dal); *pink lentils* (masar dal); *yellow split peas* (channa dal); *and yellow split mung beans* (moong dal)
3 medium-sized tomatoes
1 medium-sized aubergine
1 large courgette
½ teaspoon turmeric
1 tablespoon finely chopped fresh ginger root
1 teaspoon chopped garlic (optional)
2 green chilies, seeded and minced, or ⅓ teaspoon red pepper
4 tablespoons usli ghee *(p. 52)*
¾ teaspoon black mustard seeds
¾ teaspoon cumin seeds
⅓ teaspoon ground asafetida
2½ teaspoons coarse salt
8 kari leaves (fresh or dry), or 2 tablespoons chopped fresh coriander

1 Pick over and wash *dal* following the directions on page 235.

2 Put the pulses in a bowl, and add water to cover to a depth of 2 in/5 cm. Let soak for 2 hours. Drain and set aside.

3 Blanch and peel tomatoes, and cut into wedges. Cut aubergine and courgette into thick sticks.

4 Put the soaked pulses in a deep pot with turmeric, ginger, garlic, chilies, and 1¼ pint/70 cl of cold water, and bring to the boil. Reduce heat and cook, partially covered, for 45 minutes or until the lentils are fully cooked and tender. Turn off heat. When slightly cool, purée the mixture and measure. There should be about 1½ pints/1 litre of lentil purée. If not, add enough water to bring it up to that quantity. (The lentil purée can be made ahead and refrigerated for up to 4 days. It can also be frozen successfully. Defrost and heat thoroughly before proceeding with the recipe.)

5 Place all the spices and vegetables right next to the stove. Heat the *ghee* over high heat in a deep saucepan. When the *ghee* is very hot, carefully add the mustard seeds. Keep the lid of a pan handy, since the seeds may sputter when added. When sputtering stops and the seeds turn grey (about 5 seconds), add cumin seeds. When cumin turns dark (about 5-10 seconds), add asafetida, stir for a second or two, and add the tomatoes. Cook, stirring rapidly but carefully so as not to mash up the tomato pieces, for 3-4 minutes. Add aubergine and courgette and continue cooking for an additional 3 minutes.

6 Add lentil purée and salt, and bring to the boil. Reduce heat and cook the vegetables, covered, for 20 minutes or until the vegetables are cooked and very tender. Add kari leaves and serve.

NOTE The stew may be made ahead and refrigerated for up to 2 days. It does not freeze well.

To serve this stew, follow the menu suggestions given for Mung Bean and Cauliflower Stew on p. 206.

SIDE DISHES

VEGETABLES

SABZI

◆

It is almost impossible to imagine India without vegetables, for it is well known that India has the largest number of vegetarians in the world. For centuries whole segments of the population have been living on a meatless diet. Some cannot eat meat because it is beyond their means (meat costs seven to eight times as much as vegetables); others prefer not to eat meat for health reasons. But most do not eat meat because of religious dietary restrictions. Women in general, particularly unmarried ones and widows, are not allowed meat. Most people reaching old age give up meat as a gesture of preparation for encountering God, with the anticipation of being sent to heaven (in Hindu mythology one scores points towards heaven by practising *A-himsa*, meaning 'no killing', or nonviolence).

It is therefore natural that India grows the finest assortment of vegetables in the world, unsurpassed in quality and variety. The cooking of these vegetables is an art, so refined, sophisticated, and intricately varied from region to region that it is often referred to as a separate classic cuisine, holding its own esteemed place in the culinary world.

In India there are no such things as canned, frozen or freeze-dried vegetables for general consumption. This is partly because the techniques used for cooking vegetables, like those of Chinese cooking, require fresh produce. But the main reason is that Indians are very particular about the quality of vegetables. They will spend hours going through the mounds of green beans or okra at the vegetable shop, picking the tender ones.

Vegetables are usually grown in farms around the city. Due to the lack of adequate packing and transportation facilities, most of the produce is consumed locally. The vegetables are still sold in sunlit open-air markets called *Sabzi bazaar*, as they have been for centuries. The farmers bring their produce early every morning in bullock carts, and arrange them in an enticing array in stalls called *Sabzi ki ducan*. Walking through the narrow alleys lined with rows of these stalls is an experience one seldom forgets. The air is filled with the gentle lingering aroma of freshly picked vegetables, the earthy scent of the soil clinging to their roots, and the freshly cut stem-ends still dripping juices.

Vegetables served as side dishes with an Indian meal are cooked in just about every conceivable way. The most popular and commonly used technique, however, is *bhojia*, a process which can be described as twice stir-fried – for that is exactly what it is. The process is quick and utterly simple, some vegetables taking as little as ten minutes for total cooking.

In this process, the spices are first fried in hot oil; then the vegetables are added and quickly stir-fried until lightly seared. Some spices, such as turmeric, red pepper, ginger powder, and mango powder are often added with or after the vegetables, because they burn so easily. All this is done over high heat. The heat is then reduced and the vegetables are cooked in their own moisture and vapour. If the vegetables look dry, a little water is sprinkled on. Finally the heat is increased and the vegetables go through a second stir-frying, to get nicely browned and develop a beautiful shiny glaze. Sometimes a little oil or fat is added to the vegetables at the end, to increase the glaze. Vegetables cooked thus have a roasted flavour and very soft texture, though the pieces hold their shape.

Some vegetables, such as potatoes, yams and plaintain (green banana) are often cooked prior to stir-frying. This is done to preserve the full robust aroma of fried spices, as these vegetables require a lot of water and time to cook, and prolonged moist cooking robs the spices of much of their fried flavour.

Take a little time and care to choose vegetables that are fresh and in season. Avoid the wilted, rotting, and sad-looking. Remember, in all vegetable dishes the natural taste of the vegetables is as important as the herbs and spices flavouring them.

These recipes for preparing vegetable side dishes have been particularly selected to introduce you to some of the important and interesting cooking techniques and flavouring principles of different regions.

BROCCOLI SMOTHERED IN GARLIC OIL

HARE GOBHI KI SABZI

◆

Broccoli is not an Indian vegetable, although it lends itself amazingly well to Indian spices and flavourings. The technique for this recipe finds its roots in the classic cooking of the North, where green vegetables are briefly stir-fried with spices in oil before being cooked in their own moisture. The vegetables are stir-fried again, to coat them with the shiny glaze that is characteristic of many North Indian vegetable dishes.

FOR 4-6 PERSONS

◆

1½ lb/ 750 g broccoli
3 tablespoons light vegetable oil
8-10 garlic cloves, peeled
⅓ teaspoon turmeric
1 teaspoon coarse salt

1 Cut broccoli into spears, leaving long stems attached to the florets. Peel the stems carefully – they break easily. Rinse the spears under running cold water. Leave them for 5 minutes to drain.

2 Heat the oil over medium heat in a frying pan large enough to accommodate the broccoli in a single layer. When the oil is hot, add garlic, and sauté, turning and tossing until it turns golden (about 1-2 minutes). Add turmeric and immediately follow it with the broccoli. Spread the broccoli so that it lies in one layer. Let it sizzle undisturbed for 1 minute; then sprinkle on the salt. Turn the broccoli carefully with a flat spatula or a pair of tongs, and sauté for an additional minute.

3 Reduce heat and cook, covered, until the broccoli is cooked but still crisp and dark green (about 8-10 minutes). Uncover, and continue cooking until all the moisture evaporates and the broccoli spears are glazed with garlic oil (about 3-5 minutes). Check for salt, and serve immediately.

This garlic-scented broccoli dish goes especially well with lamb dishes, such as Royal Roast Leg of Lamb with Saffron Raisin Sauce (p. 141), Royal Braised Lamb with Spices (p. 134) or Lamb Fillets Braised in Yogurt Cardamom Sauce (p. 131).

BUTTERED SMOTHERED CABBAGE

BANDH GOBHI KI SABZI

◆

Cabbage, known as *Bandh* (closed) or *Patta* (leaf) *Gobhi*, is a popular vegetable with Indians. They cook it in many wonderful ways. The best method of all is a slow sautéeing in butter until the cabbage releases its natural sweetness. Generally a little turmeric is added to enhance the flavour and colour. This technique is common throughout India, although flavourings change from state to state. Here the cabbage is enhanced with cumin and ginger root and cooked in asafetida-laced oil, to produce a warm and refreshing taste.

FOR 6-8 PERSONS

◆

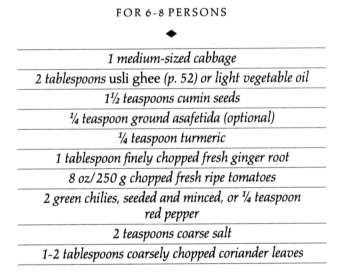

1 medium-sized cabbage
2 tablespoons usli ghee *(p. 52) or light vegetable oil*
1½ teaspoons cumin seeds
¼ teaspoon ground asafetida (optional)
¼ teaspoon turmeric
1 tablespoon finely chopped fresh ginger root
8 oz/ 250 g chopped fresh ripe tomatoes
2 green chilies, seeded and minced, or ¼ teaspoon red pepper
2 teaspoons coarse salt
1-2 tablespoons coarsely chopped coriander leaves

1 Cut the cabbage into quarters, remove the stem from each quarter and shred. Heat the *ghee* over medium-high heat in a large heavy-bottomed pan, preferably one with a non-stick surface. When the *ghee* is hot, add cumin. When cumin turns dark brown (about 10-15 seconds), add ground asafetida, if you are using it, and immediately add the shredded cabbage. Sprinkle turmeric over the cabbage, and sauté, turning and tossing rapidly until the cabbage is wilted (about 5 minutes).

3 Add ginger, tomatoes, and chilies or red pepper, and continue cooking for an additional 5 minutes. Add salt and 8 fl oz/25 cl hot water. Reduce heat to medium-low and cook the cabbage, covered, until it is tender and the water is absorbed into the vegetables (about 20 minutes). Check and stir often while it is cooking to prevent burning. Fold in chopped coriander leaves, check for salt, and serve.

NOTE This vegetable preparation may be made several hours ahead and reheated just before serving.

These buttery shreds of cabbage are good enough to be served as a first course. They are moist and juicy, hence ideal with bread. They are particularly good with Tandoori Chicken (p. 168), Fried Fillet of Sole Laced with Carom (p. 184), or Chick-pea Batter Fish (p. 185).

GLAZED CAULIFLOWER WITH GINGER

GOBHI SABZI

◆

Indians love cauliflower and this particular fondness has resulted in the creation of cooking techniques that do justice to this vegetable. Cauliflower is never boiled (if it is cooked in a liquid, the broth becomes part of the dish) because it might become mushy and lose its flavour. Instead, it is stir-fried and cooked in its own moisture. The dish, a classic from the states of Punjab and Uttar Pradesh, is seasoned with turmeric, cumin, and fresh ginger root shreds. FOR A VARIATION Substitute potatoes or green peas, or both, for a part of the cauliflower. If you use potatoes, increase the cooking time by 5 to 10 minutes, depending on how large the pieces of potato are.

FOR 4-6 PERSONS

◆

1 small head cauliflower
4 tablespoons light vegetable oil
1 teaspoon coriander seeds, or ½ teaspoon cumin
1½ tablespoons shredded fresh ginger root
1-2 green chilies, seeded and chopped (optional)
½ teaspoon turmeric
¾ teaspoon coarse salt
1 teaspoon lemon juice
2 tablespoons chopped coriander leaves

1 Separate the cauliflower into small florets cutting them with a knife if necessary. Wash under running cold water, and drain. On a surface next to the stove, place all the spices, the drained cauliflower, and 4 fl oz/12.5 cl hot water.
2 Heat 3 tablespoons of the oil over medium heat in a *kadhai* or large frying pan. When the oil is very hot, add coriander or cumin, and fry until the seeds turn dark brown (about 10 seconds). Add ginger and chilies, if using them, and stir for a couple of seconds. Immediately add turmeric and salt, and follow at once with the cauliflower. Stir rapidly to distribute the spices and to prevent burning. Add the hot water, reduce heat and cook, covered, until the cauliflower is fully cooked to crispy tenderness (about 20-25 minutes). Stir once or twice during cooking. (The cauliflower may be cooked up to this stage and set aside, covered, for several hours.)
3 Increase heat to medium, and stir-fry to evaporate any moisture remaining in the pan and to lightly brown the cauliflower (about 5-10 minutes). Stir carefully, as cooked cauliflower is usually very fragile and breaks easily. If the vegetable looks a little dry, stir in the remaining oil. Add lemon juice and chopped coriander leaves, and toss gently. Check for salt, and serve.

This dish goes well with cardamom-laced dishes, and cream and yogurt sauce dishes look subtly elegant against its sparkling yellow colour. Good choices are Moghul Braised Chicken (p. 155), Chicken Pilaf (p. 172), and Royal Braised Vegetables in Cardamom Nut Sauce (p. 198).

CAULIFLOWER AND SPRING ONIONS
WITH BLACK MUSTARD SEEDS

GOBHI KARI

◆

Indians treat spring onions as a vegetable in their own right, or mix them with another vegetable – in this case, cauliflower. *Gobhi Kari* is a speciality of the southern and southwestern regions. It is flavoured with black mustard seeds and turmeric.

Urad dal (p. 233), although not an essential ingredient, does lend a spicy aroma and an interesting texture to the dish.

FOR 4-6 PERSONS

◆

1 medium-sized cauliflower
2 bunches spring onions
4 tablespoons light vegetable oil
½ teaspoon black mustard seeds
1 teaspoon white split gram beans (Urad dal – *optional)*
½ teaspoon turmeric
1-2 green chilies, chopped, or ¼ teaspoon red pepper
1½ teaspoons coarse salt
6-8 fresh or dry kari leaves, slightly crushed (optional)

1 Separate cauliflower into very small florets, cutting them with a knife if necessary. Wash them in running cold water, and drain.
2 Trim the root ends of the spring onions, and chop them (including the green part) into ¼ in/5 mm pieces.
3 Measure out the spices and place them, the vegetables, and 5 tablespoons hot water next to the stove.
4 Heat 3 tablespoons of the oil over high heat in a *kadhai* or large frying pan. When the oil is very hot, carefully add the mustard seeds. Keep a lid handy, since the seeds may sputter when added. When the seeds are sputtering, add gram beans. When the beans turn light brown and the mustard seeds grey, add turmeric, chilies, salt, and spring onions, stirring rapidly. Sauté briefly (about 15 seconds), and add cauliflower. Stir to distribute the spices and spring onions, and add the hot water. Reduce heat to medium-low and cook, covered,

until the cauliflower is cooked to crispy tenderness (about 15-20 minutes). Uncover, increase heat to medium, and stir-fry to evaporate any moisture remaining in the pan and to lightly brown the cauliflower (about 5-10 minutes). Stir in the remaining tablespoon of oil during browning. Add kari leaves, if you are using them. Stir to mix. Check the dish for salt, and serve immediately.

SPICY BABY AUBERGINE

BAIGAN MASALEDAR

◆

This recipe calls for tiny aubergines as small as 2-3 in/5-7.5 cm and weighing about 2 oz/60 g available in both white and purple colours. In India they are prepared in many different ways: simmered with lentils in *sambaar*, cooked with spices and coconut, braised in tamarind juice, or stuffed with spices and stir-fried. Stuffed aubergines is the most popular method, and the stuffings vary from state to state. This particular recipe reflects the typical cooking of the Rajasthanis, and is very spicy.

FOR 2-4 PERSONS

◆

8-10 tiny aubergines
THE STUFFING
2 teaspoons ground coriander
1 teaspoon ground cumin
¼-½ teaspoon red pepper
½ teaspoon mango powder, or 1½ teaspoons lemon juice
½ teaspoon garam masala *(p. 42)*
1 teaspoon coarse salt
2 tablespoons light vegetable oil
½ teaspoon cumin seeds
⅛ teaspoon ground asafetida

1 Cut off the stem from the aubergines, being careful not to cut the green skirtlike top. Quarter the aubergines from the stem end, cutting through the green part, to within ¾ in/2 cm of the bottom. Put them in a bowl, add enough cold water to cover. Soak them for 15 minutes. (This will make the aubergines open up slightly like flower buds. Do not oversoak, or they will open up too much.) Drain and pat dry the outsides with kitchen towels.

2 Mix all the spices for the stuffing, and stuff the aubergines, making sure to distribute the mixture evenly. Press gently to reshape the aubergines. Do not worry if some of the spice stuffing falls out. Just be sure to reserve it.

3 Heat the oil over medium heat in a large frying pan. When the oil is very hot, add the cumin seeds. When the cumin turns dark brown (about 10 seconds), add asafetida and immediately follow with the aubergines. Stir for 10-15 seconds, then reduce heat to low. Sprinkle on any reserved stuffing mixture, and fry, turning and tossing for 3-5 minutes or until the oil coats the aubergines all over. Increase heat to medium, and fry them until they are lightly browned (about 5 minutes). Sprinkle 2-3 tablespoons of water over the aubergines, reduce heat to very low, and cook, covered, until they are tender (about 20 minutes). Watch constantly to prevent burning, and stir a few times, being very careful not to break the aubergines as they become extremely fragile when cooked. Uncover, increase heat to medium-low, and continue cooking the aubergines until all the remaining moisture evaporates and they look fried and glazed (about 5-10 minutes). Check for salt, and serve.

NOTE This dish may be prepared a couple of hours before you are ready to serve. Reheat gently but thoroughly before serving.

These aubergines offer a perfect contrast to mildly seasoned dishes. Serve them with Lamb Fillets Braised in Yogurt Cardamom Sauce (p. 131). For a lighter meal, fold the aubergines into plain cooked rice (p. 256) and serve it as spicy pilaf. Or serve them with *Paratha* (p. 285) or *Poori* (p. 293).

SMOKED AUBERGINE WITH FRESH HERBS

BHARTA

◆

Traditionally, the aubergine for *Bharta* is roasted over the ashes of a burnt down wood fire for 2-2½ hours; this process, which can be duplicated over an open fire, gives *Bharta* its special smoky flavour. The aubergine is then puréed, mixed with fragrant herbs and seasonings, and cooked. The more subtle and prolonged the roasting process, the more flavourful the *Bharta* becomes. *Bharta* cannot be cooked on a hot plate or electric stove. For the sake of convenience, I have outlined a method of roasting it in a gas oven, even though the aubergine will not develop a smoked flavour this way.

FOR 6 PERSONS

◆

2 aubergines (about 1 lb/500 g each)
4 oz/125 g shelled peas, fresh or frozen
9 tablespoons light vegetable oil
1 teaspoon minced garlic
1 tablespoon grated fresh ginger root
8 oz/250 g finely chopped onions
12 oz/375 g finely chopped fresh ripe tomatoes (or 8 oz/250 g canned tomatoes, drained and chopped)
2 green chilies, seeded and minced (optional)
2 teaspoons coarse salt
2-3 tablespoons finely chopped coriander leaves

1 Wash aubergines under running cold water, and wipe them dry with kitchen towels.

2 First, roast the aubergines. To roast, stand one aubergine on a burner of a gas stove, stem side uppermost, over a low flame, until the bottom of the aubergine is thoroughly charred (about 5 minutes). Now lay the aubergine on its side, and roast, turning it every minute with a pair of tongs until it is fully charred and very soft (about 15-20 minutes). When fully cooked, the aubergine will be quite limp, the skin blistered, and the juices beginning to ooze out. Repeat. Alternatively, the aubergines may be roasted on a baking sheet in an oven preheated to 500°F/250°C/Gas 9 for 20 minutes.

3 Let the aubergines cool briefly. Then carefully scrape the charred skin off. Rinse quickly under running cold water to wash away any skin that may still cling to the flesh. Place the aubergines in a small bowl. With paper towels, pat dry all the juices oozing out, pressing the aubergines slightly. (The juices carry the bitterness often found in aubergine. Therefore it is essential you dry them thoroughly.) Chop the pulp coarsely with a knife and put it in a small bowl, and beat with a fork for a minute. Set aside.

4 Cook the fresh peas in a little water to cover, for 5 minutes or until tender. (If you are using frozen peas, cook them following directions on the package.) Drain, and set aside.

5 Heat the oil over medium-high heat in a shallow pan, preferably one with a non-stick surface. When the oil is hot add garlic and ginger, and cook, stirring, for a minute. Add onions, and fry until they are light golden – do not let them brown – (about 8 minutes), stirring constantly to prevent burning. Reduce heat to medium, add aubergine purée, and cook for an additional 8 minutes, stirring often.

6 Add tomatoes and chilies, if you are using them, and continue cooking until the aubergines and tomatoes are fried (about 10 minutes). Add peas, and cook until a glaze forms on the purée and the fat begins to separate (about 5 minutes). Turn off heat, and stir in salt. Just before serving fold in chopped coriander leaves.

NOTE This dish may be made ahead and kept refrigerated for up to 3 days. It also freezes well. Defrost thoroughly before reheating. Taste and add more salt, if necessary, and a little chopped coriander.

This smooth purée, bursting with the fragrance of ginger root, coriander leaves, and most important of all, smoked aubergine, is best accompanied by only North Indian dishes, such as Beef in Fragrant Spinach Sauce (p. 138), Meat Smothered with Onions (p. 129), or Chicken in Onion Tomato Gravy (p. 157). For a simpler meal, serve the *Bharta* with a kebab, such as Moghul Kebabs with Raisin Stuffing (p. 91), accompanied by *Phulka* (p. 282).

GREEN BEANS WITH COCONUT AND BLACK MUSTARD SEEDS

BEANS KARI

◆

Kari is the popular southern Indian technique for preparing fresh vegetables. The dish prepared in this way is also called a *kari*. Coconut and mustard seeds are its primary ingredients.

In this *kari* of beans, freshly grated coconut is folded in during the last few minutes of cooking, so that its sweet fragrance and snow-white colour will not be overpowered. The contrast of green beans against the white coconut specked with black mustard seeds makes for a most attractive dish.

FOR 4 PERSONS

◆

1 lb/500 g fresh green beans
⅓ teaspoon turmeric
¾ teaspoon coarse salt
2 tablespoons light sesame oil, or light vegetable oil
½ teaspoon black mustard seeds
1 teaspoon white split gram beans (urad dal – optional)
1½ oz/45 g grated coconut (p. 49)
1-2 green chilies, seeded and minced, or ¼ teaspoon red pepper
1 tablespoon finely chopped fresh coriander leaves

1 Snap off the ends of the green beans, and cut into 1 in/2.5 cm long pieces.
2 Put the beans, along with turmeric, salt, and ¾ pint/45 cl water in a saucepan, and bring to the boil. Cook over medium heat, covered, until the beans are tender but still crisp (about 15-20 minutes). Drain, and set aside.
3 Heat the oil over high heat in a large frying pan. When the oil is very hot, add the mustard seeds. Keep a lid handy, since the seeds may sputter when added. When the seeds begin to sputter, add gram beans, and cook until they turn light brown.
4 Add grated coconut and green chilies or red pepper, and stir for a minute or two. Add the cooked beans, and stir-fry for 5 minutes. Turn off heat, add chopped coriander leaves and mix thoroughly. Check for salt, and serve.

STIR-FRIED OKRA

BHINDI SABZI

◆

If there is one vegetable that is grossly misunderstood and underrated it is okra. It can be truly delicious if properly cooked. In my cooking classes, I always include an okra preparation. This inevitably elicits dismay from the students. They picture the overcooked, bland stewed okra in a slimy sauce that they have tasted so often. Sliminess results when cut okra comes in contact with water. In Indian cooking, particularly North Indian, okra is never cooked with water. The North Indian technique calls for stir-frying okra in oil. After this explanation and a little persuasion, my students reluctantly give in, probably just to satisfy their curiosity. But when the dish is finally made and sampled, they are delightfully surprised and sorry to have missed out on such a delicacy all these years.

NOTE When buying okra, select deep green unblemished ones that snap easily at the end when bent. Always remember two things when cooking okra: Dry the washed okra thoroughly before cutting it. Salt it only *after* it is fully cooked, as salt will cause the okra to sweat.

FOR 4 PERSONS

◆

1 lb/500 g fresh okra
2 green chilies (optional)
3 tablespoons light vegetable oil
½ teaspoon salt

1 Wash okra under running cold water, and wipe dry with kitchen towels. Trim both ends, and slice the okra into ¼ in/5 mm rounds. Slit and seed the chilies, and slice them also into ¼ in/5 mm rounds.
2 Heat the oil over high heat in a large frying pan. When it is very hot, add the okra and chilies. Spread them into an even layer. Let the okra sizzle undisturbed for a minute, then reduce heat to medium. Cook the okra, uncovered, for 20 minutes, stirring frequently to ensure even cooking. Increase heat to high, and now fry the okra, stirring rapidly, for 5 minutes, or until it is lightly browned (the browning will be uneven). Turn off heat, sprinkle with salt, and toss the fried okra well to coat all pieces evenly.

NOTE Fried okra may be prepared a day ahead and refrigerated. To reheat, place the okra in a frying pan over low heat until heated through, stirring frequently. If it looks a little dry, add a teaspoon of oil while heating.

Stir-fried okra go well with just about any main dish. I often serve them with a *dal*, such as Spice- and Herb-Laced Split Peas (p. 237), accompanied by plain cooked rice (p. 256) for a light meal.

CRISP FRIED OKRA

BHONI BHINDI

◆

These okra are shallow-fried in oil until they turn crisp and brown. They are then drained and used in various dishes, such as Okra and Yogurt Salad (p. 249). They are delicious folded into Dry-cooked Spicy Minced Meat (*Sookha Keema*, p. 124).

MAKES 8 oz/250 g

◆

1 lb/500 g fresh okra
6 tablespoons light vegetable oil

1 Wash okra under running cold water, and wipe dry with kitchen towels. Trim both ends, and slice the okra into very thin rounds.
2 Heat the oil over high heat in a large frying pan. When it is very hot, add the okra in one even layer. Let the okra sizzle undisturbed for a minute; then reduce heat to medium-high. Fry the okra, turning and tossing until cooked and crispy brown (about 20-25 minutes). Remove with a slotted spoon, and spread over paper towels to drain and cool.

NOTE The crisp fried okra can be made several hours ahead and set aside, uncovered, until needed.

STUFFED OKRA WITH SPICES

BHINDI BHARVA

◆

Stuffing and stir-frying okra is a common technique popular in Uttar Pradesh, particularly with vegetarians. The young tender pods of the okra are slit, filled with fennel, cumin, coriander, and dry mango powder, and fried until cooked. These irresistible okra are often served just with *Paratha* (p. 285) for a light meal.

FOR 4-6 PERSONS

◆

1 lb/500 g fresh okra, preferably even-sized pods (3-4 in/7.5-10 cm long)
2 teaspoons fennel seeds, crushed
1 tablespoon ground cumin
1 tablespoon ground coriander
¼ teaspoon red or black pepper
¾ teaspoon mango powder, or 2 teaspoons lemon juice
2-3 tablespoons light vegetable oil
1¼ teaspoons coarse salt

1 Wash okra, and wipe dry. Cut off the head from the okra. Working with one pod at a time, make a slit along the length of each with a small pointed knife. Leave about ¼ in/5 mm unslit at either end. Slit all the okra pods this way, and set aside.

2 Mix fennel, cumin, coriander, red or black pepper, and mango powder (if you are using lemon juice, do not add it yet) in a small bowl.

3 Hold an okra pod in your left hand (if you are right-handed) so that the slit is facing up. Insert your left thumb into the slit to open it slightly. With your right hand, take about ¼-½ teaspoon of the spice mixture with a small spoon and insert it evenly into the slit. Press the okra by closing your palm to cover the slit; this will make the spices adhere to the inside of the pod, thus preventing their falling out. Continue with the rest of the slit okra pods the same way, until all are stuffed and all the spice mixture is used up. (The okra can be stuffed and set aside for several hours until you are ready to cook.)

4 When you are ready to cook, heat the oil over high heat in a large frying pan. When the oil is very hot, add the okra, preferably in one layer. Let it sizzle undisturbed for 1 minute. Reduce heat to medium. Then carefully turn the okra with a flat spatula, making sure the slits do not open. Fry for 5 minutes, turning now and then to prevent burning.

5 Reduce heat to low, cover the pan, and cook for 10 minutes. Uncover, and continue cooking until all the moisture evaporates and the okra is fried brown (about 15 minutes), stirring frequently and regulating heat from low to medium-low.

6 Turn off heat, and sprinkle with salt. If you are using lemon juice in place of mango powder, stir it in now. Serve immediately.

NOTE Stuffed okra can be made several hours ahead and reheated just before serving. In such a case, do not add salt and lemon juice until you reheat and are ready to serve the dish.

These are excellent accompaniments to North Indian main dishes such as Chicken in Onion Tomato Gravy (p. 157), Meat-Stuffed Cabbage Rolls with Ginger Lemon Sauce (p. 148), and Beef in Spicy Tomato Gravy (p. 133).

ROASTED ONIONS

BHONE PIAZ

◆

Here is a simple and delicious way to prepare onions — and it takes only a few minutes! The onions are thickly sliced and placed in a smoking-hot greased pan. They sizzle, roast, and become coated with a shimmering glaze. Although you can use yellow onions, I prefer the large Spanish kind because they tend to be sweeter.

FOR 6 PERSONS

◆

1 large Spanish onion (about 1 lb/500 g)
1 tablespoon light vegetable oil
2 tablespoons coarsely chopped coriander leaves (optional)

1 Peel onion, cut in half, and slice into ¼ in/5 mm thick slices. Separate the slices into shreds.

2 Heat a large heavy-bottomed frying pan over high heat. When it is very hot, add the oil, tilting the pan to coat it thoroughly. When the oil is smoking hot, add the onions. Do not stir, but let the onions sizzle and roast undisturbed for ½ minute. Now stir, and keep roasting, tossing and turning, until the onions are translucent and slightly browned (about 2 minutes). The roasted onions should be crisp, not limp, and sweet to the taste. Fold in coriander leaves and transfer to a serving platter.

NOTE Essential to preparing roasted onions is a good heavyweight frying pan that holds heat uniformly, otherwise the onions will burn instead of roasting.

These roasted onions traditionally accompany Tandoori Chicken (p. 168). They are also served with Kebab Patties Laced with Ginger and Mint (*Shamme Kabab*, p. 92).

TURMERIC POTATOES WITH GREEN PEPPERS

ALOO MIRCH

◆

Here is a popular dish from the North. Potatoes have a marvellous ability to enhance the flavour of any food cooked with them. For this reason, green vegetables are often cooked with a few pieces of potato. You can also make this lovely dish with cabbage, cauliflower, or green peas in place of the green pepper. The potatoes can also be cooked on their own.

FOR 8 PERSONS

◆

2 lb/1 kg potatoes
4 medium-sized green peppers
3-4 tablespoons light vegetable oil
1½ teaspoons turmeric
1 tablespoon coarse salt

1 Boil potatoes in their jackets until cooked but still firm. Plunge them into cold water for a minute, and peel. Cut them into 1 in/2.5 cm pieces. Cut green peppers into quarters, and core out the stem and seeds from each quarter. Cut them into 1 in/2.5 cm pieces.

2 Heat the oil over medium-high heat in a large frying pan. When the oil is very hot, add turmeric, and immediately add the potatoes and green peppers. Sprinkle with salt, and fry, turning and tossing for 3-4 minutes. Sprinkle 2-3 tablespoons of water over the vegetables, reduce heat, and cook, covered, until the green peppers are cooked but still very crisp and bright green (about 5-10 minutes).

3 Uncover, and stir-fry the vegetables to evaporate any excess moisture remaining in the pan and to brown the vegetables (about 5 minutes). Check for salt, and serve.

Except that you should avoid a main dish that contains potatoes, you can serve this with practically any dish. For a simple vegetarian meal, serve it with a *dal* – Lentils with Garlic Butter (p. 238) or Mung Beans Laced with Black Mustard Seeds (p. 240) – and plain cooked rice (p. 256). Or accompany it with Cucumber and Yogurt Salad (p. 246) and any of the plain baked breads, such as *Phulka* (p. 282).

COOKED SPINACH

OBLA SAAG

◆

This is a basic recipe for making cooked spinach. It is used in Beef in Fragrant Spinach Sauce (p. 138), Cream of Spinach Soup (p. 117), Spinach and Yogurt Salad (p. 247), and Spinach Bread (p. 291).

◆

3 lb/1.5 kg fresh spinach, or 3 × 10 oz/300 g packages frozen leaf spinach

2 tablespoons coarse salt

1 Snip the stems from the leaves of fresh spinach. For the more mature leaves, fold the leaf vertically along the stem, and with one hand pull away the stem, including that portion of it attached to the leaf's underside. Pick out and discard all rotting, wilting, or yellow leaves.

2 Wash the spinach thoroughly by swishing it around in several changes of cold water until all sand is washed away.

3 Bring about 12 pints/8 litres water mixed with the salt to the boil in a deep pot. Drop the spinach leaves into the rapidly boiling water. When the water comes to the boil again, reduce heat to medium, and let the spinach boil, uncovered, for 5 minutes. (If you are using frozen leaf spinach, defrost thoroughly, and separate the leaves. Cut off the stems, and discard. Cook the spinach, if you are using it in salad, in the boiling water, to which salt has been added, for 3 minutes.)

4 Pour the entire contents of the pot immediately into a colander or a sieve held firmly over the kitchen sink. Let cold water run through for a minute to refresh the spinach – this will preserve its bright green colour and also prevent any further cooking.

5 Squeeze as much water out of the spinach as possible by pressing it with the back of a spoon, or use your hand.

6 Place the spinach on a chopping board, and chop it as coarse or fine as called for in a recipe.

BUTTERED GREENS

SAAG

◆

For an Indian, it is not enough that any food be good for him — *it must also taste good*. Indians eat a lot of greens for this reason. Greens have a distinct, subtle, natural flavour which needs to be released and enhanced before they can be enjoyed. This is achieved by slow stir-frying in a gentle spice-laced *ghee* or oil — a common technique in India. If the spicing tends to be too overpowering, potatoes are added to right the balance. This wonderful-tasting dish can be made with a variety of different greens — as long as half of them are spinach.

SERVES 6-8 PEOPLE

◆

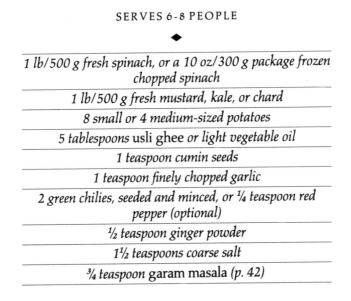

1 lb/500 g fresh spinach, or a 10 oz/300 g package frozen chopped spinach
1 lb/500 g fresh mustard, kale, or chard
8 small or 4 medium-sized potatoes
5 tablespoons usli ghee *or light vegetable oil*
1 teaspoon cumin seeds
1 teaspoon finely chopped garlic
2 green chilies, seeded and minced, or ¼ teaspoon red pepper (optional)
½ teaspoon ginger powder
1½ teaspoons coarse salt
¾ teaspoon garam masala *(p. 42)*

1 Pick over and discard all rotting, wilted, and yellow leaves. Wash the greens by dunking them into several changes of cold water until all the sand is washed away. Drain, pat the greens dry with paper towels, and place them on a chopping board. Chop the greens (leaves and stem) coarsely. If you are using frozen chopped spinach, defrost thoroughly, and squeeze out the excess water by pressing with the back of a spoon, or use your hand. Set aside.
2 Peel the potatoes, and cut small ones in half and medium ones in quarters.
3 Heat the *ghee* over medium-high heat in a large frying pan, preferably with a non-stick surface. When it is very hot, add cumin seeds. When the cumin turns dark (about 10 seconds), add garlic and chili or red pepper if you are using

them. Stir rapidly for a moment or two, and add potatoes. Reduce heat to medium and fry the potatoes, turning and tossing them until they are lightly browned all over (about 5-8 minutes). Add about a quarter of the chopped greens and stir in. When the greens get limp (about ½ minute) add another quarter of greens. Continue until all greens are incorporated. Sprinkle with ginger powder and salt. Stir well to mix. Add ½ pint/30 cl boiling water, reduce heat and cook, covered, until the potatoes are tender (20-25 minutes).

4 Uncover, and continue cooking until the excess moisture evaporates (about 15 minutes). The vegetables must be stirred very carefully at this stage, as the potatoes break easily. Increase heat to medium and continue frying, stirring the vegetables gently until the potatoes and greens look almost dry and the butter begins to coat and glaze the vegetables (about 5 minutes). Stir in *garam masala*, and turn off heat. Check for salt, and serve.

NOTE This dish may be prepared several hours before you are ready to serve. It also keeps well in the refrigerator for up to 4 days.

Buttered Greens represents the authentic peasant-style cooking in both its ingredients and its flavour. It is best served with robust dishes such as Beef in Spicy Tomato Gravy (p. 133) or Whole Eggs in Spicy Tomato Sauce (p. 175).

PULSES

DAL

♦

The use of pulses in Indian cooking is so widespread that it would be impossible to include all the pertinent information in this book. I will, however, give you an idea of the most common and important uses. There are three basic and popular ways of preparing pulses: one, they are simply boiled in water, with or without herbs and seasonings, and mashed to a smooth golden purée, which is then flavoured and enriched with spice-perfumed butter (*Tadka*, p. 68). The purée is usually used for dipping bread, or it is poured over rice and mixed. Two, they are briefly soaked in water and steamed with spice-laced butter, so that the pulses emerge with each grain separate and intact. Three, they are cooked with other ingredients, such as vegetables, meat, fish, poultry, nuts and even rice, and turned into hearty stews (see pp. 200-209). Such preparations are generally served as main dishes.

In addition to these three methods, pulses are also used in soups, stuffings for breads, turnovers, dumplings, puddings, and desserts. Pulses are ground to a flour and used to make batter for fritters and dough for wafers, as well as fudge, and other sweetmeats. They are soaked, ground into paste, and used for making dumplings which are either served as appetizers, simmered in sauces and served as main dishes or dressed with yogurt and served as a cold side dish. Mixed with herbs and seasonings, pulses are cooked into pancakes, buns, and breads.

♦

CLASSIFICATION OF PULSES

Pulses can be grouped into three broad categories; lentils, beans, and peas. Of all the varieties, the most widely used in Indian cooking are two kinds of lentil: yellow lentils (*toovar dal*) and pink lentils (*masar dal*); two kinds of beans: mung beans (*moong dal*) and black gram beans (*urad dal*); and yellow split peas (*channa dal*). The wonderful characteristic of these pulses is that they are virtually indestructible, and thus can be stored indefinitely.

Lentils are thin lens-shaped seeds ranging in colour from yellow to walnut brown. They are the most commonly consumed pulses in India. As a matter of fact, half the world's production and consumption of lentils is concentrated in India. They are among the easiest pulses to digest.

The yellow lentil (*toovar dal*, known as *toor dal* or *arhar dal*) is the seed of the plant *Cajanus cajan*. The seeds are hulled and split to yield golden yellow lentils. These yellow lentils should not be confused with the common variety, an altogether different species that, since they are sold unhulled, with the thin brown skin on, turn into a dirty brown purée when cooked instead of a golden yellow one.

The pink lentil (*Masar dal*, also known as *Masoor dal*) is the seed of the plant *Lens culinaris*. The tiny brown seeds are hulled to yield lens-shaped salmon-coloured lentils, which turn pale yellow when cooked. The pink lentils are similar to yellow lentils (in most recipes they can be used interchangeably) except that the purée is not as thick and creamy. Pink lentil purée is much lighter and thinner. It also cooks faster, in about half the time taken by yellow lentils. Red Egyptian lentils make a good substitute.

Beans are the next most common pulse consumed in India. They are cooked whole, as well as hulled and split. The tiny cylindrical seeds are rectangular in shape when split.

Mung bean (*moong dal*), technically known as green gram bean, is the seed of the plant *Phaseolus aureus*. The name *moong dal* usually refers to the hulled and split bean, yellow in colour. This is the form most widely used in Indian cooking. In this form it is the most easily digestible pulse, and is therefore cooked with rice to make a porridge called *khichari*, served to ailing people. (The boiled rice-and-fish preparation known as 'kedgeree' is not an Indian dish, for a proper *khichari* must contain *dal* and does not contain fish. Kedgeree was originally concocted by the British stationed in India to suit the Western palate.) The whole seed, dark green in colour, is called *sabat* (whole) *moong*, and is more popular in the northern and western regions of India.

Black gram bean (*urad dal*, also known as *dhooli* [washed] *urad*) is the seed of the plant *Phaseolus mungo*. The name *urad dal* usually refers to the hulled and split seed, ivory white in colour. This is the form most widely used. The whole seed, black in colour, is called *sabat* (whole) *urad*, *maan*, or *kali* (black) *dal*. This bean is popular in the North, especially in Punjab where it is cooked with onions, ginger, herbs, and butter, and turned into a rich creamy purée called *Kali Dal* (p. 242). In better quality restaurants this dish is often called 'special *dal*'.

Peas, if properly cooked with aromatic herbs and spices, can be a true delicacy. The northerners, particularly the people of Punjab, have a natural knack for turning them into ravishing main dishes. They are cooked either whole or hulled and split. The most popular and commonly used pea throughout India is the yellow split pea (*channa dal*) from the pod of the plant *Cicer arietinum*. The name *channa dal* usually refers to the hulled split peas

The whole peas known as chick-peas are called *kabuli channa* or *safaid channa* in Indian. Chick-peas are widely available in dry form or cooked and canned, either of which is suitable in Indian cooking. In India, another variety of chick-pea called black chick-peas (*kala* [black] *channa*) is also available; it is the *channa dal* chick-pea before hulling. These are particularly savoured by the people of Delhi. They cook these peas, as well as the white ones, in a pomegranate or tamarind sauce and serve them with the famous leavened potato bread, *bhatoora*. This combination, called *Channa* or *Cholle bhatoore*, is today popular throughout India and is served in restaurants specializing in North Indian food.

In addition to the above-mentioned pulses, red kidney beans (*badi rajma*), pink beans (*choti rajma*) and black-eyed peas (*lobhia*) are all available in dry or canned form, and are quite suitable for Indian cooking.

◆

PREPARING PULSES *(DAL)* FOR COOKING

CLEANING All varieties of pulses (*dal*) imported from India and sold in Indian shops need to be cleaned, because they often contain such foreign matter as pieces of stone, sticks, and mud.

To clean, put the *dal* on a large plate or simply put them on the kitchen or dining table. Spread a small portion so that the seeds are all separated and the dirt pieces are clearly visible. Pick out and discard all foreign objects, and push the cleaned *dal* to one side. Spread more of the *dal* the same way, and continue until the entire amount is cleaned.

WASHING Put the *dal* in a large fine-mesh sieve. Hold the sieve under the tap in the kitchen sink and let the cold water run through at medium speed for about 30 seconds, or until the water runs clear and the *dal* is thoroughly washed. Shake the sieve now and then to ensure proper cleaning.

◆

IMPORTANT FACTS ABOUT *DAL*

After eating *dal* some people experience stuffiness, heaviness, and even gaseousness in the stomach – a feeling that the food, even several hours after the meal, is still undigested. This feeling is of course intensified if you take a nap immediately following a meal of *dal*.

Dal is naturally rich in protein nitrogen compounds, important for muscle-building and body growth, and abundant in meat, poultry, fish, eggs, milk, and other dairy products. The proteins present in *dal*, however, are very different from those in meat, fish, milk, cheese, and eggs. The latter are much easier and quicker to digest. Vegetable proteins, particularly those present in certain types of unhulled beans and peas, such as the black gram bean, kidney bean, and chick-pea, require more time and effort to digest. They are ideal for people who work out-of-doors, especially doing heavy physical labour. That's why people around the world who work in fields and forests or on rivers are able to consume great quantities of *dal* day after day without any problem. When we transplant them to our sedentary urban setting, our digestive systems rebel. So it is imperative that you make certain adjustments when cooking with them. One is to serve them in moderate portions, no more than 4-8 oz/125-250 g of cooked *dal* per person. And always increase the quantity of digestive spices, such as asafetida and fresh ginger root, that you add to the dish.

SPICE- AND HERB-LACED SPLIT PEAS

MASALA DAL

◆

This is a lovely *dal* recipe that you can make with the common variety of yellow split peas. Since the peas cook like Indian split peas (*Channa dal*) but taste like lentils (*Arhar* or *Toovar dal*), I have slightly modified the recipe to suit its particular flavour and texture. The *dal* is seasoned with onions and cumin, a technique popular in Uttar Pradesh and Punjab, and it is divine.

In Indian cooking, split peas are traditionally accompanied by bread, and lentils by rice. The unique taste and texture of this *dal* make it suitable for serving with either staple.

FOR 4-6 PERSONS

◆

10 oz/300 g yellow split peas
⅓ teaspoon turmeric
2 teaspoons coarse salt
THE TADKA
4 oz/125 g Indian vegetable shortening, or light vegetable oil
1 teaspoon cumin seeds
8 oz/250 g finely chopped onions
¼ teaspoon red pepper (optional)
2 tablespoons finely chopped coriander leaves

1 Wash the peas following directions on page 235. Put the peas in a bowl, and add enough hot water to cover by 1 in/2.5 cm. Let soak for 1 hour. Drain.
2 Put the peas in a deep pot along with the turmeric and 2 pints/1 litre water. Bring to the boil, stirring well to keep the peas from lumping. Reduce heat to medium-low and simmer, partially covered, for 45 minutes or until the peas are thoroughly cooked and tender when pressed between your fingers. Stir now and then to ensure that they do not stick to the bottom of the pan. Turn off heat, and beat the split peas with a wire whisk or wooden spoon for a minute or until finely puréed. Measure the purée. There should be about 2 pints/1 litre; if not, add enough water to complete the measurement. Stir in salt, and set aside. (The split pea purée may be prepared and kept refrigerated for up to 4

days. It also freezes extremely well. Defrost thoroughly before proceeding with the recipe.)

3 When ready to serve, simmer the purée over low heat until piping hot. Check the consistency of the purée if you have made it ahead of time: keeping often thickens it considerably and you may need to add water. Transfer it to a warm serving bowl, and make the spiced butter (*tadka*).

4 Heat shortening or oil over medium-high heat in a frying pan. When it is very hot, add cumin seeds, and fry until they turn dark brown (about 10 seconds). Add onions, and fry until they turn dark brown (about 20 minutes), stirring constantly to prevent burning. (See directions for Brown-Frying Onions, p. 66.) Stir in red pepper if you are using it, and immediately pour the butter with its spices and onions over the split pea purée. Garnish with chopped coriander, and serve immediately in small bowls (*katoori*).

This *dal* is particularly good accompanied by main dishes served with rice, such as Meat-Stuffed Cabbage Rolls with Ginger Lemon Sauce (p. 148), Fried Fillet of Sole Laced with Carom (p. 184) or Chick-pea Batter Fish (p. 185).

LENTILS WITH GARLIC BUTTER

MASAR DAL

◆

This is my favourite everyday *dal* – a smooth and silky golden purée of pink lentils known as *masar dal*. It is laced with lightly sautéed garlic slivers, a typical example of how Punjabis prepare and flavour the *masar dal*. For a variation, you can add a teaspoon of cumin seeds to the oil and brown them before adding the garlic.

FOR 4-6 PERSONS

◆

10 oz/300 g pink lentils (Masar dal) *or yellow lentils* (Toovar dal)
¾ teaspoon turmeric
2 teaspoons coarse salt
THE TADKA
5 tablespoons Indian vegetable shortening, or light vegetable oil
5-6 large garlic cloves, peeled and sliced lengthwise

1 Pick over, clean, and wash lentils following the directions on p. 235.

2 Put the lentils in a deep pot along with the turmeric and 2 pints/1 litre water, and bring to the boil, stirring often, as the lentils have a tendency to lump together at this stage. Reduce heat to medium-low and simmer, partially covered, for 25-30 minutes (40-45 minutes for yellow lentils) or until the lentils are thoroughly cooked and tender when pressed between your fingers. Stir now and then to prevent sticking. Turn off the heat, and beat the lentils with a wire whisk or wooden spoon for a minute to smooth the purée. Measure. There should be about 2¼ pints/1¼ litres of purée. If you have less, add sufficient water to complete the measurement. Stir in the salt. (The lentil purée may be prepared ahead and refrigerated for up to 3 days. It also freezes well. Defrost thoroughly before proceeding with the recipe.)

3 When ready to serve, simmer the purée in the pot over low heat until piping hot. It thickens with keeping; therefore check the consistency and add water if necessary. It should be like a moderately thick cream soup. Keep the purée warm while you make the garlic butter (*tadka*).

4 Heat the shortening or oil over medium heat in a small frying pan. When it is hot, add the garlic slices, and fry just until they turn light brown and are still soft (about 1-2 minutes). Turn off heat and immediately pour this perfumed garlic butter with the slivers of garlic over the lentil purée. Stir to mix, and serve in small bowls.

TO SERVE Follow the menu suggestions given for Spice- and Herb-Laced Split Peas (see last recipe).

MUNG BEANS LACED WITH BLACK MUSTARD SEEDS

MOONG DAL

◆

This *dal* is very light and has a refreshing taste lent by the chopped fresh coriander and lemon juice. A classic from the state of Maharashtra, it reflects the garlic-free cooking of the Maharashtrian Brahmins, known also as Poona Brahmins.

FOR 4 PERSONS

◆

6 oz/175 g yellow split mung beans (Moong dal)
¼ teaspoon turmeric
½ teaspoon grated fresh ginger root
1 teaspoon coarse salt
2 teaspoons lemon juice
THE TADKA
3 tablespoons usli ghee *(p. 52), or light vegetable oil*
½ teaspoon black mustard seeds
1-2 green chilies, seeded and shredded (or ¼-½ teaspoon black pepper)
2 tablespoons chopped coriander leaves

1 Pick over, clean and wash mung beans following the directions on p. 235.
2 Put the beans along with the turmeric and ginger root in a deep heavy-bottomed saucepan. Add 1½ pints/1 litre water, and bring to the boil, stirring often, as the beans have a tendency to lump together at this stage. Reduce heat to medium and simmer, partially covered, for 30 minutes or until the beans are fully cooked and soft when pressed between your fingers. Stir now and then to prevent sticking. Turn off heat, and when slightly cool, beat the purée with a wire whisk or wooden spoon for a few seconds to thicken the purée. There should be about 1½ pints/1 litre of purée; if not, add enough water to increase it to that level. (It may be prepared ahead and refrigerated up to 2 days.)
3 Simmer the bean purée gently until piping hot. Stir in the salt and lemon juice. Keep it hot while you make the perfumed butter (*tadka*).

4 Heat the *ghee* over high heat in a small frying pan. When it is very hot, carefully add black mustard seeds. Keep a lid handy, since the seeds may sputter. When the seeds stop sputtering and turn grey, add the shredded chilies or black pepper. Stir rapidly for a moment, and turn off heat. Pour the *ghee* with its seasonings over the bean purée. Fold in the chopped coriander. Check for salt, and serve immediately in small bowls.

To serve, follow the menu suggestions given for Spice- and Herb-Laced Split Peas on p. 237-8. This dish is excellent with almost any vegetable and cheese main dish.

LUCKNOW SOUR LENTILS

LAKHNAWI KHATTI DAL

◆

Khatti Dal, a classic from the city of Lucknow in the state of Uttar Pradesh, is indeed a superbly flavoured lentil dish. It is fragrant with garlic and fresh ginger root and black cumin seed. The characteristic feature of this *dal* is the tamarind juice added to perk up the flavours and provide a tang.

FOR 6 PERSONS

◆

10 oz/300 g pink lentils
1 tablespoon finely chopped fresh ginger root
½ teaspoon turmeric
2 oz/60 g tamarind pulp, or 1 teaspoon mango powder, or 1 tablespoon lemon juice
8 fl oz/25 cl boiling water
2 teaspoons coarse salt
THE TADKA
5 tablespoons Indian vegetable shortening, or light vegetable oil
1 teaspoon black cumin seeds, or ½ teaspoon white cumin seeds
1 tablespoon mashed or minced garlic
¼-½ teaspoon red pepper

1 Pick over, clean and wash lentils following the directions on page 235.

2 Put the lentils in a deep saucepan along with the ginger, turmeric and 2¼ pints/1¼ litres water, and bring back to the boil, stirring often, as the lentils have a tendency to settle at the bottom of the pan. Reduce heat to medium-low and simmer, partially covered, for 25 minutes, stirring now and then.

3 While the lentils are cooking, put the tamarind pulp in a small bowl, add 8 fl oz/25 cl of boiling water, and let soak for 15 minutes. Mash the pulp with the back of a spoon or using your fingers. Strain the liquid into another bowl, squeezing out as much juice as possible from the pulp. Discard the stringy fibrous residue.

4 Add the tamarind juice to the cooked lentils, and continue cooking for an additional 15 minutes (if you are using mango powder or lemon juice in place of tamarind, do not add yet). Turn off the heat, and beat the lentils with a wire whisk or wooden spoon for 1 minute to smooth the purée. Measure the purée and, if necessary, add enough water to make 2½ pints/2½ litres. If you are using mango powder or lemon juice, stir it in now with the salt. (The lentil purée may be prepared ahead and refrigerated for up to 3 days. It also freezes well. Defrost thoroughly before proceeding with the recipe.)

5 When ready to serve, simmer the purée over low heat until piping hot. It thickens with keeping, so check the consistency again. You may need to add 4 fl oz/12.5 cl water to bring it to the right consistency. Check for salt and transfer to a serving bowl while you make the spice-perfumed butter (*tadka*).

6 Heat the shortening over medium-high heat in a small frying pan. When it is very hot, add cumin seeds, and fry for a moment or two (white cumin seeds will take about 10 seconds). Remove the pan from the heat, add red pepper and the mashed garlic, and stir rapidly for 10 seconds or until the garlic loses its raw smell and begins to colour – do *not* let it brown. Pour the butter with its seasonings over the lentil purée. Stir once or twice – just enough to lace the purée with ribbons of perfumed butter. Serve immediately in small bowls.

To serve, follow the menu suggestions given for Spice- and Herb-Laced Split Peas on p. 237-8.

BUTTERED BLACK BEANS

KALI DAL

◆

Kali dal, popularly known as Butter *dal* or Special *dal,* is a Moghul classic. It is made with black whole gram beans, known as *sabat urad* or *maan dal.* The beans are traditionally cooked in the leftover oven heat of the *tandoor.* Its consistency, which resembles a thick *chili con carne*, comes from the slow, prolonged cooking of beans with yogurt, tomatoes, and onions. The important ingredients that give the *dal* its velvet-smooth texture and satiny sheen are butter and cream. In India, *Kali dal* is not an everyday dish. Partly because it tastes rich and mainly because it contains such expensive ingredients, *Kali dal* is usually reserved for special occasions. A favourite with Indians, this *dal* is a standard feature in better-quality restaurants that serve North Indian specialities, particularly *tandoori* food.

NOTE It is important to cook the beans over a very slow fire so that they can expand and become plump without breaking. *Kali dal* takes 5 hours to cook, although most of the cooking requires little or no supervision, rather like simmering stock, and the results will more than compensate for the time.

FOR 8 PERSONS

◆

8 oz/ 250 g black whole gram beans (Sabat urad dal *or* Kali dal)
2 tablespoons red kidney beans
FOR COOKING BEANS
6 oz/ 175 g finely chopped onions
2 tablespoons finely chopped fresh ginger root
6 oz/ 175 g chopped fresh tomatoes, or 4 oz/ 125 g canned drained tomatoes
8 fl oz/ 25 cl plain yogurt
½ teaspoon ground cardamom
1 tablespoon ground coriander
½ teaspoon red pepper
2 teaspoons coarse salt
4 oz/ 125 g unsalted butter, *or 6 tablespoons* usli ghee *(p. 52)*
THE TADKA
4 tablespoons usli ghee, *or light vegetable oil*
1½ teaspoons cumin seeds
6 oz/ 175 g minced or finely chopped onions
4 fl oz/ 12.5 cl double cream
4 tablespoons chopped coriander leaves

1 Pick over, clean and wash gram beans following the directions on page 235.
2 Put the gram beans and the kidney beans in a deep saucepan. Add 1½
pints/1 litre water, and bring to the boil. Turn off heat, and let the beans soak,
covered, for 2 hours. *Do not drain*, as the beans will cook in the water they are
soaking in.

3 Add all the ingredients for cooking the beans, and stir to mix. Bring to the
boil. Reduce heat and simmer, partially covered, for 4½-5 hours. Stir the beans
very carefully every ½ hour during cooking. (The heat should be as low as
possible so that the beans barely simmer during the entire 5 hours of cooking.
At no point should they ever boil rapidly, or the beans will crack and become slimy.)

5 Take out about a third of the cooked beans from the pan, and finely purée
them in a blender or food processor and return the purée to the pan. Or mash a
third of the cooked beans in the pan itself, with the back of a spoon. (This will
give the bean mixture a smoother, creamier consistency.) Keep the *dal* on a low
simmer while you make the perfumed butter (*tadka*).

6 Heat the *ghee* or oil over medium-high heat in a frying pan. When it is hot,
add the cumin seeds. When the seeds turn dark brown (about 10 seconds), add
the onions, and cook until they turn light brown (about 10 minutes), stirring
constantly so they do not burn. Pour the entire contents of the frying pan over
the simmering bean mixture. Add the cream and chopped coriander leaves,
and stir well to mix thoroughly. Simmer until heated through. Check for salt,
and serve.

NOTE This dish can be made several hours before you are ready to serve it. It
also keeps in the refrigerator for up to 4 days, and freezes extremely well.
Defrost thoroughly before reheating. To reheat, simmer over low heat until
warmed through, stirring often but very carefully. Check for salt. Fold in a little
ground roasted cumin seeds and fresh chopped coriander leaves to perk up the
flavours.

This *dal* traditionally accompanies all *tandoori* food. Because of its consistency,
Kali Dal is served with bread as well as rice. Its rich wholesome quality makes it
an ideal vegetarian main dish for days when you are planning a light meal. It is
excellent with Lamb Pilaf (p. 143), Emperor's Layered Meat and Fragrant Rice
Casserole (p. 146) or Chicken Pilaf (p. 172).

YOGURT SALADS

RAITA

An Indian meal, especially a vegetarian meal, is never considered complete without a dish containing yogurt, a primary source of protein. In yogurt salads, yogurt is an ingredient; therefore its rich flavour and texture are of prime importance. Indian yogurt is thick, creamy, and sweet, almost like cheese. This is because it is made from buffalo's milk, which has a high fat content, and also because it is sometimes poured into several layers of muslin and hung for a few minutes to drain off the moisture – a process which makes it even creamier. When you make *raita*, you should use homemade yogurt made with whole milk (p. 51). The commercially available plain yogurt, with some minor modifications, makes a satisfactory substitute: first taste the commercial yogurt to be sure it doesn't taste too tangy, then add a little cream (preferably sour or double) to enrich its flavour and texture.

Yogurt salads, though more popular in the summer, are eaten all year round in all parts of India. The spices naturally vary from region to region. However all *raitas* can be grouped under three broad categories:

1 *Raitas* made with raw vegetables, the easiest and fastest to make. Raw vegetables are peeled, grated, or chopped, and then folded into seasoned yogurt, as in Tomato and Yogurt Salad (p. 248).

2 *Raitas* made with cooked vegetables. The vegetables are cooked separately and folded into the seasoned yogurt just before serving, as in Spinach and Yogurt Salad (p. 247).

3 *Raitas* made with dumplings, fruits, nuts, and such. These salads are often a little sweet. Since they require either special preparations or expensive ingredients, they are usually reserved for weddings, formal dinners, and other special occasions. A classic example is Sweet Banana and Yogurt Salad (p. 251).

CUCUMBER AND YOGURT SALAD

KHEERE KA RAITA

◆

This cool refreshing yogurt salad is both easy and quick to put together. For best results, use only young cucumbers.

FOR 4-6 PERSONS

◆

2 medium-sized cucumbers (about 1½ lb/750 g)
1 medium-sized ripe tomato
1 green chili, seeded and sliced (optional)
12 fl oz/37.5 cl plain yogurt
4 fl oz/12.5 cl sour cream
½ teaspoon ground roasted cumin seeds (p. 62)
2 tablespoons finely chopped mint or coriander leaves
½ teaspoon salt

1 Peel the cucumbers and cut them in half lengthwise. If the seeds look hard and mature, scrape them out with a spoon, and discard. Using the coarse blade of the grater or a food processor, grate the cucumbers into a bowl.
2 Wash the tomato and wipe dry. Cut it in quarters and using a spoon, scrape out the pulp with the seeds (reserve them for some other use). Slice the tomato into thin shreds, and add them to the bowl.
3 Slit and seed the chili, cut it into thin shreds, and add.
4 Put the yogurt, sour cream, cumin, and mint or coriander leaves in another bowl, and mix thoroughly. (The vegetables and the yogurt mixture can be prepared several hours ahead and refrigerated separately until needed.)
5 When ready to serve, stir the salt and prepared vegetables into the yogurt mixture. Check for salt, and transfer to a serving bowl. Sprinkle with additional cumin, if desired.

On a hot summer day, the addition of a cool yogurt salad to the meal is essential. For a refreshingly light lunch or supper, serve yogurt salad with a stuffed bread, such as Cauliflower Stuffed Bread (p. 287), Spinach Bread (p. 291), or Potato- and Herb-stuffed Bread (p. 290).

SPINACH AND YOGURT SALAD

PALAK RAITA

◆

This is a simple yet tasty yogurt salad made with cooked spinach. All you need to do is mix the cooked spinach with the spices and yogurt. You can substitute cooked potatoes, peas, mixed vegetables or smoked aubergine pulp for the spinach if desired.

FOR 4-6 PERSONS

◆

⅓ recipe Cooked Spinach (p. 229)
12 fl oz/37.5 cl plain yogurt
4 fl oz/12.5 cl sour cream
1 teaspoon ground roasted cumin seeds (p. 62)
1 teaspoon ground roasted coriander seeds (p. 62)
¼ teaspoon each black and red pepper
½ teaspoon salt
Paprika (optional)

1 Coarsely chop the spinach in a food processor, or on a chopping board, using a knife.
2 Put the yogurt, sour cream, cumin, coriander, and black and red pepper in a bowl, and mix thoroughly. (Both these items can be prepared several hours ahead and refrigerated.)
3 When ready to serve, stir the salt and the spinach into the seasoned yogurt, and transfer to a serving bowl. If desired, sprinkle with additional cumin, coriander, and a little sweet paprika.

Follow serving suggestions given in previous recipe.

TOMATO AND YOGURT SALAD

TAMATO PACHADI

◆

This simple yogurt salad is a universal favourite – red ripe tomatoes chopped and folded into thick creamy yogurt, streaked with mustard-seed-flavoured oil. For this salad you need fully ripe sweet tomatoes with firm flesh; otherwise the tomato pulp will scatter into the yogurt, making the salad look rather unappealing.

FOR 4-6 PERSONS

◆

4 medium-sized ripe tomatoes
12 fl oz/37.5 cl plain yogurt
4 fl oz/12.5 cl sour cream
½ teaspoon salt
2 tablespoons light sesame oil, or light vegetable oil
⅓ teaspoon black mustard seeds
1 green chili, seeded and shredded (optional)

1 Wash tomatoes and wipe dry. Dice them into neat ½-in/1 cm pieces.
2 Mix yogurt, sour cream, and salt in a serving bowl. Add tomatoes but do not stir. Cover and refrigerate until needed. (This may be prepared several hours ahead and kept refrigerated until you are ready to serve the dish.)
3 Heat the oil over high heat in a small frying pan. When the oil is very hot, add the mustard seeds. Keep a lid handy, since the seeds may splutter. When the mustard seeds stop sputtering and turn grey, add the chili, if you are using it. Stir rapidly for a moment, and pour the entire contents of the pan over the vegetable-yogurt mixture. Stir the salad carefully to mix the ingredients. Do not overstir; the salad must remain a little lumpy. Serve immediately.

Try to serve southern and southwestern specialities with the salad, such as Goanese Hot and Pungent Curry (p. 150), Spicy Brussels Sprouts, Green Beans, and Lentil Stew (p. 204), or Mixed Lentils and Vegetable Stew (p. 208).

OKRA AND YOGURT SALAD

BHINDI PACHADI

◆

Whether or not you like okra, you will love this yogurt salad made with crisp crunchy pieces of okra. The only thing to remember is that you should fold the okra into the yogurt just prior to serving, because fried okra loses its crisp texture and becomes limp if it sits too long in yogurt, and also turns the yogurt brown and unpleasant-looking.

FOR 4-6 PERSONS

◆

12 fl oz/ 37.5 cl plain yogurt
4 fl oz/ 12.5 cl sour cream
½ teaspoon salt
1 tablespoon oil, preferably light sesame oil
⅓ teaspoon black mustard seeds
1 green chili, seeded and shredded
8 oz/ 250 g Crisp Fried Okra (p. 225)

1 Put the yogurt, sour cream, and salt in a bowl, mix thoroughly, and set to one side.
2 Heat the oil over high heat in a small frying pan. When the oil is very hot, carefully add the mustard seeds. Keep a lid handy, since the seeds may sputter. When the seeds stop sputtering and turn grey, add the shredded chili. Stir rapidly for a moment, and pour the entire contents of the pan over the yogurt. Add the fried okra, folding all the ingredients into the yogurt. Do not overmix. The salad should be a little lumpy. Serve immediately.

Follow serving suggestions given on p. 227 or those in previous recipe.

DUMPLINGS IN FRAGRANT YOGURT

DAHI BHALLE

◆

This recipe is from the state of Punjab, where the salad is flavoured with cumin, coriander, and fresh ginger root, and wrapped in the fragrance of fresh coriander leaves. The dish takes a little time to make, since you first have to make the bean dumplings, but the results are rewarding.

FOR 8-12 PERSONS

◆

24 Silky Bean Dumplings (Bade, p. 103)
1½ pints/ 1 litre plain yogurt
4 fl oz/ 12.5 cl sour cream
4 fl oz/ 12.5 cl cold water
1¼ teaspoons ground roasted cumin seeds (p. 62)
¼ teaspoon black pepper
¼ teaspoon red pepper
¾ teaspoon salt
2 green chilies, finely chopped
2 tablespoons chopped coriander leaves

1 Put the bean dumplings in a bowl, and cover with hot water. Let them soak for 15 minutes, and drain. Pick up one dumpling at a time, and press very gently between your palms to squeeze out as much water as possible. Do not overpress, or the dumpling will fall apart. Repeat the same process with the rest of the dumplings. Set aside.

2 Blend the yogurt, sour cream, and water in a bowl, beating with a fork for 1 minute or until the ingredients are thoroughly mixed. Add 1 teaspoon of the cumin, ⅛ teaspoon each of the black and red pepper, and salt. Mix again.

3 Dip the dumplings, one at a time, in the seasoned yogurt, and lay them in a shallow serving dish big enough to hold the dumplings in one slightly overlapping layer. Pour the remaining yogurt over the dumplings, distributing it evenly, and cover. Chill for at least 4 hours. (During this period the dumplings will soak up the yogurt sauce.)

4 When ready to serve, uncover, sprinkle with the remaining cumin and black and red pepper. Scatter the chopped chilies and coriander over all and serve accompanied by Sweet and Sour Tamarind Relish (*Imli Chutney* – p. 315), if desired.

Dahi Bhalle is fairly filling; therefore, for a light meal, serve it accompanied by a stuffed bread or a plain fried bread and a pickle like Sweet Lemon Pickle with Cumin (p. 318).

SWEET BANANA AND YOGURT SALAD

KEELA RAITA

◆

This is a luscious salad traditionally reserved for special occasions in India. Usually bananas are used, but you can substitute pineapple, peaches, apricots, or grapes. Just remember to adjust for sweetness, as all these fruits are more tart than bananas.

FOR 4-6 PERSONS

◆

2 tablespoons slivered blanched almonds
2 tablespoons seedless raisins
8 fl oz/ 25 cl plain yogurt
8 fl oz/ 25 cl sour cream
3-4 tablespoons honey or sugar
⅛ teaspoon ground cardamom or grated nutmeg
1 medium-sized ripe banana, peeled and thinly sliced

1 Put almonds and raisins in a small bowl, and add about 4 fl oz/12.5 cl boiling water. Soak for 15 minutes, and drain.
2 Mix the drained almonds and raisins with the yogurt, sour cream, honey or sugar, and cardamom or nutmeg in a serving bowl. Add the banana slices and gently fold them into the yogurt mixture. Cover, and chill thoroughly before serving. If desired, sprinkle with additional cardamom or nutmeg.

This yogurt salad with its sweet nutty overtone is ideal with such pilafs as Emperor's Layered Meat and Fragrant Rice Casserole (p. 146), Chicken Pilaf (p. 172), Sweet Saffron Pilaf (p. 264), and Saffron Pilaf with Peaches (p. 266).

ACCOMPANYING STAPLES

RICE

CHAWAL

◆

Rice is one of the oldest grains known to mankind. In India it has been cultivated for some six thousand years. Today it is the staple of more than two thirds of the country's population. This long and close association with rice has resulted in a classic Indian cuisine that makes full use of it.

To begin with, Indians cook the rice itself to perfection — in a way that is unbeatable anywhere in the world. It is ground and turned into flour or roasted into flakes, and in one or the other of these forms, is used in making pancakes, fritters, buns, cakes, dumplings, wafers, desserts, puddings, and sweetmeats. Rice flour dissolved in water is considered holy and is used as a paint for decoration during religious festivals. Raw rice grains are thrown on newly married couples as a symbol of fertility; this ancient Hindu custom is observed in many cultures around the world.

Even though there are thousands of different varieties of rice grains in the world, they basically fall into two categories — long grain rice and short grain rice. The short grain variety with fat oval grains is popular in southern Europe and parts of eastern China. When cooked, the starchy grains become plump and creamy, and adhere to each other. They are used in such Italian dishes as *risotto* and in the Spanish *paella*. Short grain rice is particularly suited for making puddings and cakes.

The long grain variety is more popular and is eaten widely around the world. This cooks to light fluffy grains that are non-sticky. In India several varieties of long grain rice, known as *arwa chawal*, are cultivated in the southern and eastern regions, where they grow abundantly. There the staple is rice, and it is usually served plain — steamed or boiled.

There is one particular variety of long grain rice grown in limited quantity along the foothills of the Himalayas in the North and this is considered the best rice in the world. Its generic name is *basmati*. Cooked *basmati* has long thin grains, is tender and spongy to the touch, and exudes a special nutty-milky aroma. As a result, even plain cooked *basmati* has the aroma, and flavour of an exquisite pilaf. This is why it is essential to use *basmati* to make authentic-tasting *pullao*, *biriyani*, and other Indian rice preparations. The two most commonly available varieties of *basmati* are *Patna basmati* from the state of Bihar, and *Dehradun basmati* from the state of Uttar Pradesh. *Dehradun basmati* is considered to be superior. All *basmati* rice is processed and then graded by the percentage of whole, unbroken grains in each batch. The number one grade contains no broken grains. The *basmati* is then aged for several years in *godowns*; this process enhances its aroma and flavour. The best quality *basmati* commercially available in India today is well-aged *Dehradun basmati*. It is this variety that is generally recommended for making pilafs. Presently there is no shortage of *basmati* in India, especially in New Delhi and other big cities in the North. However, the supply of the best grade of *basmati* is limited to the *Dehradun* region.

    Basmati requires no special skill to cook. It is like any other long grain rice, requiring twice as much water as short grain and about twenty-five minutes to cook. There is, however, one major difference between regular long grain rice cooking and *basmati* cooking: *basmati* is always soaked in cold water prior to being cooked. Also there are a few special techniques that ensure fluffy tender rice grains that come out looking like lace.

◆

PREPARING *BASMATI* RICE FOR COOKING

CLEANING When you buy *basmati* rice you may notice that it contains a few unhulled rice grains, pieces of stones, and sticks. These should be removed. Put the rice in a large plate or simply spread it on the kitchen table. Gather a small portion aside so that the grains are all separated and the foreign objects clearly visible. Pick out and discard all the dirt pieces, and push the cleaned rice to one side. Spread more of the rice the same way, and continue cleaning until the entire amount is clear of foreign particles. (There is no need to remove the husk and bran pieces, since they will disappear when the rice is washed.)

WASHING No matter which quality *basmati* you use, as long as it is *basmati*, and cooked the Indian way, *it must be washed*. Washing removes light foreign objects, which will float. It also removes the starch clinging to the rice grains, which could make the cooked rice sticky and gummy.

    To wash the rice, put it in a large bowl, and fill with cold water. The water will grow milky, and several pieces of bran, husk, and other objects will float to the top. Let the rice settle to the bottom for 2-3 seconds. Then tilt the bowl and pour off the water. Repeat this process 8 or 9 times, until the water runs clear.

SOAKING This is an essential step, unique to *basmati* rice cooking. The only other rice in the world that is soaked before being cooked is the Persian rice called *Domsia*. But *Domsia* requires a much longer soaking, usually overnight. In the soaking process, the rice grains absorb moisture and thereby 'relax' prior to being cooked. As a result, they expand to long thin grains that will not crack or break when water is added during cooking.

    To soak the rice, add twice the volume of cold water as there is raw rice.

Let the rice soak exactly ½ hour, and drain, reserving the water. (In Indian cooking, unless otherwise specified, the rice is always cooked in the water in which it is soaked.) The soaked rice will be chalk-white in colour and very fragile. Therefore be careful when you handle it.

COOKING *BASMATI* RICE

The *basmati* rice can be cooked plain in one of three ways: steamed, boiled, or baked, all referred to as *sada chawal* or *obla chawal*. All three methods produce excellent results. It can be cooked with fat or oil, spices, herbs, vegetables, and all types of meat and cheese. When it is cooked with other ingredients the dish is called *pullao, biriyani,* or *tahari.* No matter what rice dish you are preparing, each is created from one of these three basic techniques.

PLAIN STEAMED *BASMATI* RICE

In this process the rice is simmered, in the same water it has been soaking in, until it is almost tender and the water is absorbed. It is then steamed gently over very low heat until the rice grains are all separated and become tender, springy, and fluffy.

1 Put the reserved water into a large heavy-bottomed pan with a tight-fitting lid, and bring to the boil. Add the soaked rice, and stir carefully with a narrow stirring implement such as a fork or knife (so that the rice grains are not crushed) until the water comes to a second boil. (Stirring will keep the rice from settling or lumping.)

2 Reduce the heat to low and simmer, partially covered, until most of the water is absorbed and the surface of the rice is full of steamy holes (about 10-15 minutes). There is no need to stir the rice but if you wish to do so, use a fork or a knife.

3 Cover the pan tightly, reduce heat further to the lowest possible level, and raise the pan about 1 in/2.5 cm away from the source of the heat. (This can be achieved by placing a pair of tongs or a Chinese wok ring over the burner and resting the pot on it.) Let the rice steam for 10 minutes.

PLAIN BOILED *BASMATI* RICE

Here the rice is boiled briskly for a short time in a large quantity of water until almost tender. Then it is drained and rinsed, and returned to the pot. The pot is then placed over the lowest possible heat. The rice is steamed until it is fluffy and tender, and the grains are all separated. The water for soaking the rice is not used for cooking.

1 Bring a large quantity of water (about 6-7 times the volume of rice) to the boil in a deep pot. Add the soaked rice, and stir immediately for ½ minute (this prevents the rice from settling) being careful not to break the fragile rice grains. Bring the water to a second boil (it will take about 3 minutes), and cook the rice for 2 minutes.

2 Pour the entire contents into a large sieve held over the kitchen sink. Hold the sieve under the tap, and let cold water run through the rice at medium speed for 3-5 seconds. Shake the sieve to drain the rice thoroughly.

3 Return the rice to the pot, and cover it tightly. Place the pot over the lowest possible heat, raised above the burner with a pair of tongs, or a Chinese wok ring. Let the rice steam for 10 minutes.

PLAIN BAKED *BASMATI* RICE

In this process the rice is first boiled quickly until almost tender, then drained, and baked in the oven to finish the cooking. A little butter or oil is folded into the rice before baking it. Rice cooked in this way expands fully and the grains become long and a little dry.

1 Preheat the oven to 300°F/150°C/Gas 2.

2 Bring a large quantity of water (about 6-7 times the volume of rice) to the boil in a deep pot. Add the soaked rice, and stir immediately for ½ minute (this will prevent the rice from settling), being careful not to break the fragile grains. Bring the water to a second boil, and cook the rice for 2 minutes.

3 Pour the entire contents into a large sieve held over the kitchen sink, and drain the rice thoroughly.

4 Return the rice to a heavy oven-proof casserole with a tight-fitting lid. Add a little fat or oil, and mix carefully but thoroughly to coat all the grains. Put a piece of foil on top of the casserole, and cover tightly with the lid.

5 Bake the rice for 25 minutes.

RESTING THE COOKED *BASMATI* RICE

No matter which of the three basic cooking techniques is followed for the *basmati* rice, it must rest undisturbed, covered, on top of the stove or in the turned-off oven for a short period (about 5 minutes) before being handled. During this time the pan should not be opened and the contents never stirred. This is an essential step that causes the firm, springy separate grains to retain their shape, even with repeated handling. This is because freshly cooked rice, just like a fresh roast, is moist, steamy, and very fragile; when handled it becomes sticky and mushy. Just before serving, the rice should be fluffed with a fork or knife. Cooked rice generally remains warm for up to 25 minutes, covered with a lid.

PREPARING RICE DISHES AHEAD OF TIME

Except for *biriyani* and certain *pullao*, most rice preparations should be made just before serving, because the fragrance of such spices as cinnamon, cloves, and cumin is much more pronounced in a freshly made pilaf. Storing, especially refrigeration, makes these dishes lose much of their delicate aroma and flavour. It is possible to reheat rice dishes, however, either on top of the stove or in a low oven.

TO HEAT IN THE OVEN Place the rice in a large sheet of heavy-duty foil, sprinkling a little cold water over the rice if it looks somewhat dry. Cover, wrap and seal tightly. Bake in an oven preheated to 300°F/150°C/Gas 2 for 25-30 minutes or until heated through.

TO HEAT ON TOP OF THE STOVE Place the rice in a heavy-bottomed pan. Add a few tablespoons of cold water. Heat the pan over medium heat, stirring and tossing the rice constantly until enough steam builds up. Cover the pan tightly, reduce heat, and let the rice steam until heated through (about 10-15 minutes).

ABOUT SUBSTITUTIONS

There is no substitute for *basmati* rice, not even the Persian *domsia* rice, for that does not have the *basmati* aroma or flavour. Therefore, if you want to cook *basmati* rice, you have to use *basmati* rice. In the event you are unable to get *basmati*, or your supply has run out, you may substitute ordinary long grain rice but remember it will taste, smell, and look quite different. When substituting regular long grain rice for *basmati*, the following modifications have to be made in the recipe:

1 Ordinary long grain rice may not need cleaning; it depends on the packing.

2 The washing and soaking steps can be omitted, as the regular long grain rice no longer contains a starch coating.

3 The cooking process is practically the same, except that regular long grain rice takes a little longer to cook (partly because the *basmati* grains are much thinner, but mainly because they have been soaked, which is comparable to a partial cooking).

RICE COOKED IN MEAT BROTH

YAKHNI CHAWAL

◆

Yakhni Chawal is traditionally used for making *Shah Jahani Biriyani*, the famous Emperor's Layered Meat and Fragrant Rice Casserole (p. 146), but it is equally good with all Moghul lamb or beef preparations.

FOR 8-10 PERSONS

◆

20 oz/600 g basmati *rice*
4 tablespoons usli ghee *(p. 52) or light vegetable oil*
*1½ pints/1 litre homemade meat broth (*Yakhni, p. 47*)*
2 teaspoons coarse salt

1 Wash *basmati* rice following directions on page 255.

2 Place rice in a bowl, and add enough cold water to cover the rice by 1 in/2.5 cm. Let it soak for exactly ½ hour. (The rice grains will turn opaque and chalk-white in colour.) Drain the rice, and set aside. Discard the water in which the rice was soaking.

3 Heat the *ghee* over medium heat in a heavy-bottomed pan. When it is hot, add the drained rice, and fry, stirring with a spatula for 3 minutes or until the rice turns translucent again. Add broth and salt, and stir carefully to keep the rice from lumping. Bring to the boil.

4 Reduce heat to low and simmer, partially covered, until the water is almost absorbed and the surface of the rice is full of steamy holes (about 12-15 minutes).

5 Cover the pan tightly and reduce heat to the lowest possible level. If possible, also raise the pan about 1 in/2.5 cm from the source of heat by placing a pair of tongs or a Chinese wok ring over the burner. Let rice steam for 10 minutes. Turn off the heat, and let the rice rest undisturbed, covered, for 5 minutes before serving. The rice should not be stirred during the final steaming and resting, as the grains of rice are sticky and very fragile, and will break easily if handled. The rest process firms and separates them; as a result they retain their shape no matter how often they are handled. The rice will remain warm for 20 minutes, covered. Uncover, and if desired, fluff the rice, and serve.

INDIAN FRIED RICE

GHEE CHAWAL

◆

This delicious fried rice takes only a few minutes to prepare. The onions and cauliflower are cooked first, and then the rice is folded in. *Ghee Chawal* is a southern speciality; it can also be made with a combination of peas, green peppers, spring onions, shallots, and potatoes.

FOR 8 PERSONS

◆

3 tablespoons light vegetable oil
6 oz/175 g coarsely chopped onions
1 small cauliflower, cut into ¾ in/2 cm pieces
10 oz/300 g leftover plain cooked rice (basmati or *ordinary long grain)*
2 teaspoons ground roasted cumin seeds (p. 62)
1 teaspoon ground roasted coriander seeds (p. 62)
1¼ teaspoons coarse salt
2-3 tablespoons finely chopped fresh coriander leaves

1 Heat the oil over medium-low heat in a large frying pan, or any large shallow pan, and add the onions and cauliflower. Fry the vegetables until they are lightly browned (about 5 minutes), stirring constantly to prevent burning. Add 5 tablespoons of cold water, cover, and cook for 15 minutes or until the vegetables are cooked but still crisp and there is *some water* left in the pan.
2 Add the cooked rice, mix well, replace the cover, and continue cooking for an additional 2 minutes or until the rice is heated through.
3 Uncover, sprinkle in the cumin, coriander, salt, and chopped coriander leaves, and mix thoroughly to distribute the herbs and spices.

You can serve this rice by itself for a light lunch, accompanied by a yogurt salad. To expand the meal, serve it with other fried fish-based foods, such as Chick-pea Batter Fish (p. 185), Fried Fillet of Sole Laced with Carom (p. 184), or Prawn Fritters (p. 98).

CUMIN AND TURMERIC RICE

PEELE CHAWAL

◆

The Punjabis don't like to colour their rice dishes; they prefer to display the white grains. This hearty, peasant-style northern speciality is the one exception. The golden yellow colour is lent by the turmeric.

FOR 4-6 PERSONS

◆

2 medium-sized potatoes
10 oz/300 g basmati *rice, or ordinary long grain rice*
4 tablespoons Indian vegetable shortening, or light vegetable oil
1 teaspoon cumin seeds
¾ teaspoon turmeric
2 teaspoons coarse salt, or to taste

1 Peel the potatoes, and dice them into neat ½-in/1 cm pieces. Put them in a bowl, cover with cold water, and set aside.

2 Wash *basmati* rice following directions on page 255.

3 Place the rice in a bowl, add 1¼ pints/75 cl cold water, let soak for half an hour, and drain, reserving the water. (Omit this step if you are using ordinary long grain rice.)

4 Heat the shortening or oil over medium-high heat in a heavy-bottomed pan. When it is very hot, add the cumin seeds. When the cumin turns dark brown (about 10 seconds), add the potatoes and turmeric, and fry until potatoes are slightly browned (about 3 minutes). Add the rice, and continue cooking until the rice is slightly fried (about 2 minutes), stirring constantly to prevent burning. Add the reserved water (or 1¼ pints/75 cl cold water if you are using ordinary rice) and salt. Stir for a moment to mix all the ingredients, and bring to the boil. Reduce heat to medium-low and simmer, covered, for 10 minutes (15 minutes for regular long grain rice), or until most of the water is absorbed and the surface of the rice is full of steamy holes. There is no need to stir the rice, but if you wish to do so, use a fork or a knife and be very careful.

5 Reduce the heat to the lowest point, and raise the pan about 1 in/2.5 cm away from the source of heat. (This can be done by placing a pair of tongs or a

Chinese wok ring on the burner and resting the pan on it.) Let the rice steam for 10 minutes. Turn off heat, and let the rice rest undisturbed, covered, for 5 minutes before serving. Do not stir the rice during these last 15 minutes, as the grains are moist, steamy, and very fragile, breaking easily when handled. The resting process firms and separates the grains; as a result they retain their shape no matter how often they are handled. The rice remains warm for 20 minutes, if left covered. Uncover, and if desired, fluff the rice with a fork, and serve.

Peele Chawal is usually served as a light luncheon dish, along with a yogurt salad, such as Cucumber and Yogurt Salad (p. 246), or Dumplings in Fragrant Yogurt (p. 250). For a more substantial meal, serve it with Chick-pea Batter Fish (p. 185) or Moghul Kebabs with Raisin Stuffing (p. 91).

FRAGRANT PILAF BANARAS STYLE

BANARASI PULLAO

◆

Located along the river Ganges, Banaras is the holy city of the Hindus. The people here adhere strictly to Hindu dietary principles, which means, among other things, no onions or garlic in the food. Banaras pilaf gets its fragrance, therefore, from a variety of spices and fresh ginger root. The spices are left in the pilaf; however they are not to be eaten.

FOR 6-8 PERSONS

◆

12 oz/375 g basmati *rice*
3 tablespoons Indian vegetable shortening, or light vegetable oil
4 black (or 8 green) cardamom pods
10 whole cloves
1 bay leaf
1 stick cinnamon, 3 in/7.5 cm long
24 black peppercorns (optional)
2 teaspoons grated fresh ginger root
2 teaspoons coarse salt

1 Wash *basmati* rice following directions on page 255.
2 Place the rice in a bowl, add 1½ pints/1 litre cold water, and let soak exactly ½ hour (the rice grains will turn opaque and chalk-white in colour). Drain the rice, reserving the water, and set aside.
3 Heat the shortening over medium heat in a heavy-bottomed pan and add all the spices except the ginger. Fry until the spices are slightly brown and puffed (about 2 minutes). Add rice, and continue frying until the rice turns translucent and begins to brown (about 3 minutes), stirring constantly to prevent burning.
4 Add the reserved water, ginger, and salt, stir well to keep the rice from settling, and bring to the boil. Reduce heat and simmer, partially covered, for 10 minutes or until the water is almost totally absorbed and the surface of the rice is covered with several steamy holes. There is no need to stir the rice, but if you wish to do so, use a fork or knife, being very careful not to break the fragile rice grains.
5 Cover the pan tightly, reduce heat to the lowest point, and if possible, raise the pan about 1 in/2.5 cm above the source of heat (this can be done by placing a pair of tongs or a Chinese wok ring on the burner and resting the pan on it). Let the rice steam for 10 minutes. Turn off the heat and let the rice rest undisturbed, covered, for 5 minutes. Do not stir the rice during the last 15 minutes of steaming and resting; the grains are very moist and fragile, thus breaking easily. The rice remains warm for 20 minutes, if left covered. Uncover, and fluff the rice with a fork before serving.

This pilaf goes with practically all North Indian and Moghul dishes. It is particularly good with cream-braised dishes, such as Lamb Braised in Aromatic Cream Sauce (p. 127) and Lamb Fillets Braised in Yogurt Cardamom Sauce (p. 131). It also combines well with seafood preparations.

SWEET SAFFRON PILAF

ZARDA

◆

Zarda is traditionally prepared by the Moslems in India for their religious festival *Muharram*. Many cooks substitute a yellow vegetable colouring known as *Zarda* colouring for a part of the saffron, mainly to economize, and thus produce a less fragrant *Zarda*. To enjoy this dish to its fullest, you must use only the pure thing and no substitutes.

This pilaf is slightly sweet. The whole spices are not meant to be eaten, but if you do bite into one, no harm will come to you.

FOR 6-8 PERSONS

◆

12 oz/375 g basmati *rice*
1 teaspoon saffron threads
4 tablespoons usli ghee *(p. 52), or light vegetable oil*
10 whole cloves
8 green cardamom pods
1 stick cinnamon, 3 in/7.5 cm long
2 oz/60 g seedless raisins
4 tablespoons sugar
1¼ teaspoons coarse salt

1 Wash *basmati* rice following the directions on page 255.

2 Place the rice in a bowl, add 1½ pints/1 litre cold water, and let soak for ½ hour. Drain the rice, reserving the water, and set aside.

3 Place the saffron threads in a small plate, and using the back of a spoon or your fingertips, powder it. Add 2 tablespoons of water, and continue mashing until thoroughly dissolved. Set aside.

4 Heat the *ghee* over medium heat in a heavy-bottomed pan. When it is hot, add the cloves, cardamom, and cinnamon, and fry until they are lightly browned and puffed (about 1 minute). Add rice, and fry until the rice is thoroughly coated with the *ghee* and begins to brown (about 3 minutes), stirring constantly to prevent burning.

5 Add reserved water, saffron water, raisins, sugar, and salt, and stir well to keep the rice from settling. Bring to the boil. Reduce heat, and simmer partially covered for 10 minutes or until most of the liquid is absorbed and the surface of the rice is filled with steamy holes. There is no need to stir, but if you wish to do so, use a fork or knife so that the rice grains are not crushed.

6 Cover the pan tightly, reduce heat to the lowest possible point and, if possible, raise the pan 1 in/2.5 cm away from the source of heat by resting the pan on a pair of tongs or a Chinese wok ring placed over the burner. Let the rice steam for 10 minutes, and turn off the heat. Now let it rest undisturbed, covered, for 5 minutes. Do not stir the rice during these final 15 minutes of steaming and resting, as the grains are still very moist and fragile at this stage. The rice remains warm for 20 minutes if left covered. Uncover, and fluff the rice with a fork before serving.

This saffron-perfumed pilaf is best served with *Tandoori* foods such as

Tandoori Chicken (p. 168), and with Moghul braised dishes such as Royal Braised Lamb with Spices (p. 134) or Lamb in Garlic Cream Sauce (p. 137). For an interesting contrast in flavour, serve Fried Fillet of Sole Laced with Carom (p. 184) or Chick-pea Batter Fish (p. 185).

SAFFRON PILAF WITH PEACHES

ZAFFRANI PULLAO

◆

This beautiful orange-yellow pilaf is studded with raisins, almonds, and pistachios, and is served enclosed in a ring of butter-glazed peaches. Its sweet flavour is imparted by the sweet spices: cinnamon, cardamom, and of course, saffron. The cinnamon stick is included only for aroma and is not intended to be eaten.

FOR 6-8 PERSONS

◆

12 oz/375 g basmati *rice*
3-4 fresh ripe peaches or 1 can peach slices in syrup
6 tablespoons usli ghee *(p. 52), or light vegetable oil*
2 tablespoons slivered blanched almonds
2 tablespoons unsalted blanched pistachios
3 oz/90 g finely chopped onions
1 stick cinnamon, 3 in/7.5 cm long
½ teaspoon ground cardamom
1 teaspoon saffron threads, powdered
1½ teaspoons coarse salt
2 oz/60 g seedless raisins
8 fl oz/25 cl milk

1 Wash the *basmati* rice following the instructions on page 255.
2 Put the rice in a bowl, add 1¼ pints/75 cl cold water, and let soak for ½ hour. Drain the rice, reserving the water, and set aside.
3 Drop fresh peaches in rapidly boiling water, and blanch for ½ minute. Take the peaches out, and immediately put them into a bowl of cold water (this will

loosen the skin and make peeling easier). Peel the peaches, and cut them lengthwise into ½ in/1 cm thick slices. If you are using canned peach slices, soak them in cold salted water (1 teaspoon salt to 1½ pints/1 litre of water) for ½ hour. This will remove the excess sweetness. Drain, pat dry with paper towels, and set aside.

4 Heat the *ghee* over medium heat in a heavy-bottomed pan. When it is hot, add the peach slices, and sauté until they are lightly browned on both sides (about 2-3 minutes). Remove them with a slotted spoon, and put them in a bowl. Set aside.

5 Add slivered almonds to the same *ghee*, and sauté, turning and tossing until lightly browned (about 1-2 minutes). Transfer them to paper towels to drain. Repeat with the pistachios the same way. Set nuts aside for the garnish.

6 Increase heat to medium-high, and add onions to the *ghee*. Fry until they turn pale and limp (about 2 minutes), stirring constantly to prevent burning. Add cinnamon, and fry for an additional minute or until the cinnamon is fried and puffed. Add drained rice, and continue frying until the rice is thoroughly coated with butter and begins to brown (about 2 minutes). Add cardamom, saffron, salt, raisins, reserved water, and milk, and bring to the boil, stirring rapidly to keep the rice from settling. Reduce heat and simmer, partially covered, for 10 minutes or until most of the liquid is absorbed and the surface of the rice is filled with steamy holes. There is no need to stir, but if you wish to do so, use a fork or knife so that the rice grains are not crushed.

7 Cover the pan tightly, reduce heat to the lowest point and, if possible, raise the pan 1 cm/2.5 cm away from the source of heat by resting the pan on a pair of tongs or a Chinese wok ring placed over the burner. Let the rice steam gently for 10 minutes. Turn off the heat, and let the rice rest undisturbed, covered, for 5 minutes. Do not stir the rice during these last 15 minutes of cooking, as the rice grains are very moist and fragile, and will break easily when handled. The rice remains warm for 20 minutes, if left covered. Uncover, and transfer to a heated serving platter. Surround the rice with a ring of peach slices, sprinkle almonds and pistachios on top, and serve.

To serve, follow the menu suggestions given for previous recipe.

THE EMPEROR'S PILAF
WITH BLACK MUSHROOMS

BADSHAHI PULLAO OR GOCHIAN PULLAO

◆

When people in the West think of India, mushrooms are probably the last thing that comes to mind. Yet in the Kashmir region, the beehive-shaped mushrooms called morels grow.

Morels are wild mushrooms that are occasionally available in shops in the spring or you may be lucky enough to pick your own. Dried morels can be substituted if desired.

Except for the cumin, whole spices in pilafs are not eaten, but no harm will come to you if you bite into them.

FOR 6-8 PERSONS

◆

8 oz/250 g fresh morels or 24 dry morels, about ¾ oz/20 g
4 medium-sized onions
12 oz/375 g basmati rice, or ordinary long grain rice
8 tablespoons Indian vegetable shortening, or light vegetable oil
1½ teaspoons black (or white) cumin seeds
1½ teaspoons minced garlic
3 black (or 6 green) cardamom pods
6 whole cloves
1 stick cinnamon, 3 in/7.5 cm long
1 bay leaf
2 teaspoons coarse salt

1 Put the dry mushrooms in a bowl, add enough boiling water to cover, and let soak for 1 hour. Drain, wash the mushrooms thoroughly in several changes of water, drain again and pat dry. Cut the large mushrooms in half. If you are using fresh mushrooms, cut them in half, rinse them under running water, drain and pat dry. Set aside.
2 Peel onions, and finely chop 2 of them. Slice the remaining 2 into paper-thin shreds, and set aside.

3 Wash the *basmati* rice following instructions on page 255.

4 Place the rice in a bowl, add 1½ pints/1 litre cold water, let soak for ½ hour. Drain the rice, reserving the water, and set aside. (Omit this step if you are using ordinary rice.)

5 Heat the shortening in a heavy-bottomed pan, and add the 2 shredded onions. Over medium high heat, fry until the onions turn dark brown (about 20 minutes), stirring constantly to ensure even browning. Take the onions out with a slotted spoon, and drain them on paper towels. (See Crispy Fried Onions, p. 69.) When cool, these fried onion shreds will become crackling crisp. Set them aside for the garnish.

6 Turn the heat to medium-high, add the cumin seeds, and stir for a moment or two (if you are using white cumin seeds, fry until they turn brown – this may take about 10 seconds). Add the two chopped onions, and fry until they turn caramel brown (about 15-20 minutes), stirring constantly to prevent burning. Add garlic, and cook for an additional ½ minute. Add mushrooms and sauté for 3 minutes or until lightly fried. (Fresh mushrooms take a little longer, because they exude a lot of water in the beginning which has to evaporate before they can be fried.) Add cardamom, cloves, cinnamon, and bay leaf, and continue frying until the spices are slightly fried and puffed.

7 Add the drained rice, and as soon as it is thoroughly coated with the fat and begins to brown, add the reserved water (or 1½ pints/1 litre cold water if you are using ordinary rice) and salt. Stir rapidly to prevent the rice from settling, and bring to the boil. Reduce heat and simmer, partially covered, for 10 minutes (15 minutes for ordinary rice) or until most of the water is absorbed and the surface is covered with steamy holes. There is no need to stir, but if you wish to do so, use a fork or a knife so that the fragile rice grains do not break.

8 Cover the pan tightly, reduce heat to the lowest possible level, and if possible raise the pan 1 in/2.5 cm away from the source of heat by resting the pan on a pair of tongs or a Chinese wok ring placed over the burner. Let the rice steam for 10 minutes, and turn off the heat. Now let it rest undisturbed, covered, for 5 minutes. Do not stir the rice during these last 15 minutes, as the grains are extremely fragile, breaking easily with every touch. Resting firms and separates the grains, making them easier to handle. The rice remains warm for half an hour, if left covered. Uncover, and fluff the rice. Transfer to a heated serving platter, cover with the fried onion shreds, and serve immediately.

You can make a meal with this pilaf alone. For a light lunch, serve it with a cool yogurt salad, such as Dumplings in Fragrant Yogurt (p. 250) or Spinach and Yogurt Salad (p. 247). It is also good with dishes that have reddish brown gravies, such as Beef in Spicy Tomato Gravy (p. 133) or Prawns with Mild Spices (p. 179).

MINT PILAF

HARI CHUTNEY KA PULLAO

◆

This delicious pilaf with its appealing pale green colour is a speciality of Hyderabad, a city in the southern state of Andhra Pradesh. It is made with fresh grated coconut and green chilies, and flavoured in the Moghul tradition – with cinnamon, cloves, and mint.

FOR 6-8 PERSONS

◆

2 medium-sized potatoes
12 oz/375 g basmati rice, or ordinary long grain rice
5 tablespoons water
1½ oz/45 g fresh grated coconut (p. 49)
2 oz/60 g mint leaves
2 green chilies
⅓ teaspoon ground cloves
½ teaspoon ground cinnamon
8 tablespoons usli ghee (p. 52) or light vegetable oil
1 tablespoon coarse salt

1 Peel the potatoes, and dice them into ½-in/1 cm pieces. Put them in a bowl, add water to cover, and set aside.

2 Wash *basmati* rice following directions on page 255.

3 Place the rice in a bowl, add 1½ pints/1 litre cold water, and let soak for ½ hour. Drain the rice, reserving the water, and set aside. (Omit this step if you are using ordinary rice.)

4 While the rice is soaking, put the water, coconut, mint, chilies, cloves and cinnamon into the container of an electric blender or food processor, and purée the mixture finely.

5 Heat the *ghee* over medium-high heat in a heavy-bottomed pan, preferably one with a non-stick surface. Drain the potatoes, pat them dry, and add them to the pan. Fry the potatoes, turning and tossing until golden brown (about 7-10 minutes), stirring constantly to ensure even browning. Put in a bowl.

6 To the same pan, add coconut-mint purée, and cook until it is slightly fried and the fat begins to separate (about 8-10 minutes). Add the rice, and continue frying until the grains are thoroughly coated with the herb purée (about 3 minutes), stirring constantly to prevent the rice from sticking to the bottom of the pan and burning. Add the reserved water (or 1½ pints/1 litre of cold water if you are using ordinary rice), salt, and fried potatoes. Stir for a moment to prevent the rice from settling, and bring to the boil.

7 Reduce heat and simmer, partially covered, for 10 minutes (20 minutes for ordinary rice) or until most of the water is absorbed by the rice and its surface is covered with steamy holes. There is no need to stir the rice, but if you wish to do so, use a fork or knife so that you don't break the rice grains.

8 Cover the pan tightly, reduce heat to the lowest possible level, and raise the pan 1 in/2.5 cm away from the source of heat by resting the pan over a pair of tongs or a Chinese wok ring placed over the burner. Let the rice steam for 10 minutes, and turn off heat. Let it rest undisturbed, covered, for an additional 5 minutes. Do not stir the rice during these last 15 minutes, as there is a danger of breaking the moist and fragile rice grains and potato pieces. The rice remains warm for 20 minutes, if left covered. Uncover, fluff the rice with a fork, and then serve.

This pilaf, like most Hyderabad food, is on the hot side, so always serve it with a cool salad, such as Tomato and Yogurt Salad (p. 248) or Okra and Yogurt Salad (p. 249). For the most authentic flavour, include Hot Hyderabad Tomato Relish (p. 314).

VEGETABLE AND RICE CASSEROLE WITH HERBS

TAHARI

◆

Tahari, a speciality of Uttar Pradesh, is a bright yellow casserole made with rice, potatoes, and peas. It is like a pilaf, but much spicier because of the addition of cumin, *garam masala*, green chilies, and fresh coriander leaves. Its distinguishing feature is the yellow colour, which the turmeric imparts.

This is a favourite dish among Indian vegetarians, who traditionally serve it for a Sunday lunch, sometimes accompanied by a Cucumber and Yogurt Salad (p. 246).

FOR 4-6 PERSONS

◆

6 oz/175 g basmati *rice, or ordinary long grain rice*
2 tablespoons Indian vegetable shortening or light vegetable oil
¾ teaspoon white cumin seeds
1 medium-sized potato, peeled and diced into ½ in/1 cm pieces
6 oz/175 g fresh or frozen green peas
½ teaspoon turmeric
¾ teaspoon garam masala *(p. 42)*
⅓-¼ teaspoon red pepper
1¾ teaspoons coarse salt
2 tablespoons chopped coriander leaves
1 green chili, seeded and sliced (optional)

1 Wash *basmati* rice following directions on page 255.
2 Place the rice in a bowl, add 1 pint/60 cl cold water, and let soak for ½ hour. Drain the rice, reserving the water, and set aside. (Omit this step if you are using ordinary long grain rice.)
3 Heat the shortening or oil over medium-high heat in a heavy-bottomed pan. When the oil is very hot, add the cumin seeds. When the seeds turn dark brown (about 10 seconds) add the potatoes and peas, and fry for 3 minutes, stirring rapidly. Add rice, and fry for an additional minute or until the rice grains are thoroughly coated with the fat. Add turmeric, *garam masala*, red

pepper, salt, and reserved water (or 1 pint/60 cl cold water if you are using ordinary rice). Stir for a moment to prevent the rice from settling, and bring to the boil. Reduce heat to medium and simmer, covered, for 10 minutes (15 minutes for ordinary rice) or until most of the water is absorbed by the rice and the surface is filled with steamy holes. There is no need to stir the rice, but if you wish to, use a fork or a knife so that you don't break the fragile rice grains.

4 Reduce the heat to the lowest point, and raise the pan about 1 in/2.5 cm away from the source of heat by resting the pan on a pair of tongs or a Chinese wok ring placed over the burner. Let the rice steam for 10 minutes, and turn off heat. Let it rest undisturbed, covered, for 5 minutes. Do not stir the rice during these last 15 minutes, as the grains are very moist and fragile, breaking easily if stirred. The rice will remain warm for half an hour, covered. Uncover, and fluff the rice with a fork. Transfer it to a warm serving platter, and serve sprinkled with the chopped coriander leaves and sliced chili.

BREADS

ROTI

◆

There is nothing more enticing than the wholesome-tasting breads of India. The honesty of ingredients and the simplicity of the cooking techniques make these natural breads the best in the world.

Indian breads can be put into two categories: commercial and homemade.

Commercial, or bakery breads are those made in a *tandoor*, the Indian clay oven. These are the breads most popular in Indian restaurants. They are particularly suited for mass production, since they are cooked in large ovens in which several can be baked simultaneously. Also they are not rolled but are formed by patting, folding, and stretching with the hands. This is a quick process, developed for turning out large quantities of bread. The bakery or commercial Indian breads include *nan, kulcha, tandoori roti, tandoori paratha,* and *roomali roti.*

Homemade breads are in a category by themselves. Once you try them, you will become an addict. These breads are lighter and more flavourful and nutritious than bakery breads. There is an incredible variety of homemade breads, and listing all of them is not possible. But they all have one thing in common: they are uncomplicated, and therefore quick and easy to make.

Most of the breads eaten every day in Indian homes are made with unleavened stone-ground whole-grain flour. Leavened breads are cooked on special occasions. Breads, as a general rule, accompany dishes that are substantially dry, roasted, fried, or those whose thick gravies can be scooped up with a piece of bread. There is no hard and fast rule as to which bread accompanies which main dish. Much depends upon personal taste and how rich and elaborate the meal is.

This chapter on breads deals mainly with the homemade varieties – making them is an art, and not much light has been shed upon the process. Homemade breads can be classified in three general categories: griddle-baked breads, griddle-fried breads, and deep-fried breads.

GRIDDLE-BAKED BREADS

These breads are by far the most popular and widely eaten in India. They are made with whole-grain flour, such as wheat, corn (or maize), chick-pea, and millet. Only water is incorporated into the flour to make the dough. The bread is then baked on the griddle or over an open flame. These breads are traditionally made with the rest of the meal and served while still warm. This category includes *Chapati* or *Roti* (p. 279), *Phulka* (p. 282), and *Besan ki Roti* (p. 283).

GRIDDLE-FRIED BREADS

These breads are made with wholemeal flour. The dough is usually enriched with a little fat and salt. They are often referred to as 'flaky' or 'layered' breads, because they are brushed with fat or oil and folded several times before being rolled and fried. This bread is called *Paratha* (p. 285). They are also stuffed with a variety of ingredients, such as herbs, spices, cooked vegetables, chopped greens, lentils, and meat. The stuffing is either used as a filling or mixed with the dough before it is rolled and fried. These breads are called *bhara* (stuffed) *paratha* in general. Examples include *Phool Gobhi Paratha* (p. 287), *Aloo Paratha* (p. 290), and *Palak Paratha* (p. 291).

DEEP-FRIED BREADS

Indian deep-fried breads are known for their spectacular appearance and delicate taste. The dough for these breads is similar to the dough made for griddle-fried breads. The only difference is that instead of being fried on the griddle, these are deep-fried in hot oil, where they puff up like balloons. They are also nonperishable; they stay fresh and moist for several days at room temperature. These breads are often called 'travel breads' in India, and are carried by people on long journeys because they survive prolonged exposure to heat without spoiling or any change in taste. Deep-fried breads are traditionally served at wedding banquets and other festive occasions. This category of breads includes *Poori* (p. 293), and *Kachauri* (p. 295).

◆

FLOUR

The flour used in most Indian homemade breads is wholemeal. In Indian wholemeal flour, the entire kernel of wheat is ground to a very fine powder. Indians usually sift it through a fine sieve to remove the few remaining coarse bran flakes. The resulting flour is like a very fine powder loaded with ground bran and germ. This flour is called *aata* and is widely available under the label 'chapati flour'. The dough made with it has a silky smooth texture and little resistance to kneading and rolling.

To get good results with baking, however, it is not essential to have this flour. Ordinary wholemeal flour, although too coarse-textured to be used straight, can give exceedingly good results with slight modifications. You will, however, need to do one of two things:

1, Sift the flour through a fine sieve to remove the bran flakes. (If it shocks and distresses you to see all that bran thrown away, then this method is not for you.) Or 2, substitute strong plain flour, preferably unbleached, for a portion of the wholemeal flour. This will reduce the proportion of bran in the flour, thus decreasing the coarseness. The amount of strong plain flour to be added depends on the quality of the wholemeal flour. Generally 8 oz/250 g of wholemeal mixed with 4 oz/125 g of plain flour should give good results.

Because wholemeal flour contains bran and germ, which have natural oils, it will become musty and turn rancid if stored in a warm place. To keep your flour smelling sweet and fresh, store it in airtight containers in a cool place.

◆

PREPARING THE DOUGH

The dough for all homemade breads, whether griddle-cooked or deep-fried, is prepared in the same way. The technique is exclusively Indian. It is important to understand and follow it carefully; otherwise the bread will not come out right.

There are three steps in this process: mixing the dough, kneading the dough, and resting the dough.

◆

MIXING THE DOUGH

This is the most important of all the steps in the process of preparing the dough. Unlike European breads, to which the liquid is added without fine precision (since the dough is finally firmed and dried with flour), when making Indian breads the water added is exactly the amount specified – or a little less. This does not mean the water is measured to an exact amount and then added; but rather that the amount added is precisely what will form a firm, kneadable dough. This is important, because once too much water is added, the dough becomes sticky and impossible to knead. Another reason for caution is that instead of incorporating a little extra flour during kneading, you will be kneading a little extra water into this Indian dough. If, on the other hand, you are overcautious and add too little water, you will end up with a very firm dough that is too hard and rubbery to knead. No matter how much water is later sprinkled over it, it will not become properly soft and pliable.

Therefore, while mixing, pay careful attention to the way the dough feels to the touch.

THE PROCESS Place the flour in a bowl. With your left hand if you are right handed, add the water in a stream, pouring it fast at first. Simultaneously mix the flour with the fingers of your right hand, in a rotating motion, to moisten it enough so that it gathers into a mass. As the flour begins to lump up, add water more and more slowly until all the flour forms a mass, and the dough is firm but soft enough to be kneaded. In most instances you will need only the amount of water suggested in the recipe. But if you find that for any reason the dough looks and feels a little dry, simply add a few extra spoonfuls of water. Do not, however, add more water than necessary, as you will be using water, not flour, to knead the dough. Also, the dough will be allowed to rest before being rolled, which further softens and moistens it. Gather the dough into a rough ball, place it on the work surface, and wash your hands clean.

◆

KNEADING THE DOUGH

The Indian method of kneading dough is completely different from any other method used elsewhere in the world. It is mostly wrist work. Also, instead of being dusted with flour and folded, the Indian dough is sprinkled with water and kneaded.

THE PROCESS First put about 4 fl oz/12.5 cl of water in a small shallow bowl, and place it close to the work surface where the dough is to be kneaded. Clench your right hand into a fist (if you are right handed), and dip your knuckles into the water. Knead by pressing your knuckles repeatedly into the dough, as though punching it, while simultaneously pushing and spreading it away from you, to form an approximately 9 in/23 cm round. Lift one edge of the round, and fold the dough over. Continue kneading, punching, and spreading the same way, dipping your knuckles in water from time to time, until you have a very soft, pliable dough. This will take about 10 to 15 minutes. (You will have incorporated about 1 tablespoon of water into the dough.) Press your index finger lightly and quickly about ¼ in/5 mm into the kneaded dough. If the dough springs back, it is fully kneaded. Replace the dough in the bowl.

NOTES

1 Instead of dipping your knuckles in the water, you can sprinkle water directly over the dough. However, this should be done after spreading the dough into a round.

2 You can use the heel of your palm instead of your knuckles to knead the dough.

3 The dough can be kneaded in an electric mixer, with the dough hook attachment in place, for 3-4 minutes at medium speed.

Mixing and Kneading in the Food Processor

To mix the dough, attach the metal cutting blade, and put the flour (or combination of flours), seasonings, and spices if you are using them, into the container. Cover. Run the machine until all the ingredients are blended well (about 10 seconds). Add fat or oil, and greens or herbs as the recipe suggests, and process for another 10 seconds to mix. Now, with the machine running, start to add the water. Add about half the suggested amount in a steady stream. Be careful not to run the machine too long at one stretch. Turn it off and on every 5 to 10 seconds, and add water only while the machine is running. As the flour begins to adhere into a mass, slow the speed of water to dribbles. Process the dough between additions of water, and stop adding water as soon as a ball of dough forms on the blades.

To knead the dough, turn on the processor and continue processing for 40-50 seconds, turning the machine on and off every 5 to 10 seconds. If your processor overheats or shows signs of strain, divide the ball of dough and knead half at a time. The dough is kneaded when it looks smooth and shiny and feels soft and pliable to the touch. With your hands, carefully take the dough from the container and place it in a bowl.

CAUTION Most mixers will not knead dough made with less than 12 oz/375 g of flour: therefore, if you are making bread with less than that amount, you may not be able to use the machine.

◆

RESTING THE DOUGH

The final step in the preparation of the dough is letting it rest before it is rolled. This is a very important step because it relaxes the dough, thus making it less resistant to stretching and rolling. Also, the temperature in kitchens in India generally ranges between 100°-120°F/38-50°C, which, even though quite unbearable for human beings, is ideal for the dough. The warm temperature ferments it and causes it to rise, thus making the dough light, airy, and spongy, as though it has been leavened slightly. The cooked bread will therefore be moist and soft.

THE PROCESS To rest the dough, cover the bowl with a moist towel or a plastic film and let it rest, preferably in a warm place, for at least ½ hour. The dough can be made a day ahead and refrigerated, tightly covered and sealed in foil. Remove the dough from the refrigerator about 30 minutes before you are ready to roll it.

Baking Indian breads is an art that you learn and perfect, with practice and patience, in time. The preparation of dough described earlier and the rolling techniques for each different bread are special skills that need to be developed. To do this you need to learn the techniques first and then practise until you are fully familiar and comfortable with them. As I mentioned earlier, the process itself is simple; all you need is the confidence that comes with practice.

BAKED WHOLEMEAL BREAD

CHAPATI OR ROTI

◆

This is the basic bread of India – it is made every day in North Indian homes. Its smooth, soft, and very pliable texture comes from the finely ground wholemeal flour. Only water is added to make the dough. It is then rolled into thin rounds ranging in size from 4-8 in/10 cm-20 cm and baked on a griddle. It takes a bit of practice to learn to roll the dough properly. Don't worry if your first few batches are not perfectly round, or if they don't roll out to the full size indicated. With practice you will soon master this technique. In the meantime, the bread will still taste good, even if it doesn't look perfect.

MAKES 24 7 in/18 cm CHAPATI
FOR 6-8 PERSONS

◆

12 oz/375 g chapati *flour (or 8 oz/250 g wholemeal flour mixed with 4 oz/125 g strong plain flour)*
8 fl oz/25 cl warm water
2-3 oz/60-90 g chapati *flour, or plain flour, for dusting*

1 Place *chapati* flour (or wholemeal mixed with plain flour) in a bowl. Add water, pouring it fast at first, to moisten the flour enough that it adheres into a mass; then slowly, little by little, until the dough is formed and can be kneaded. (See Mixing and Kneading the Dough, pp. 276-277.)

2 Place the dough on the work surface and knead for 10-15 minutes, or mix and knead the dough in the food processor (p. 278). This will be a very soft and pliable dough, quite sticky to the touch. Put the dough back in the bowl, cover with a moist towel or plastic film, and let it rest, preferably in a warm place, for at least ½ hour. (The dough may be made a day ahead and refrigerated, tightly sealed in foil. Remove from the refrigerator about 30 minutes before you are ready to roll it.)

ROLLING THE BREAD

3 Put the flour for dusting in a plate or a shallow bowl and keep it close to the work surface where you are rolling the dough. Knead the dough again for a minute, and divide it into 2 equal portions. Using your hands, roll each into a rope, cut into 12 equal parts, and roll the small pieces into smooth balls (or pinch off small pieces of dough from the rope, and roll them into 1 in/2.5 cm balls). Dust the balls lightly with flour to prevent their sticking to each other, and put them back in the bowl. Keep the bowl covered loosely with a damp towel or plastic film to prevent the dough drying out.

4 Start heating the griddle or frying pan over medium heat. Working one at a time, pick up a ball and place it on the dusting flour. Press the ball lightly but firmly, both to flatten it into a round pillow and simultaneously to coat the underside with flour. Turn and repeat, to coat the other side with flour. Pick up the patty with your fingers, shake it gently to release any excess flour, and place it on the work surface.

5 Roll the patty into a very thin 8-9 in/20-22 cm circle, pressing and stretching with the rolling pin with a brisk back-and-forth motion, going from edge to edge to keep it circular. Dust the dough from time to time to prevent its sticking to the work surface or rolling pin. (Bear in mind that this method of rolling is altogether different from the familiar technique used for pies and tarts. There you position the rolling pin in the centre and roll the dough away or towards you, thus spreading and not stretching the dough.)

BAKING THE BREAD

6 Lift the bread gently, place it on the hot griddle, and bake until the side in contact with the griddle is cooked and several tiny brown spots appear. Flip the bread, using a pair of unserrated tongs, and bake the other side the same way. (Generally, when the griddle temperature is right, the first side of the bread will take about 20-30 seconds and the second side 8-10 seconds. But if it is too hot, the bread will brown too fast and burn before cooking; if it is not hot enough, it will take too long to brown, by which time the bread will become dry, tough, and leathery. Therefore it is essential to check and keep the griddle at the right temperature at all times.) Take the bread out, and if desired, brush with clarified butter or shortening. Place it in a covered dish, preferably lined with a kitchen towel. Repeat with the rest of the dough the same way. As the breads are baked, pile them one on top of the other in the dish. (The dish is lined because as more and more breads are piled in the dish, the steam from the breads begins to condense and accumulate at the bottom, which could cause the bottom few breads to be soft. The towel absorbs the moisture, preventing such a disaster.)

NOTE If the breads are to be served immediately, simply stack them up as they are baked on a thick napkin placed in a small round bread basket. Keep the napkin folded on top, enclosing the bread fully, to keep it warm. (The *chapati* can be made a couple of hours ahead and warmed up, wrapped and sealed in foil, in a preheated 300°F/150°C/Gas 2 oven for 12 minutes.)

BAKED WHOLEMEAL PUFFY BREAD

PHULKA

◆

Phulka dough is similar to *chapati* dough. The texture and taste are also very similar, except *phulka* is baked for a second time over flame, after it has been griddle-baked. This method is generally used for breads made with a dense flour, such as chick-pea or millet. Since these breads are also rolled thicker than *chapati*, the griddle-baking process is usually not sufficient to cook them thoroughly, so they are held over the flame for a few seconds and baked until completely cooked. Don't be afraid to do this. The bread will not burn, it will puff up like a balloon (hence the name *phulka*, meaning puffed) and freckle.

MAKES 24 6 in/15 cm PHULKA
FOR 6-8 PERSONS

◆

12 oz/375 g chapati flour (or 8 oz/250 g wholemeal flour mixed with 4 oz/125 g strong plain flour)
8 fl oz/25 cl warm water
2-3 oz/60-90 g flour for dusting

Follow the preceding recipe's instructions for making *chapati*, from Step 1 to Step 6, except that instead of storing the *chapati* after baking them on the griddle, place them directly on a burner with a high flame on, and bake until the bread is puffed and several brown spots appear on the underside (about 5-10 seconds). Turn and bake the other side until the bread is puffed up like a balloon and covered with brown spots.

NOTE The *phulka* should be rolled thicker than *chapati*, only to a 6 in/15 cm round. Also the bread should be handled very carefully during the rolling and baking processes, as any crack or tear in the bread will prevent it puffing up.

To enjoy the full aroma and taste of these puffy breads, they must be eaten soon after they are baked. They also make an attractive and dramatic entrance when brought to the table although this is not always possible. Often all the breads are made and gently deflated before being placed in a covered dish or napkin-lined basket and served immediately. The bread can be made a couple of hours ahead, brushed with *usli ghee* or shortening and kept wrapped and sealed in foil. To reheat, place the sealed foil package in a 300°F/150°C/Gas 2 preheated oven for 12 minutes.

CHICK-PEA FLOUR BREAD

BESAN KI ROTI

◆

Chick-pea flour bread is generally very fragrant and pleasantly spicy. Like all breads made with a dense flour, it is first griddle-baked and then cooked over a flame. Chick-pea flour by itself is too rich and heavy to digest, so it is mixed with wholemeal flour.

MAKES 24 6 in/15 cm ROTI
FOR 8-12 PERSONS

◆

8 oz/250 g wholemeal flour
4 oz/125 g strong plain flour
2 oz/60 g chick-pea flour (besan)
¼-½ teaspoon red pepper (optional)
½ teaspoon salt
½ pint/30 cl (or more) warm water
2 oz/60 g flour for dusting

1 Place the wholemeal flour, plain flour, and chick-pea flour in a bowl. Mix in red pepper if you are using it, and salt. Add water, pouring it fast at first, to moisten the flour enough that it adheres into a mass; then slowly, little by little, until the dough is firm and can be kneaded. (See Mixing and Kneading the Dough, pp. 276-277.)

2 Place the dough on the work surface and knead for 10-15 minutes (or mix and knead in the food processor, see p. 278). This will be a soft, pliable dough, slightly sticky to the touch. Cover and let it rest for ½ hour. (The dough can be made a day ahead and refrigerated, tightly sealed in foil. Remove from refrigerator about 30 minutes before you are ready to roll.)

3 Put the flour for dusting in a plate or a shallow bowl, and keep it close to the work surface where you are rolling dough.

4 Knead the dough again for a minute, and divide into 2 portions. Using your hands, roll each portion into a rope, and cut into 12 equal portions. Roll the small pieces into smooth balls, dust them lightly with flour to prevent their sticking together, and keep them loosely covered with plastic film or a moist tea towel.

5 Start heating a griddle or frying pan over medium heat. You will need another burner next to it to puff the bread, so make sure the burner is free. Working one at a time and dusting generously with flour, place 1 ball on the work surface, and roll it into a 6 in/15 cm round. Dust the dough from time to time to prevent its sticking to the work surface or rolling pin.

6 Lift the bread gently, place it on the hot griddle, and bake until the bottom is cooked and a few brown spots appear (about ½ minute). Flip the bread, and cook the other side about 15-20 seconds.

7 Lift the bread, using a pair of unserrated tongs, and place the bread flat on the other burner with the high flame on. Cook the bread for 10 seconds, then turn it and cook the other side for an additional 10 seconds. (Because of the dense chick-pea flour this bread does not puff up as much as *phulka*.)

These breads are generally served brushed with *usli ghee* or shortening. They taste best hot off the burner, still warm and full of chick-pea aroma. They can, however, be served after all the breads are baked. When serving them this way, place the breads as they are baked on the work surface, and press each gently to deflate. Brush them generously with *ghee* or shortening, and stack them in a covered dish or napkin-lined basket.

NOTE This bread does not take well to reheating, principally because the breads are cooked over direct flame, which dries them somewhat; further heating only makes them crisp and leathery.

WHOLEMEAL FLAKY BREAD

PARATHA

◆

This bread is known for its exquisite flakiness. Since it is folded three times, and oiled with each fold, the layers separate and flake while they fry. Also, the dough itself is enriched with oil, which causes the bread to taste crisp and rich. It is almost a simple version of puff pastry.

MAKES 16 7 in/17.5 cm PARATHA
FOR 6-8 PERSONS

◆

8 oz/250 g chapati *flour, or wholemeal flour*
4 oz/125 g *strong plain flour*
1 *teaspoon coarse salt*
¼ *teaspoon carom seeds (optional)*
3 *tablespoons Indian vegetable shortening, or light vegetable oil*
8 fl oz/25 cl *warm water*
2 oz/60 g *flour for dusting*
4 oz/125 g *melted Indian vegetable shortening, or oil for brushing*

1 Combine *chapati* flour or wholemeal flour with strong plain flour, salt, and carom seeds in a bowl. Save about 1 teaspoon of shortening, and rub the remainder into the flour. Add water, fast at first, to moisten the flour enough that it adheres into a mass; then slowly, little by little, until the dough is formed and can be kneaded. See the instructions on Mixing and Kneading the Dough, pages 276-277.

2 Brush the work surface and your fingers with the reserved teaspoon of shortening. Place the dough on the greased surface, and knead for 10-15 minutes. (Or mix and knead the dough in the food processor, see p. 278.) This will be a very soft and pliable dough. Put the dough back in the bowl, cover with a moist towel or plastic film wrap, and let it rest, preferably in a warm place, for at least ½ hour. (The dough can be made a day ahead and refrigerated, tightly sealed in foil. Remove from refrigerator about 30 minutes before you are ready to roll it.)

3 Put the shortening for brushing in a shallow bowl and the flour for dusting in a plate or another bowl, and keep them close to the work surface where the dough is to be rolled.

4 Knead the dough again for a minute, and divide it into 2 equal portions. Using your hands, roll each portion into a rope, and cut each rope into 8 equal parts. Roll the small pieces into smooth balls, dust them lightly with flour, and put them back in the bowl. Keep them loosely covered with a damp towel or plastic film to prevent a crust forming.

5 Working one at a time, take a ball from the bowl and place it on the dusting flour. Press lightly but firmly, both to flatten it into a pillow and simultaneously to coat the underside with flour. Turn and repeat, to coat the other side with flour. Pick up the patty, shake off excess flour, place it on the work surface, and roll it into a 5 in/12.5 cm circle. Brush the top with melted shortening, using a pastry brush or your fingers, and fold the circle in half. Brush the top of the semicircle with fat and fold in half again. You will now have a triangle of dough. Pick up this folded dough, and place it on the dusting flour. Press lightly with your fingers so that the flour sticks to the underside of the dough. Turn and press again to flour the other side. Return the floured dough to the work surface, and roll it out to a 6-7 in/15-17.5 cm triangle. Keep dusting with flour from time to time, to prevent sticking. (These breads can be rolled out about an hour ahead of time, as long as they are kept covered with plastic film or a damp towel to keep the dough from drying out. Don't stack them, or they will stick together and be impossible to separate. They may be kept slightly overlapping, provided the surfaces in contact are generously dusted with flour and separated by plastic film.)

6 When ready to fry, heat the griddle or frying pan over medium heat for 2 minutes or until hot. Put one bread at a time on the griddle. Cook for 2 minutes or until the side in contact with the griddle is baked and brown spots appear. Flip the bread upside down with a broad spatula, such as a pancake turner, and bake the other side for a short period (10-15 seconds).

7 Meanwhile brush the baked side lightly but thoroughly with fat, and flip the bread again. Now the baked side in contact with the griddle is frying. Cook for ½ minute, then brush the other baked side with fat, and flip the bread to fry the second side for ½ minute. Take it off the griddle, and keep it warm in a covered dish or tightly wrapped with foil. Repeat with the remaining triangles of bread. Serve hot.

NOTE *Paratha* can be made several hours ahead and reheated, loosely covered with foil, in a preheated 300°F/150°C/Gas 2 oven for 10-12 minutes.

CAULIFLOWER-STUFFED BREAD

PHOOL GOBHI PARATHA

◆

This is the classic recipe for making stuffed bread, in which the dough is stuffed with the filling before being rolled into flat circles and griddle-baked. The bread is stuffed with sautéed cauliflower and ginger shreds. And it is delicious beyond words.

MAKES 12 7 in/17.5 cm STUFFED PARATHA
FOR 6 PERSONS

◆

THE CAULIFLOWER STUFFING
1 small cauliflower
3 tablespoons Indian vegetable shortening, or light vegetable oil
1 tablespoon finely chopped or grated fresh ginger root (optional)
½ teaspoon red pepper
1¼ teaspoons coarse salt
THE BREAD
8 oz/250 g chapati flour, or wholemeal flour
4 oz/125 g strong plain flour
1 teaspoon coarse salt
3 tablespoons Indian vegetable shortening, or light vegetable oil
8 fl oz/25 cl warm water
2 oz/60 g flour for dusting
4 oz/125 g melted Indian vegetable shortening, or light vegetable oil for brushing

1 Cut off the outer leaves and stems from the cauliflower, and discard. Wash the cauliflower thoroughly under running cold water, and pat dry with kitchen towels. Using the coarse blade of a grater, or a food processor, grate the cauliflower into a bowl.

2 Heat the shortening over medium heat in a large frying pan for 2 minutes or until very hot. Add the grated cauliflower, and cook until most of its moisture i₊ evaporated and it begins to look limp and fried (about 5 minutes). Turn off heat. Add the remaining stuffing ingredients. Mix well and set aside. (This filling can be made ahead and refrigerated for a day. There is no need to warm the stuffing before filling the breads.)

3 Combine *chapati* flour or wholemeal flour with plain flour and salt in a bowl. Reserve about 1 teaspoon of shortening, and rub the remainder into the flour. Add water, initially fast, to moisten the flour enough that it adheres into a mass; then slowly, little by little, until the dough is formed and can be kneaded. (See Mixing and Kneading the Dough, pp. 276-277.)

4 Brush the work surface and your hands with the reserved teaspoon of fat. Place the dough on the greased surface, and knead for 10-15 minutes. (Or mix and knead the dough in the food processor, see p. 278.) This will be a very soft pliable dough. Put the dough back in the bowl, cover with a moist towel or plastic film and let it rest, preferably in a warm place, for at least ½ hour. (The dough can be made a day ahead and refrigerated, tightly sealed in foil. Remove from refrigerator about 30 minutes before you are ready to roll.)

5 Put the shortening for brushing the bread in a shallow bowl and the flour for dusting in a plate or another bowl. Keep them, and the filling, close to the work surface where the dough is to be rolled.

6 Divide both *paratha* dough and filling into 12 equal portions. Take 1 piece of dough, and flatten it into a round 4 in/10 cm pillow with your hand. Depress the centre slightly, and place a portion of the filling into the depression. Bring the sides of the dough over the filling and enclose it completely. Press lightly but firmly to flatten it into a pillow, either between your hands or on the workboard. With the fingers, pinch the edges slightly, so that the filling is in the centre and not near the edge where it could break through the dough. Repeat with the rest of the patties the same way, and keep them covered with plastic film or a moist towel to prevent drying out.

7 Pick up a filled patty, and place it on the dusting flour. Press lightly with fingers so that some flour sticks to the underside of the patty. Turn and repeat to dust the other side with flour. Return the patty to the work surface.

8 Hold the handles of the rolling pin firmly, and smack or pat the filled patty all over. (This will make the filling adhere to the inside of the bread, so that the filling spreads evenly with the bread when rolled.) Roll the patty into a 6 in/15 cm circle. Keep dusting with flour from time to time to prevent sticking. (These stuffed breads can be rolled out an hour ahead of time and kept covered with a moist towel to prevent the dough drying out. Be careful not to stack them one on top of the other, as they will stick together and be impossible to separate. They may be kept slightly overlapping, provided the surfaces in contact are dusted generously with flour.)

9 When ready to fry, heat the griddle or frying pan over medium heat for a couple of minutes or until hot. Put one bread at a time onto the griddle. Cook for 2 minutes or until the side in contact with the griddle is baked and brown spots begin to appear. Flip the bread over with a broad spatula, such as a pancake turner, and bake the other side for a short period (about 30 seconds).
10 Meanwhile brush the baked side, lightly but thoroughly, with melted shortening or oil, and flip the bread again. Now the baked side in contact with the griddle is frying. Cook for ½ minute, then brush the other baked side with fat, and flip the bread to fry the other side for ½ minute. Take it off the griddle, and keep it warm in a covered dish or tightly wrapped with foil. Repeat with the remaining stuffed breads.

NOTE These stuffed breads can be made several hours ahead and reheated, loosely covered with foil in a 300°F/150°C/Gas 2 preheated oven for 10-12 minutes.

POTATO- AND HERB-STUFFED BREAD

ALOO PARATHA

◆

Aloo Paratha is similar to the previous recipe, except that here the *paratha* is filled with mashed potatoes.

MAKES 12 7 in/17.5 cm STUFFED PARATHA
FOR 6 PERSONS

◆

THE POTATO AND HERB STUFFING
4 medium-sized potatoes
½ teaspoon red pepper
1 teaspoon ground cumin
1 teaspoon ground coriander
1¼ teaspoons salt
3 tablespoons chopped fresh coriander leaves
THE BREAD
8 oz/250 g chapati *flour or wholemeal flour*
4 oz/125 g strong plain flour
3 tablespoons Indian vegetable shortening, or light vegetable oil
1 teaspoon salt
8 fl oz/25 cl warm water
2 oz/60 g flour for dusting
4 oz/125 g melted Indian vegetable shortening, or light vegetable oil for brushing

1 Boil the potatoes in their jackets until very soft. Peel, and mash them thoroughly. Add the remaining stuffing ingredients. Mix well and set aside. (This filling can be prepared ahead and refrigerated for a day. There is no need to warm the stuffing before filling the bread.)

2 To prepare the dough and make the bread, follow all the instructions, from Step 3 on, given for making stuffed breads in the preceding recipe.

SPINACH BREAD

PALAK PARATHA

◆

This is another technique for making stuffed bread. Here the filling is mixed in the dough before the bread is rolled. Since the bread is also oiled and folded several times, it is flakier than the conventional stuffed bread.

MAKES 8 PARATHA

◆

6 oz/175 g strong plain flour
3 oz/90 g wholemeal flour
½ teaspoon cumin seeds, slightly crushed
1 teaspoon salt
3 tablespoons Indian vegetable shortening or light vegetable oil
⅓ recipe Cooked Spinach (p. 229)
4 tablespoons warm water
2 oz/60 g plain flour for dusting
4 oz/125 g melted Indian vegetable shortening, or light vegetable oil for brushing

1 Finely chop the spinach in a food processor or on a chopping board, using a knife. (Skip this step if you are making the dough in a food processor.)

2 Combine strong plain flour, wholemeal flour, cumin, and salt in a bowl. Rub 2 tablespoons of the oil or shortening into it. Add spinach, and mix thoroughly. Add water, little by little, until the dough can be gathered into a firm ball and kneaded (it will be very sticky, so do not try to knead it yet). Clean your hands thoroughly, and dip your fingers and knuckles in the remaining oil to grease them (this will prevent the dough from sticking to your hands while you knead it). Apply a little oil to the work surface. Lift the dough, and place it on the oiled surface. Knead the dough for 10 minutes, coating your fingers with more oil from time to time. Make sure to work all the remaining oil into the dough. Place the dough in a bowl.

IN THE FOOD PROCESSOR To make the dough in a food processor, first attach the steel cutting blade. Put both flours, cumin, and salt in the container, cover, and process for 10 seconds to mix the ingredients. Add 2 tablespoons of the oil, and spinach, and process for another 20 seconds, turning the machine on and off every 5 seconds, until the spinach is thoroughly mixed with the flour. Add the water, little by little (about 1 tablespoon at a time), through the feed tube. As soon as the flour begins to adhere into a mass, stop adding water. Very soon a ball will form on the blades. (Be careful not to run the machine too long at a stretch, which causes the machine to heat up.)

To knead the dough, turn on the processor and continue processing for 40-50 seconds, turning the machine on and off every 5-10 seconds. Add the remaining tablespoon of oil through the feed tube, little by little, during kneading. The dough is kneaded when it looks smooth and shiny and feels very soft and silky to the touch. This is an extremely soft and pliable dough. Carefully remove the dough from the container and place it in a bowl.

3 Cover the bowl with plastic film or a moist towel, and let it rest for ½ hour. (The dough may be made a day ahead and refrigerated, tightly covered. Remove from refrigerator about 30 minutes before you are ready to roll.)

4 Put the oil for brushing in a shallow bowl, and flour for dusting in a plate, and keep them close to the work surface where the dough is to be rolled.

5 Knead the dough for another minute, and divide into 8 equal portions.

6 Working one at a time, place 1 ball, generously dusted with flour, on the work surface, and roll it (or spread it with your fingers) into a 6 in/15 cm circle, dusting from time to time to prevent sticking. Brush the top with oil (about 1 teaspoon), using a pastry brush or your fingers.

7 Make a cut from the centre to the edge of the circle (1). Then roll it from one edge of the cut, all the way around into a cone (2). Stand the cone up vertically (3), with its apex at the top, and gently press down on the tip to compress the cone into a patty. Dust the patty generously with flour, and roll it into a 7 in/17.5 cm disc. (The bread can be rolled out an hour ahead of time, and kept covered with a moist towel to keep the dough from drying out. Be careful not to stack the patties one atop another, as they will stick together.)

8 When ready to fry, heat the griddle or frying pan over medium heat for 2 minutes or until hot. Put one bread on the griddle. Cook for 2 minutes or until the side in contact with the griddle is baked and brown spots appear. Flip the bread over with a broad spatula, such as a pancake turner, and bake the other side for a short period (about 10-15 seconds).

9 Meanwhile, brush the baked side lightly but thoroughly with oil, and flip the bread again. Now the baked side in contact with the griddle is frying. Cook for ½ minute, then brush the other side with oil, and flip the bread for the final time, to fry the second side for ½ minute. Take it off the griddle, and keep it warm in a covered dish or tightly wrapped in foil. Repeat with the remaining breads the same way. Serve hot.

NOTE *Palak Paratha* can be made several hours ahead and reheated, loosely wrapped in foil, in a 300°F/150°C/Gas 2 preheated oven for 10-12 minutes.

DEEP-FRIED PUFFY BREAD

POORI

In appearance, *poori* looks very much like *phulka*, the puffy bread baked over flame, except that *poori* has a beautiful sheen and is flakier than *phulka* because it is deep-fried.

A WORD OF CAUTION If you are planning to serve *poori* in a puffed-up state, you have to be sure to plan your menu carefully so that no other dish requires last-minute preparation, because *poori* will take about twenty to thirty minutes to roll and fry. Once fried, it *must* be served immediately.

MAKES 16 5 in/12.5 cm POORI
FOR 6-8 PERSONS

4 oz/125 g chapati flour plus 2 oz/60 g plain flour; or 3 oz/90 g wholemeal flour plus 3 oz/90 g plain flour

¼ teaspoon salt

2 tablespoons, plus 1 teaspoon light vegetable oil

4 fl oz/12.5 cl warm water

2 oz/60 g plain flour for dusting

Peanut or corn oil, enough to fill a fryer to a depth of 3 in/7.5 cm

1 Combine *chapati* flour and plain flour (or wholemeal and plain flour) with salt in a bowl. Rub 2 tablespoons of oil into it. Add water, fast at first, to moisten the flour so that it adheres into a mass; then slowly, little by little, until the dough is formed and can be kneaded. (See Mixing and Kneading the Dough, pp. 276-277.)

2 Place the dough on the work surface, brush your fingers and knuckles with the remaining teaspoon of oil (this will prevent the dough from sticking to your hand), and knead for 10 minutes or until you have a soft and pliable dough that is smooth and silky in appearance. (Or mix and knead the dough in the food processor, see p. 278.)

3 Cover the bowl with plastic film or a moist towel, and let it rest for ½ hour. (The dough may be made a day ahead and refrigerated, tightly covered. Remove from refrigerator about 30 minutes before you are ready to roll.)

4 Put the flour for dusting in a plate, and keep it close to the work surface where the dough is to be rolled.

5 Knead the dough again for a minute, and divide into 2 equal portions. With your hands, roll each portion into a rope, and cut each rope into 8 equal portions (or pinch off small pieces of dough and roll them into 1 in/2.5 cm balls). Roll the small pieces into smooth balls, dust them lightly with flour to prevent their sticking to each other, and put them back in the bowl. Keep the balls covered loosely with a damp towel to prevent their drying out.

6 Working one at a time, place a ball, generously dusted with flour, on the work surface, and roll it into a 1 in/2.5 cm circle, pressing and stretching it with the rolling pin. Dust the dough from time to time to keep it from sticking to the work surface or rolling pin. (All the breads may be rolled ahead of time and kept covered with a moist towel until you are ready to fry them.)

7 While the last few breads are being rolled, start heating the oil in a *kadhai* or a deep-fryer. When the oil is very hot and begins to smoke (400°F/200°C), drop one bread at a time into the oil. The bread will sink to the bottom. Immediately hold a slotted spoon flat over the bread, as though keeping it from rising, but not quite touching the bread. As the bread begins to sizzle and rise to the surface (about 3-5 seconds), press the bread very gently, as though patting it, for 2-3 seconds. This will puff the bread. Once the bread begins to puff up, be careful not to press the puffed part too hard, or the bread will break and oil will seep in. Let the bread cook until it stops sizzling and the underside is slightly brown. The entire process of puffing and cooking the first side should take about 15 seconds. Gently flip the bread, and let the other side cook for about 15 seconds. Take it out, and drain it briefly on kitchen towels. Repeat with the rest of the rolled bread the same way. Serve immediately; or deflate them by placing them on the work surface and pressing gently, and put them in a covered dish or wrap in foil. Just before serving, warm them in a 300°F/150°C/Gas 2 preheated oven for 15-20 minutes.

DEEP-FRIED BREAD WITH SPICY STUFFING

KACHAURI

◆

This bread is similar to *poori*, except it is filled with a spicy bean stuffing. It is traditionally served with *poori* at the wedding banquets of the Hindu Brahmins of North India. It is also stuffed with different ingredients, such as spices, potatoes, and other vegetables. When it has a stuffing other than the one in this recipe, it is referred to not as *Kachauri*, but as *Masala-poori*, meaning Spicy Deep-fried Puffy Bread.

MAKES 16 5 in/12.5 cm KACHAURI
FOR 8 PERSONS

◆

THE SPICY STUFFING
3 oz/90 g white split gram beans (Urad dal)
4 teaspoons usli ghee *(p. 52), or light vegetable oil*
⅛ teaspoon ground asafetida
¼ teaspoon red pepper
¼ teaspoon cumin seeds, slightly crushed
1 teaspoon salt
THE BREAD
3 oz/90 g wholemeal flour
3 oz/90 g plain flour
2 tablespoons plus 1 teaspoon light vegetable oil
4 fl oz/12.5 cl warm water
2 oz/60 g plain flour for dusting
Peanut or corn oil, enough to fill a fryer to a depth of 3 in/7.5 cm

1 Pick over, clean, and wash beans following directions on p. 235.

2 Put the beans in a bowl, add enough water to cover the beans by 1 in/2.5cm and let soak for 24 hours. Drain, discard the water, and set aside.

3 Put the beans in the container of an electric blender or food processor, and grind them to a fine paste. (Use a little water if necessary. However, be careful not to add too much water. The bean paste should be fairly thick, like a soft dough.)

4 Heat the *ghee* in a frying pan over medium heat. When it is hot, add asafetida, stir for a moment or two, and immediately add the bean paste. Reduce heat to medium-low, and fry until the paste begins to look a little dry (about 3-5 minutes). Add the remaining ingredients, and mix well. Turn off heat, and set aside.

5 Follow Steps 1-5 in preceding recipe, Deep-fried Puffy Bread (p. 293).

6 Divide the spicy stuffing into 16 equal portions. Working one at a time, place a ball, generously dusted with flour, on the work surface, and roll it into a 4 in/10 cm circle, or flatten it into a 4 in/10 cm pillow with your hand. Depress the centre slightly, and place a portion of the filling into the depression. Bring the sides of the dough over the filling to enclose it completely. With your fingers, slightly pinch the edges so that the filling is in the centre and not near the edge where it could break through the dough. Repeat with the rest of the balls the same way, and keep them covered with a moist towel.

7 Place a filled patty on the dusting flour. Press it lightly with your fingers so that some flour sticks to the underside. Turn and repeat, to dust the other side with flour. Return the patty to the work surface, and roll into a 5 in/12.5 cm circle. Keep dusting with flour from time to time to prevent sticking. (These breads can be rolled out an hour ahead of time and kept covered with a moist towel to prevent the dough drying out. Be careful not to stack them one atop another, as they may stick together. They may, however, be overlapped slightly, provided the surfaces in contact are generously dusted with flour.)

8 When ready to fry, heat the oil in a *kadhai*, or deep fryer. When the oil is very hot and begins to smoke (400°F/200°C), drop 1 bread into the oil. It will sink to the bottom of the pan. Immediately hold the slotted spoon flat over the bread, as though to keep it from rising to the top. As the bread begins to sizzle and rise to the surface (about 5-8 seconds), press the bread gently for 3-5 seconds. This will make it puff slightly. Let the bread cook for ½ minute. Gently flip the bread, and let the other side cook for an additional ½ minute or until nicely browned. Take it out, and drain briefly on paper towels. Repeat with the rest of the breads the same way. Serve immediately; or deflate them by pressing gently, and place in a covered dish or wrap in foil. Just before serving, warm them, wrapped in foil, in a 300°F/150°C/Gas 2 preheated oven for 15-20 minutes.

TRADITIONAL ACCOMPANIMENTS TO AN INDIAN MEAL

◆

An Indian meal, whether formal or just for the family, always has accompaniments. The significance of serving them has been grossly misunderstood by people around the world. Many think accompaniments are garnishes, and serve grated coconut, chopped nuts, cardamom pods, chopped onions, and herbs — something never ever done in Indian homes. The accompaniments are generally served to provide extra pep to the dishes and to enhance their flavour. This could mean adding an extra tang, a bitter, sweet, or peppery taste, or crackling textures against smooth sauces. They are not an essential part of a meal, but for an Indian who grew up on these crisp wafers, fragrant relishes, and delicious pickles, meals taste quite incomplete without them.

WAFERS

PAPAD AU PHOOL BADI

◆

These crackling wafers are a delight by themselves. Since they are so easy to cook and to serve, they are often served as hors d'oeuvres with cocktails. All the varieties of wafer mentioned here are commercially available in their uncooked state.

The most popular of all wafers is *papad*, especially those made with beans. They are popularly known as lentil wafers, although that is an inaccurate description. The wafers are made with tapioca, potatoes, and rice, as well as with beans. All have two things in common: they take long hours to make, and they cook in no time at all — about 2 or 3 seconds. Since they are so time consuming, the responsibility for wafer making, which was a household art a generation ago, has been left to the rural cooperatives who now mass-produce them.

The wafers are made by grinding the soaked beans to a paste, then beating the paste to a smooth, elastic dough that can be kneaded and rolled. Various flavourings are added to the dough, which is then rolled into paper-thin discs, and left to dry in the shade for several days, or weeks. The dried discs, still very flexible to the touch, are called *papad*, and will keep indefinitely if properly sealed in airtight containers.

The most commonly served wafer around the country is the one made with white split gram beans (*urad dal*). To provide contrast to the mildly spiced, subtle food, the northerners season their wafers fiercely, with cracked black pepper, red pepper flakes, garlic flakes, cumin seeds, and carom. The southerners, on the other hand, prefer plain wafers to lend a mellow accent to their highly spiced food.

The *puppadam*, originally from Malabar along the west coast, are very different from *papad*, yet they are wafers all the same. The *papad* is a large wafer, usually 7-10 in/17.5-25 cm in diameter, as compared to the tiny *puppadam*, about 3 in/7 cm in diameter. *Papad* contains a moderate amount of baking soda and a generous amount of salt whereas *puppadam* contains a large portion of soda and just a tiny pinch of salt. It is the baking soda that gives the *puppadam* its characteristic flavour and light porous texture. The dough for *papad* is rolled paper-thin, while *puppadam's* comparative thickness enables the wafers to puff up, giving them their resemblance to *Poori* (p. 293). That is why many people confuse these wafers with bread and serve them as just that — a gross error. *Poori* is a soft bread eaten as part of the meal, to scoop up meat and vegetables. *Puppadam*, on the other hand, is a crunchy crisp wafer, to be munched on the side, with the meal, for contrasting texture and flavour.

The *Phool badi* is made by cooking tapioca and rice flour into a very thick custard. A little salt and a few chopped green chilies are folded into the custard – or paste – before it is spread into thin discs on a large sheet of cloth. They are left to dry in the sun for several days. The dried discs, or *phool badi*, are crisp and fragile, breaking easily if roughly handled. These wafers also keep indefinitely if stored in airtight containers.

LENTIL WAFERS

PAPAD OR APPALAM

◆

FOR 8 PERSONS

◆

8 *lentil wafers* (Papad *or* Appalam)
*Peanut or corn oil, enough to fill a frying pan to a depth
of 1½ in/4 cm*

Heat the oil in a *kadhai* or frying pan. When the oil is hot (350°-375°F/175°-190°C), hold one wafer at a time with a pair of tongs, lower it into the oil, and gently release it. Push the wafer down and swirl it around, using the tips of the tongs, pressing it gently to keep it submerged at all times during cooking. The wafer will expand to double its original size. The entire cooking takes about 3-5 seconds. Lift the wafer out, holding it at one end to prevent it curling, and give it a gentle shake over the pan to remove excess oil. Drain on a baking sheet lined with several layers of paper towels. Continue with the rest of the wafers the same way.

This is the traditional method of draining fried wafers in Indian cooking. Wafers fried this way have a little oil, even though not visible, clinging to them, thus making them slightly richer and heavier. I have therefore devised a method for degreasing the wafers.

DEGREASING WAFERS

1 While the oil is heating, make preparations for draining the wafers. Place 2 or 3 thicknesses of paper towels on the kitchen counter beside the stove. Keep another set of towels handy to use as a blotting pad.

2 Transfer the fried wafer to the paper towels on the counter, and cover it with the other set of towels. Press the wafer through the towels, using moderate pressure to blot up the excess oil. Do not apply too much pressure or you will break the wafer. Repeat with the remaining wafers the same way. The whole process should be carried out without interruption, while the wafers are still warm and pliable, because once they cool (in about 5 seconds) they turn brittle. Any pressure from that point on will instantly and most definitely crumble the wafers.

The wafers may be made ahead, and reheated just before serving, uncovered, in a preheated 375°F/190°C/Gas 5 oven for 2 minutes. To keep them warm, turn off the oven and leave the wafers inside, covered, until needed. They may be left uncovered on the kitchen counter provided there is no humidity in the air to make the wafers limp. Just to be on the safe side, I would advise you to store them either in airtight containers or loosely wrapped and sealed in foil.

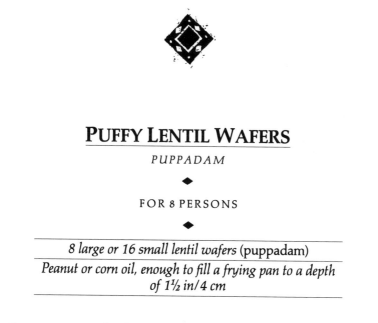

PUFFY LENTIL WAFERS

PUPPADAM

◆

FOR 8 PERSONS

◆

---

8 large or 16 small lentil wafers (puppadam)
Peanut or corn oil, enough to fill a frying pan to a depth
of 1½ in/4 cm

Follow the instructions for frying Lentil Wafers opposite. Since these wafers puff up when fried, the alternative method for degreasing suggested in the Lentil Wafers recipe cannot be used.

SNOWFLAKES OR TAPIOCA WAFERS

PHOOL BADI

◆

FOR 8 PERSONS

◆

---

16 Sago wafers (phool badi)

Peanut or corn oil, enough to fill a frying pan to a depth of 1½ in/ 4 cm

---

Follow the recipe for Lentil Wafers (p. 300), using tapioca wafers instead of lentil wafers. The alternative method for degreasing the wafers will not work with tapioca wafers, because of their uneven textured surface.

RELISHES

CHUTNEY

◆

Relishes can be grouped into three general categories: vegetable relishes, herb relishes, and preserved relishes.

Vegetable relishes are the quickest and simplest to make. They are nothing but chopped or grated vegetables flavoured with a little salt, pepper, and lemon juice. Sometimes a spice or two is added to enhance the flavour. Vegetable relishes are usually very mild and frequently take the place of a green salad. They are often assembled just before serving.

Herb relishes are made with highly fragrant herbs, such as mint, coriander, and basil, that are combined with raw ingredients such as mango, grated coconut, and spices. They range from mild and highly aromatic to spicy and peppery hot. These relishes keep well for a couple of days in the refrigerator, after which they begin to lose their fragrance and turn dark.

Preserved relishes are made by cooking pulpy fruits, such as apples, pears, peaches, apricots, bananas, guava, and mangoes, or such vegetables as carrots, tomatoes, and tamarind. They are minced or chopped, cooked with sugar, vinegar, and spices, and turned into a sort of sweetish-sour spicy conserve. Since preserved relishes, particularly those made with fruits, contain expensive ingredients, they are reserved for special occasions like wedding banquets. Because of their saucelike consistency, they make ideal dips to be served with fried fish fillets (pp. 184 and 185) and Prawn Fritters (p. 98). If properly cooked and bottled in sterilized jars, these relishes can be kept up to a year. Once opened, they must be stored in the refrigerator.

There are no rules as to which relish should accompany which appetizer. Some combinations, however, have become classics. Savoury Pastries with Spicy Potato Filling (p. 105) are generally served with Sweet and Sour Tamarind Relish (p. 315), Onion Fritters (p. 95) with Fresh Mint Relish (p. 309) or Mint Coriander Dip (p. 310), and Silky Bean Dumplings (p. 103) with Coconut Relish (p. 311).

RAW ONION RELISH

KACHE PIAZ

◆

In India, most dry meat preparations such as kebabs, *tandoori* food, and cutlets are eaten with raw onions, because the onions provide moisture against the dry meat. The onion slices are often squeezed slightly to extract and remove some of the juices; this is done to reduce the impact of too sharp and hot a taste. The onions are washed in several changes of water to rid them of any clinging juices; this also makes them taste less sharp. If you want the onions even milder, soak the squeezed onions in salted water to cover (about ¼ teaspoon of salt per ½ pint/30 cl of water) for ½ hour, and drain. This will make the onions taste sweet, and best of all, there will be no onion odour lingering in your mouth. To make this salad more aromatic, add leaves from 2 or 3 sprigs of fresh coriander.

FOR 6-8 PERSONS

◆

3 medium-sized onions
1 green chili, seeded and sliced (optional)
Juice of ½ lemon, or 2 teaspoons cider vinegar
Coarse salt, to taste

Peel onions, and cut them in thin slices. Separate the shreds, and wash them in several changes of cold water, squeezing them slightly. Be careful not to squeeze the shreds too hard, or you may crush them. Put them in a bowl, add chili, and sprinkle them with lemon juice or vinegar, and salt. Toss and serve immediately.

ONION VEGETABLE RELISH

KACHOOMAR

◆

Kachoomar is a classic North Indian relish. It is made with onions, tomatoes, green peppers, and usually flavoured with lemon juice, coriander leaves, and green chilies. Sometimes a little ground roasted cumin seed is sprinkled on top to give it an interesting texture and flavour. *Kachoomar* goes well with all North Indian dishes.

FOR 6-8 PERSONS

◆

2 medium-sized onions, or 1 large Spanish onion
½ teaspoon cider vinegar (optional)
1 small green pepper
1 small ripe tomato
1 oz/ 30 g fresh coriander leaves
1-2 green chilies
Juice of 1 small lemon
Salt, to taste

1 Peel the onions, and cut them in half from the top. Cut off the ends, and slice each half into ⅛ in/3 mm slices. Separate the shreds, and put them in a bowl. Add enough iced water to cover them. Stir in the vinegar, and then refrigerate until needed.

2 Wash green pepper in cold water, and wipe dry. Cut off the stem and discard. Cut the pepper in half, and discard the seeds and spongy white interior. Slice the pepper into shreds, and put in a bowl.

3 Wash tomato in cold water, and wipe dry. Cut the tomato in half, and scrape the interior, removing the pulp (save it for some other use, such as making gravy for meat dishes). Slice the tomato halves into thin shreds, and add them to the bowl with the shredded pepper.

4 Chop coriander leaves coarsely. Seed and shred the green chilies. Add both to the tomato and pepper.

5 Do not mix the vegetables. Simply cover the bowl, and refrigerate until needed. (The vegetables and onions can be prepared ahead and refrigerated for up to 2 hours.)

6 When ready to assemble the relish, drain the onions thoroughly and add them to the other vegetables. Squeeze the juice of the lemon over them, and add salt to taste. Toss the vegetables briefly, and serve immediately. The *kachoomar* must be served soon after it is assembled, or it will lose its appetizing crunchy texture.

ONION AND ROASTED TOMATO RELISH

TAMATARWALE PIAZ

◆

This is my favourite relish. It is made with onions and the pulp of roasted tomato. Because of its gentle smoky flavour, it is served with Lamb Pilaf (p. 143) and Emperor's Layered Meat and Fragrant Rice Casserole (p. 146).

FOR 6-8 PERSONS

◆

2 medium-sized onions
1 medium-sized ripe tomato
Coarse salt

1 Preheat the oven to 500°F/260°C/Gas 9.
2 Peel the onions, and cut them in half from the top. Cut off the ends, and slice each half into ⅛ in/3 mm slices. Separate the shreds, and wash them in several changes of water, squeezing them slightly. Be careful not to squeeze too hard, or you may crush the shreds. Put them in a bowl, and set aside.
3 Wash the tomato, wipe dry, and smear a little oil over it. Place the tomato in a small oven-proof dish. Bake, uncovered, for 15 minutes or until the tomato is fully cooked and very soft and the skin is cracked and charred. Take the dish from the oven, and let the tomato cool briefly. Then carefully peel off the skin. Mash the pulp with a fork or spoon. Be careful not to overmash; the pulp must remain a little lumpy.
4 Mix onions and tomato pulp in a small serving bowl. Add salt to taste, and then serve.

GRATED CUCUMBER RELISH

KHEERE KE LACHE

◆

This simple yet very refreshing relish of grated cucumber is a marvellous snack for any time of the day. It is also good with any Indian meal.

FOR 6-8 PERSONS

◆

3 medium-sized cucumbers
1 tablespoon lemon juice
Black pepper, to taste
Coarse salt, to taste

1 Peel the cucumbers and cut in half. If the seeds look hard and mature, scrape them out and discard. Grate the cucumber into a bowl, using the coarse blade of the grater or food processor. Cover and refrigerate. (This can be done up to 4 hours in advance.)

2 When ready to serve, add lemon juice, and black pepper and salt to taste. Toss well, and serve.

SHREDDED CARROT
AND MUSTARD SEED RELISH

KOOSMALI

◆

This is a popular relish in the southern and southwestern parts of India. It is made with grated carrot (you may substitute cucumber) and mustard-seed-flavoured oil. The carrots are briefly cooked in oil to remove their raw taste.

FOR 6-8 PERSONS

◆

6 medium-sized carrots
3 tablespoons usli ghee (p. 52), or oil (preferably light sesame)
½ teaspoon black mustard seeds
1-2 green chilies, seeded and sliced (optional)
6-8 fresh or dry kari leaves, or 2 sprigs fresh coriander leaves
Coarse salt, to taste

1 Wash the carrots, scrubbing them under running cold water, and pat them dry. Grate them, using the coarse blade of the grater, or finely shred them.
2 Heat the *ghee* in a frying pan over medium-high heat. When it is very hot, carefully add the mustard seeds. Keep a lid handy, since the seeds may sputter. When they stop sputtering and turn grey, add the chilies, stir rapidly for a moment or two, and follow at once with the grated carrots. Fry the carrots briefly to remove the raw taste (about 5 minutes), stirring constantly to prevent burning. Turn off heat, sprinkle with salt, and mix. When slightly cool, transfer the relish to a small serving bowl. Bury the kari leaves or coriander sprigs in the pile of shredded carrots. Cover and refrigerate. When ready to serve, discard the kari leaves or coriander sprigs, and check for salt. Fluff the shreds, and serve.

NOTE This relish can be made several hours ahead and refrigerated until you are ready to serve.

FRESH MINT RELISH

PODINA CHUTNEY

◆

This relish is made year-round in North India since mint flourishes in the North all year. This relish has the consistency of a thick *pesto* (the Italian basil sauce) and is generally served with fried foods.

MAKES ABOUT ½ pint/30 cl

◆

8 oz/250 g mint leaves (without stems)
2-3 green chilies, seeded
3 tablespoons finely chopped onions
¾ teaspoon grated fresh ginger root
¾ teaspoon coarse salt
1½ teaspoons sugar
1½ tablespoons lemon juice
3 tablespoons water

Put all the ingredients in the container of a food processor or electric blender, and blend until reduced to a fine, smooth purée. (This will take a few minutes more in the blender because of the lack of liquid. You will need to push the ingredients down, scraping the sides of the container from time to time.) Cover, and chill thoroughly before serving. Taste for flavouring, and if desired, add more salt and sugar.

NOTE This relish keeps well in the refrigerator for a week. It also takes well to freezing, except that the liquid separates from the pulp. Therefore, be sure to stir the relish thoroughly before serving.

MINT CORIANDER DIP

DHANIA-PODINA CHUTNEY

◆

This relish is made with coriander and mint, and thinned with yogurt so that its consistency resembles that of a sauce. It is ideal served as a dipping sauce with fried appetizers.

MAKES ABOUT ½ pint/30 cl

◆

5 tablespoons plain yogurt
2 tablespoons cold water
1 tablespoon finely chopped onions
⅓ teaspoon finely chopped fresh ginger root
1-2 green chilies, seeded
1 teaspoon coarse salt
¾ teaspoon sugar
¼ small green pepper, cored and chopped
1 oz/30 g mint leaves
3 oz/90 g coriander leaves

Put all the ingredients in the container of a food processor or electric blender, and blend until finely puréed and reduced to a creamy sauce. Check for salt, and pour into a small bowl. Cover and chill thoroughly before serving.

COCONUT RELISH

NARIAL CHUTNEY

◆

This is the most popular relish of South India. Although its flavour will vary from state to state, it consists essentially of freshly grated coconut and mustard seeds. The mustard seeds are sizzled in hot oil and folded into the coconut. Some Indians season the relish with ground roasted yellow split peas (*bhona channa dal ka aata*); others with tomato. But the most refreshing and fragrant is the *Malayali* version from Kerala, which adds chopped fresh coriander. This herb also tints the relish a very appealing pale green colour.

MAKES ABOUT ½ pint/30 cl

◆

3 oz/90 g fresh grated coconut (p. 49)
4 oz/125 g plain yogurt
2 tablespoons finely chopped coriander leaves (optional)
2 green chilies (or ¼ small green pepper plus ¼ teaspoon red pepper)
½ teaspoon coarse salt
2 tablespoons hot water
4 tablespoons usli ghee *(p. 52), or oil (preferably sesame)*
1 teaspoon black mustard seeds

1 Put coconut, yogurt, coriander leaves, chilies, salt, and hot water into the container of an electric blender, and blend until finely puréed. Put into a small serving bowl.

2 Heat the *ghee* or oil over medium-high heat in a small frying pan. When it is very hot, carefully add mustard seeds. Keep a lid handy, since the seeds may sputter. When they stop sputtering and turn grey, immediately pour the *ghee* and seeds over the coconut purée. Mix thoroughly, check for salt, and serve.

NOTE This relish may be prepared ahead and refrigerated for up to 2 days. Remove from refrigerator at least 15 minutes before serving.

SOUR MANGO RELISH

AAM CHUTNEY

◆

This is a relish commonly seen on North Indian tables during the summer, when mangoes are in season. The traditional recipe is fairly hot, so serve only a few teaspoons per person. This relish may accompany a North Indian meal, particularly a vegetarian one.

MAKES ABOUT ¾ pint/45 cl

◆

1-2 very green raw mangoes (about 1½ lb/750 g altogether)
3 oz/90 g mint leaves
2 teaspoons ground cumin
2 tablespoons ground coriander
¼ teaspoon red pepper
¼ teaspoon ground cloves
¼ teaspoon grated nutmeg
1 teaspoon dry ginger powder
1 teaspoon salt
3 tablespoons sugar or molasses

1 Peel and seed the mango, and cut the pulp into ½ in/1 cm pieces.
2 Put the mango, with all the other ingredients, in the container of an electric blender, and blend until reduced to a fine purée. Taste, and if desired, add more salt and sugar. Pour the relish into a serving bowl, and then chill thoroughly before serving.

NOTE For best results, the relish must be served within a couple of hours after being prepared, as the spices seem to lose much of their fragrance if kept for too long.

SWEET TOMATO RELISH

TAMATAR CHUTNEY

◆

This bright-red tomato relish is perfumed with ginger and cloves. Its consistency is like ketchup, and it is excellent served with fried foods.

MAKES 1 pint/60 cl

◆

2 lb/1 kg ripe tomatoes, blanched, peeled, and coarsely chopped
1 medium-sized onion, peeled and finely chopped
1½ teaspoons finely chopped garlic
5 tablespoons cider vinegar
¼ teaspoon ground cloves (optional)
1½ teaspoons ginger powder
½ teaspoon paprika
¼-½ teaspoon red pepper
4 oz/125 g sugar
2 teaspoons coarse salt

1 Put tomatoes, onion, and garlic in a heavy-bottomed enamel-coated pan, and bring to the boil. Reduce heat and simmer, uncovered, until the tomatoes are soft and reduced to a thick purée (about 45 minutes). Stir from time to time to prevent sticking and burning.

2 Strain the purée through a sieve into a small bowl. Discard seeds and any residue that remain in the sieve.

3 Return the strained purée to the pan, add the remaining ingredients, and bring again to the boil. Reduce heat and simmer, uncovered, for 30 minutes or until the sauce turns thick and glossy and coats a spoon. Stir often throughout this time, especially during the last few minutes, when the sauce becomes quite thick and sticks to the bottom of the pan. Turn off heat, and, if storing, pour immediately into sterilized jars, and seal. Alternatively, cool thoroughly, and freeze in airtight plastic containers. The relish may be refrigerated. Let the relish rest at least 2 days before serving.

HOT HYDERABAD TOMATO RELISH

HYDERABADI TAMATAR CHUTNEY

◆

This relish is a speciality from the city of Hyderabad; it goes well with Moghul dishes containing a cream and yogurt sauce. You can step up the peppery taste in this recipe by increasing either the red peppers or the green chilies, or both, to the desired amount.

MAKES ABOUT ½ pint/30 cl

◆

1 lb/500 g ripe tomatoes
5 tablespoons light vegetable oil
⅓ teaspoon cumin seeds
8 small garlic cloves, peeled
6-8 green chilies, slit open and seeded
1-2 teaspoons red pepper
1 teaspoon paprika
1 teaspoon coarse salt

1 Wash tomatoes in cold water, and wipe dry. Slice them into ¼ in/5 mm thick wedges, and set aside.

2 Heat oil over medium heat in a heavy-bottomed enamel-coated pan. When the oil is very hot, add cumin seeds. When the cumin turns dark (about 10 seconds), add garlic and whole chilies, and fry for 1 minute. Add the tomato wedges and remaining ingredients, stir to mix, and cook for 2-3 minutes. Reduce heat, and let the tomatoes cook, uncovered, for 1 hour or until the tomatoes are reduced to a thick pulpy sauce and oil has separated. Stir 3 or 4 times during this period to ensure that the sauce does not burn. The stirring should be very slow and gentle, as the tomato pieces break easily if roughly handled. Cool thoroughly, and serve at room temperature.

NOTE This relish keeps well for up to a day if left at room temperature. In the refrigerator it keeps for a week, and it also freezes well. Defrost thoroughly, and bring to room temperature before serving.

SWEET AND SOUR TAMARIND RELISH

IMLI CHUTNEY

◆

This tamarind relish has a sweet, sour, and hot taste. Its consistency is like a cream sauce.

MAKES ABOUT ¼ pint/15 cl

◆

4 oz/125 g tamarind pulp
4 oz/125 g molasses, or brown sugar
1 oz/30 g golden raisins
2 oz/60 g finely chopped pitted dates
1½ teaspoons ground roasted cumin seeds (p. 62)
1 teaspoon Mughal garam masala (p. 41), or garam masala (p. 42)
1 teaspoon dry ginger powder
¼-½ teaspoon red pepper
2 teaspoons coarse salt
1 teaspoon black salt (kala namak – optional)

1 Put the tamarind in a bowl and add 8 fl oz/25 cl boiling water. Cover and let soak for ½ hour. Mash the pulp with the back of a spoon, or use your fingers, to make it into a thick pulpy sauce. Add ½ pint/30 cl of boiling water, mix well, and let stand until lukewarm. When cool enough to handle, mash the pulp again for a minute. Strain the juices through a sieve or muslin into another bowl, squeezing as much juice out of the tamarind pulp as possible. Discard the fibrous residue.

2 Stir in the remaining ingredients. Cover and let rest at least 4 hours at room temperature, or overnight in the refrigerator before serving.

NOTE This relish keeps well in the refrigerator for a week. It can also be frozen successfully. Defrost slowly and thoroughly before serving.

VARIATIONS

◆

BANANA TAMARIND RELISH

Follow the instructions for making basic Sweet and Sour Tamarind Relish, except add 1 large ripe banana, thinly sliced, and reduce molasses or sugar by half.

◆

GINGER TAMARIND RELISH

Follow the instructions for basic Sweet and Sour Tamarind Relish, but add 2-3 tablespoons shredded fresh ginger root and 4 oz/125 g thinly sliced onions, and omit the dates.

PICKLES

ACHAR

◆

The Indian vegetarian meal almost always contains a pickle or two – a phenomenon not as common with nonvegetarian meals. In India, for poor farmers and labourers whose lunch consists of several thick breads, or rice mixed with a little plain yogurt, either staple accompanied by a chunk of spicy pickle, the pickle often takes the place of the side dish. Pickles are a very popular accompaniment for picnics and long journeys away from home. There are vast numbers of orthodox Indians who won't eat food cooked by people not of their sect. When they have to go on trips for two or three days, they would often go hungry if it weren't for the pickles they take along, with a stack of bread.

Indians pickle just about every vegetable, meat, fruit, nut, and berry. The most common, of course, are the vegetable and berry varieties, because they are inexpensive and plentiful. Except for a few sweet ones, most pickles range from mild to very hot. All contain fragrant spices. For many pickles the ingredients are left whole or cut into large chunks. For this reason, the pickles may take as long as half a year to mature in a strong brine solution.

Exposure to sunlight is an essential step in preparing pickles. This is done during the initial maturing period, because sunlight kills off bacteria, thus preventing mould and mildew from forming. To take advantage of the strong sunlight, pickles are generally prepared in summer.

Pickling is an art flourishing in the kitchens of Indian house-wives, with whom the commercial establishment dares not compete. Each family has a special method and recipe for preparing pickles, a secret seldom divulged to outsiders.

The lemon pickle recipes included in this chapter have been particularly chosen for their simplicity and superb flavour and appearance. Packed in attractive jars, they make excellent gifts.

SWEET LEMON PICKLE WITH CUMIN

MEETHA SABAT NIMBOO ACHAR

◆

MAKES ABOUT 1½ pints/1 litre

◆

9 lemons
4 tablespoons coarse salt
1 tablespoon ground cumin
1 tablespoon black pepper
1 lb/500 g sugar
2 tablespoons seedless raisins (optional)
1 teaspoon black peppercorns (optional)
5-6 dry red chili pods (optional)

1 Wash the lemons in running cold water and wipe completely dry. (If there is moisture on the surface of the lemon, the pickle will spoil.)

2 Quarter 6 lemons from the top to within ½ in/1 cm of the bottom. Extract the juice from the other 3 lemons in a small bowl.

3 Mix salt, cumin, and black pepper in a small dish, and stuff the 6 cut lemons with it, making sure not to separate the wedges so much that lemons break open. Press the lemons slightly, to reshape them, and place in a ceramic or glass jar so that they fit snugly without crushing each other. Pour the lemon juice over them. Cover the jar with a piece of muslin, and tie a cord or elastic around the jar so that the cover does not slip or blow away. (During this stage, the pickle should not be covered with the lid of the jar, or it may rot. The porous muslin excludes dust and other foreign matter, while allowing full air circulation.) Let the lemons marinate in the salt and spices for 7 days. For best results, place the jar during the day in the sun (a sunny window sill is ideal).

4 On the eighth day, pour all the juices from the jar into an enamel pan, squeezing and pressing the lemons slightly. Add the sugar to the juices, and bring to a gentle simmer over low heat. Stir often to prevent sticking and burning. When the sugar has fully dissolved, add the lemons, and gently boil for 10 minutes or until the lemons are cooked and tender. Turn off heat, and if desired, stir in the recommended amounts of raisins, black peppercorns, and chili pods. Transfer the pickle to sterilized jars. When thoroughly cooled, cover jars with their lids. Let the pickle rest for at least 3 weeks before serving. (For full flavouring, the pickle should rest for 10 weeks.)

HOT LEMON PICKLE

GARAM NIMBOO KA ACHAR

◆

MAKES ABOUT 1½ pints/1 litre

◆

1½ *teaspoons black mustard seeds*
1 *teaspoon fenugreek seeds*
2 *tablespoons red pepper*
1 *tablespoon turmeric*
½ *teaspoon ground asafetida*
6 *tablespoons coarse salt*
8 *fl oz/25 cl light sesame or peanut oil*
6 *lemons*

1 Heat a small frying pan over medium heat. When it is very hot, add the mustard and fenugreek seeds, and roast until the mustard seeds turn grey and the fenugreek dark brown (about 5 minutes), stirring constantly to keep them from browning unevenly. Add red pepper, turmeric, and asafetida, all at once, and stir rapidly for 10-15 seconds to roast the ground spices slightly. Transfer the spices to a small plate or bowl, and let them cool briefly. Grind the spices to a fine powder in a coffee grinder, or use a mortar and pestle. Return the spices to the bowl, stir in salt, and set aside.

2 Wash lemons in running cold water, and wipe dry. (Make sure there is no moisture on the surface of the lemons that could cause the pickle to spoil). Cut each lemon into 8 slices, and set aside.

3 Heat the oil in an enamel pan until very hot; then turn off heat. Add the spices, stir for a second or two, and follow at once with the lemon pieces. Stir to coat all the lemon pieces with the spices, and transfer to a sterilized jar. When thoroughly cooled, cap the jar with its lid. Let the pickle stand for 15 days, stirring once every day, before use.

QUICK MANGO AND SHREDDED GINGER PICKLE

AAM KA ACHAR

◆

MAKES ABOUT 1¼ pints/75 cl

◆

2-3 very green raw mangoes
5 tablespoons shredded fresh ginger root
1 tablespoon coarse salt
1½ teaspoons red pepper
3 tablespoons light sesame oil or light vegetable oil
1½ teaspoons black mustard seeds

1 Wash the mangoes in running cold water, and wipe completely dry. (If there is moisture on the surface of the mango, the pickle will spoil.)

2 Cut the pulp, including the skin, into ½ in/1 cm cubes, and put it in a small bowl. Add ginger root, salt and red pepper, and mix well.

3 Heat the oil in a small frying pan until very hot, and add mustard seeds. Keep a lid handy, since the mustard seeds may sputter. When they stop sputtering and turn grey, pour the oil with the seeds over the mango pieces. Mix well. Let the pickle rest ½ hour before serving.

DESSERTS

Indian desserts are primarily milk based, and their consistency is much like creamy pudding or foamy custard. Some are served fresh while they are still warm, others are frozen into ice cream, but most are served at room temperature or chilled.

Indian restaurants often serve sweetmeats instead of desserts. Sweetmeats are easy to prepare in bulk, and will keep well for several weeks without refrigeration. Indian desserts, on the other hand, are delicate preparations that stay fresh for only two to three days, properly refrigerated. Restaurants do not always clarify the distinction between desserts and sweetmeats, and many people are led to believe that Indian desserts are rich, syrupy, candylike concoctions, rather than the actual creamy puddings scented with cardamom, rose essence or saffron. All this by no means suggests that Indian sweetmeats are something less than Indian desserts. On the contrary, they are some of the finest confections in the world. It only means that each should be served at the appropriate occasion to be enjoyed to the fullest.

CREAM PUDDING

BASOONDI

◆

Basoondi, a popular dessert in Uttar Pradesh and Rajasthan, is essentially sweetened *rabadi* (see p. 55) studded with pistachios and almonds. In India this dessert is served at room temperature, but I prefer to chill it before serving so that it will taste subtler and mellower.

FOR 4-6 PERSONS

◆

3 pints/2 litres milk
3 tablespoons honey or sugar
2 tablespoons blanched almonds, cut into thin slivers
2 tablespoons unsalted pistachio nuts, blanched and cut into thin slivers
2-3 sheets silver foil (vark – optional)

1 Make *rabadi* following the directions on page 55.

2 Stir honey or sugar and 1 tablespoon each of the almonds and pistachios into the *rabadi*.

3 Carefully spoon the pudding into individual dessert dishes. Garnish each dish with the remaining almond and pistachio slivers. If you are using the silver foil, decorate each serving with a small piece of it. Place the dishes in the refrigerator, and chill thoroughly before serving.

As a variation, fold in 8 oz/250 g fresh pineapple chunks or cantaloupe balls, or stir in ½ teaspoon crushed saffron threads.

CARROT PUDDING WITH CARDAMOM AND PISTACHIOS

GAJAR KI KHEER

◆

You don't have to be a carrot lover to like this luscious pistachio-laced pudding. Although this dessert is popular throughout the North, it is really the favourite of the Punjabis. It is made by cooking grated carrots with thick, creamy milk until the mixture reduces to the consistency of rice pudding. Sometimes a little rice is added to provide puffiness and body. This dessert is at its best when thoroughly chilled.

FOR 6-8 PERSONS

◆

3 pints/1 litre milk
2 tablespoons long grain rice
1 lb/500 g grated carrots
3 oz/90 g sugar
2 tablespoons slivered blanched almonds
⅓ teaspoon ground cardamom
1 teaspoon rose water
4 tablespoons double cream
2 tablespoons chopped blanched raw pistachios

1 Bring the milk to the boil in a heavy-bottomed pan. Add the rice, and stir for a few minutes to prevent it settling. Reduce heat to medium-low, and cook the milk at a bubbling boil for 20 minutes. The rice will be thoroughly cooked and the milk reduced by half. Stir often to ensure that no skin forms.
2 Add carrots, and continue cooking, uncovered, for 15 minutes or until the carrots are cooked and most of the milk has been absorbed by the carrots, stirring often to prevent burning. (The contents of the pan should reduce to a thick, pulpy sauce.)
3 Add sugar and almonds, and cook, stirring constantly, until the pudding is very thick and begins to stick to the bottom of the pan (about 10 minutes). Turn off heat, and let the pudding cool to room temperature.
4 Stir in cardamom, rose water, and cream. Cover with plastic film, and chill thoroughly. Check the consistency of the pudding before serving. It should be slightly thinner than rice pudding, but not runny. If it looks very thick, add a little milk. Serve in individual dessert dishes, sprinkled decoratively with chopped pistachios.

SAFFRON ALMOND PUDDING

BADAAM KHEER

◆

This silky-looking dessert, popular in the South, is made with a purée of almonds, milk, sugar, and semolina. Its lovely sweet fragrance is due to the crushed saffron added at the end. This pale-yellow pudding has a consistency similar to *zabaglione* (the Italian Marsala dessert), but its texture is grainy. It is served either hot or chilled. I prefer it chilled, because the flavours of saffron and almond are too intense in a hot pudding.

FOR 8 PERSONS

◆

4 oz/ 125 g blanched almonds
1½ pints/ 1 litre milk
2 tablespoons usli ghee (p. 52), or light vegetable oil
3 tablespoons sliced or slivered almonds for garnish (optional)
3-4 tablespoons semolina
4 oz/ 125 g sugar
½ teaspoon saffron threads

1 Put almonds in a bowl, add enough boiling water to cover by 1 in/2.5 cm, and soak for a minimum of 2 hours. Drain, reserving 6 fl oz/20 cl of the almonds' soaking water.

2 Put the almonds with the reserved water into the container of a blender, and grind to a fine paste. Add the milk, run the machine for a moment or two to blend, and set aside.

3 Heat the *ghee* over medium heat in a deep enamel pan, and add the slivered almonds. Sauté, tossing the nuts until they are golden (about 1 minute). Take them out with a slotted spoon, drain on paper towels, and set aside for the garnish. (If you are not using garnish, omit this step.)

4 Add the semolina to the pan, and fry over medium heat for 5 minutes or until lightly browned, stirring constantly to ensure even browning. Add the almond-milk mixture in a stream, stirring rapidly to prevent lumping and bring to the boil. Lower heat and cook, uncovered, for 20 minutes, stirring often to keep the milk from sticking and burning. Stir in the sugar, and continue cooking gently for an additional 5 minutes. Turn off heat. The pudding at this stage will have the consistency of a thin, grainy custard sauce. It will thicken considerably with cooling and chilling.

5 Crush the saffron threads to a powder with your fingers, and stir into the pudding until thoroughly blended. When the pudding is cool, transfer to the refrigerator and chill thoroughly. Before serving, check the consistency of the pudding. If it is too thick, thin with a little milk. Serve the pudding in individual dessert dishes sprinkled with the roasted slivered almonds.

NOTE This pudding may be prepared ahead and refrigerated for up to 5 days.

COCONUT WEDDING PUDDING

PAYASAM

◆

This dessert is traditionally served at wedding banquets in the South. It is made with mung beans, yellow split peas, and coconut milk. *Payasam,* generally flavoured with crushed cardamom, is of the consistency of a light cream soup. This dessert is served warm (mostly because of the lack of refrigeration in India). I prefer it chilled, because the coconut tastes sweeter and more delicate.

FOR 6-8 PERSONS

◆

4 tablespoons yellow split mung beans (moong dal)
1 tablespoon yellow split peas (channa dal)
2 tablespoons usli ghee (p. 52), or butter
1 pint/60 cl milk
8 fl oz/25 cl coconut milk (p. 50)
3 oz/90 g light brown sugar
¼ teaspoon ground cardamom
2 teaspoons cornflour dissolved in 2 tablespoons of milk or water

1 Pick over, clean, and wash mung beans and split peas following instructions on page 235. Pat them dry.

2 Heat the *ghee* in a heavy-bottomed pan, and add mung beans and split peas. Over medium heat, sauté the *dals*, stirring rapidly, for 2 minutes. Add 1 pint/60 cl boiling water, and cook over medium heat, partially covered, for 35 minutes or until the beans and peas are tender. Check often to make sure the water is not evaporating too fast.

3 Increase heat to high, add half the milk, and continue cooking, uncovered, for an additional 5 minutes. Stir occasionally to prevent sticking. Turn off heat. Let the mixture cool briefly, then purée the *dals* to a smooth paste in an electric blender or food processor.

4 Return the purée to the pan, and stir in the coconut milk, brown sugar, cardamom, the remaining milk, and the cornflour mixture until thoroughly mixed. Simmer gently until the pudding is slightly thickened, stirring rapidly to prevent lumping. When the pudding is cool, transfer to the refrigerator and chill thoroughly. A skin will form over the pudding which is natural. Simply stir it in with a wire whisk. Serve in individual dessert dishes.

NOTE This dessert keeps well in the refrigerator for up to 4 days, after which time the coconut milk in the dessert begins to develop a rancid smell.

ALMOND AND RICE DESSERT

FIRNI

◆

This is not the usual run-of-the-mill *firni* made with milk and rice-flour and tasting like a starchy, oversweet rice pudding. It is instead made with almond milk and cream and turned into a velvety smooth custard. Its sweetness is just enough to satisfy. This *firni*, perfumed with rose water, is garnished with slivered almonds and pistachios and crowned with red pomegranate fruit. It looks stunning and tastes exquisite.

FOR 8 PERSONS

◆

THE ALMOND MILK
2 oz/60 g blanched almonds
¼ pint/15 cl boiling water
5 tablespoons rice flour
½ pint/30 cl milk
1 pint/60 cl single cream
10 tablespoons sugar
2 teaspoons rose water
2 tablespoons finely chopped or ground unsalted pistachios
2 tablespoons finely chopped or ground blanched almonds
8 tablespoons fresh pomegranate fruit, or 8 firm ripe fresh strawberries

1 Make almond milk: Place blanched almonds in a small bowl, and pour the boiling water over them. Cover, and soak for at least 15 minutes. Put the almonds with their soaking water in the container of an electric blender, and finely purée. Strain the almond milk through a double layer of muslin into a small bowl, squeezing the cloth to extract as much almond milk as possible.

2 Add the rice flour to the almond milk, stir well to mix thoroughly, and set to one side.

3 Combine the milk, cream, and sugar in a heavy-bottomed saucepan, and bring to the boil, stirring constantly. As the milk comes to the boil, reduce the heat. Give the rice and almond mixture a stir, because rice flour has a tendency to separate from the liquid and settle at the bottom. Add it to the milk and cream in the saucepan in a steady, slow stream, stirring rapidly with a wire whisk to prevent lumping. Cook over low heat until the mixture thickens and a thin custard is formed on the spoon. Continue cooking the custard, uncovered, for an additional 5 minutes. The custard should be quite thin. As it chills, it will thicken considerably. (If the custard should accidentally stick and burn, turn off the heat, and immediately pour it into another saucepan. *Do not scrape out the burnt residue*; if you do, it will release the burnt custard smell and texture into the pudding.)

4 Cool the custard thoroughly. Check to make sure there are no lumps. If there are, pass the custard through a fine sieve. (Do not blend it in the electric blender or food processor, or it will become runny.) Stir in the rose water, cover, and refrigerate to chill thoroughly. A skin will form on the custard. No need for alarm. Simply stir it in with a wire whisk. To serve, pour into individual dessert dishes, sprinkle with chopped almonds and pistachios, and place a tablespoon of pomegranate or a strawberry in the centre.

NOTE This dessert can be made ahead and refrigerated for up to 4 days. It does not freeze well.

WHOLEMEAL PANCAKES LACED WITH FENNEL

MALPOORA

◆

Traditionally, *malpoora* batter contains no eggs and is deep-fried, but, I prefer to add an egg (it helps to bind the batter) and to cook it like a pancake (since the batter is essentially a pancake batter), because deep frying makes it taste greasy and overly rich.

FOR 6-8 PERSONS

◆

2 oz/60 g wholemeal flour
2 oz/60 g plain flour
6 fl oz/20 cl double cream
8 fl oz/25 cl milk
4-5 tablespoons sugar
1 large egg
1 teaspoon fennel seeds, crushed
2 tablespoons melted usli ghee (p. 52), Indian vegetable shortening, or butter
Pinch of coarse salt
4 oz/125 g usli ghee, Indian vegetable shortening, or butter for frying crêpes

1 Mix all the ingredients, except the 4 oz/125 g *ghee*, in an electric blender or food processor, and process until thoroughly blended. Or blend the ingredients thoroughly with a wire whisk. Cover with plastic film, and let stand at room temperature for ½ hour, or refrigerate for 2 hours. (The batter may be prepared ahead and refrigerated for up to 1 day.)

2 When ready to fry the pancakes, heat a small frying pan (about 8 in/20 cm in diameter) over medium heat, and add a teaspoon of the *ghee*. Tilt the pan to coat the bottom and sides thoroughly. When the *ghee* begins to sizzle, add 2-3 tablespoons of batter to the pan. Lift the frying pan and tilt it from side to side until the entire bottom is covered with the batter. Return the pan to the heat, and cook until the edges begin to curl and brown (about 2 minutes). Turn the pancake with a non-stick spatula, to lift and turn it. Cook the second side for ½ minute. Lift the pan and invert it quickly to drop the pancake onto a plate or a piece of foil. The serving side will be at the bottom; therefore fold the pancake in half to bring the serving side up. Continue with the rest of the batter.

NOTE These pancakes can be made several hours ahead and reheated briefly in the frying pan just before serving.

They can be served in one of the following ways:
● Arrange the folded pancakes in a heated serving platter, and sprinkle them with a little cardamom and chopped pistachios.
● Brush each one lightly with molasses or honey, before folding and sprinkling with nuts.
● Dip the pancakes in sugar syrup until they are fully soaked. Fold them in half, and arrange them on a serving platter. Serve sprinkled with chopped pistachios, and pass double cream on the side.

TO MAKE SUGAR SYRUP

Combine 6 oz/180 g sugar and 6 green cardamom pods with 1 pint/60 cl water. Boil briskly, uncovered, for 5 minutes. Let the syrup cool to room temperature before dipping the pancakes.

CHEESE DUMPLINGS IN PISTACHIO-FLECKED CREAM SAUCE

RAS MALAI

◆

Ras Malai has a very intricate flavour, yet it is made with the most basic of ingredients – milk and sugar. Bengalis, known for their famous milk desserts, believe *Ras malai* is another of their wonderful creations, while the Punjabis claim it as *their* contribution to the culinary world. But one thing is certain – it is the most delicate dessert in Indian cooking.

The milk is used in two forms in *Ras malai*: as cheese (*chenna*) and as a thick milk sauce (*rabadi*). The cheese is formed into patties, simmered in syrup until they swell up and look like dumplings. These dumplings are served with the *rabadi* and garnished with pistachios and almonds. *Ras malai* tastes best when it is chilled.

For a fuller description of the uses of *chenna* and *rabadi*, see pages 53 and 55.

FOR 8 PERSONS

◆

THE CREAM SAUCE
1½ pints/1 litre milk

Bring the milk to the boil in a shallow pan, such as a frying pan. (This will hasten the process of evaporation.) Reduce heat to medium, and let the milk boil for about 1 hour and 15 minutes or until it reduces to ½ pint/30 cl. Stir now and then to prevent it sticking to the bottom of the pan and forming a skin on the surface. A skin will prevent steam from escaping; it also slows the evaporation process. To reduce the milk quickly the skin should either not be allowed to form, or be broken as often as possible. (See more on *rabadi*-making on p. 55). Cool the sauce briefly. If you want a smoother sauce, put it in the container of an electric blender or food processor, and blend until it is smooth. Transfer to a small bowl, cover, and refrigerate until needed. The cooling and chilling will further thicken the *rabadi*.

THE CHEESE DUMPLINGS
3 pints/2 litres milk
3-4 tablespoons lemon juice
2 teaspoons plain flour
⅛ teaspoon baking powder
THE SYRUP
3 lb/1.5 kg sugar
⅛ teaspoon cream of tartar
3½ pints/2½ litres cold water
1 tablespoon cornflour, dissolved in 2 tablespoons water

1 Bring the milk to the boil in a large heavy-bottomed pan. Reduce heat, and add 3 tablespoons of lemon juice. Stir gently until a white curd forms and separates from the greenish-yellow whey, about 10 seconds. If no curd forms, add a little more lemon juice.

2 Drain the curd through 3 or 4 layers of muslin or a thin fabric, placed in a colander or sieve in the kitchen sink. Hold the colander or sieve under the tap, and let cold water run at medium speed through the curd for 10 seconds. Bring up the four corners of the muslin and tie them together. Gently twist to extract as much water as possible, and hang the cheese to drain for 1½ hours. There should be 10½ oz/315 g of cheese.

3 Remove cheese from its cloth, and transfer to a work top or a marble surface. Working with the heel of your hand, break the lumps very gently. Knead the cheese for 5 minutes, or until it becomes somewhat doughy. Use moderate pressure; it is important not to destroy the grains of the cheese so that the curd does not become a paste. Form the cheese into a thin circle. Mix the flour and baking powder together and sift several times. Sprinkle the mixture evenly over the cheese and knead again for a few minutes to mix thoroughly. The kneaded cheese dough will be very soft, moist, and sticky.

4 Divide the cheese dough into 16 equal portions, and roll the small pieces into balls. Flatten the balls into round 1¼ in/3 cm pillows with your hand, and set aside on the work surface while you make the sugar syrup.

5 Mix the sugar and cream of tartar with the cold water in a large heavy-bottomed pan with a tight-fitting lid (a casserole is ideal). Bring to the boil, stirring now and then to dissolve the sugar. Boil the syrup rapidly, uncovered, until it registers 220°F/104°C on a sugar thermometer (about 10 minutes). Add the cornflour solution, stirring rapidly. Reduce heat to settle the syrup to a gentle boil.

6 Gently slip the cheese patties into the syrup, being careful not to crack them. Let them simmer in the syrup, uncovered, for ½ minute. (This process heats the patties and cooks the outer layer so that they hold their shape and do not fall apart during the boiling which is to follow.)

7 Increase the heat to maximum, and bring the syrup to a vigorous boil. Cover the pot with the lid, and let the patties cook in the boiling syrup for 20 minutes. It is essential to keep the temperature constant during these 20 minutes of cooking so that the syrup does not get too thick. This is done by adding 3-4 tablespoons of cold water every 3 minutes (you will use about 8 fl oz/25 cl of cold water in all). If the syrup boils over, you may have to add cold water every 2 minutes, or turn down the heat just a little so that the syrup continues to boil vigorously without boiling over. The cooked patties will puff up like dumplings, and float just beneath the surface of the syrup. Turn off heat.

8 Gently remove ½ pint/30 cl of the syrup from under the floating dumplings, being careful not to break any, and pour it into a deep bowl. Thin this syrup with 1 pint/60 cl of cold water. Transfer the dumplings to this diluted light syrup. When slightly cool, cover, and refrigerate until ready to assemble.

FOR ASSEMBLING THE RAS MALAI
16 cheese dumplings in light syrup (see above)
½ pint/30 cl cream sauce
6 blanched almonds, sliced or powdered
1 tablespoon slivered unsalted pistachios
2 × 3 in/7.5 cm square pieces of silver foil (vark — optional)

Carefully take the dumplings out of the syrup, one at a time, pressing them lightly to extract excess syrup. Dip them in cream sauce, and arrange them in one layer in a shallow serving dish. Stir the almonds into the remaining cream sauce, and pour it over the dumplings. Cover, and refrigerate for at least 2 hours to cool thoroughly, turning the dumplings in the sauce a few times. Just before serving, sprinkle with pistachios, and if desired, decorate with silver foil.

NOTE The assembled *Ras malai* will keep in the refrigerator, if tightly sealed, for up to 5 days, after which time the cream sauce will begin to taste sour. The cream sauce usually thickens with keeping; therefore, always check the consistency, and if necessary, add 2-3 tablespoons of syrup or milk.

Hundreds of batches of *Ras Malai* are usually prepared every day in pastry shops in India. The syrup — gallons of it — is continuously used for subsequent batches of dumplings by thinning it with water to the appropriate consistency. When a certain amount of syrup has been used up, it is replenished with fresh syrup. With the syrup in this recipe, no more than two batches of dumplings can be made. Before starting a second batch, you first need to thin the syrup. Measure the remaining heavy syrup in the pot. To each 8 fl oz/25 cl syrup add 4 tablespoons of cold water. After cooking the second batch, the remaining syrup may be strained through a double layer of muslin and used to make *Lassi* (p. 348), *Barfi* (p. 339) or use it in fresh lemonade, in place of sugar.

MANGOES WITH CREAM

MALAI AAM

◆

This is a light and refreshing dessert, particularly if you are fond of mangoes.

FOR 8 PERSONS

◆

2 large ripe mangoes (about 1½-2 lb/750 g-1 kg each), or 2 × 20 oz/600 g cans of mango slices in syrup
3 tablespoons chopped unsalted pistachios or walnuts
8 fl oz/25 cl thickened milk sauce (rabadi, pp. 55 and 331)
2 tablespoons sugar

1 Peel mangoes, cut the pulp into large pieces, and put them in a shallow serving bowl. (If you are using canned mangoes, drain, and arrange the slices in the shallow serving bowl.) Sprinkle with the pistachios or walnuts, cover with cling film, and chill thoroughly.

2 Put the *rabadi* and the sugar in the container of an electric blender or food processor, and process until reduced to a smooth sauce. Transfer to a small bowl, cover, and chill thoroughly. Serve mango slices, and pass the *rabadi* sauce on the side.

VARIATION Substitute for the *rabadi* 4 oz/125 g sour cream diluted with 4 tablespoons drained juices from canned mangoes (or any fresh or canned fruit juice), and sweetened with 2 tablespoons of sugar.

MANGO FOOL

◆

Mango fool is made with mangoes, milk or cream, and sugar. Its consistency may vary from thin milkshake to thick custardlike dessert. This particular recipe produces a consistency similar to thin custard sauce. Generally, mango fool does not contain liquor, but I like to add peach or apricot brandy because it enhances the flavour of the mangoes, and livens up the dessert.

FOR 8 PERSONS

◆

1 lb/500 g canned mango pulp, or the pulp of 1 large ripe fresh mango weighing about 2 lb/1 kg
8 fl oz/25 cl milk
3 tablespoons sugar
1½ tablespoons cornflour, dissolved in 3 tablespoons milk or water
8 fl oz/25 cl double cream
½ teaspoon almond extract
4 tablespoons apricot or peach brandy
1 tablespoon lemon juice
8 small pieces of canned or fresh mango for garnish (optional)

1 Pass the mango pulp through a fine sieve to remove all the stringy fibre, and put it into a small bowl. Set aside.

2 Heat the milk and 2 tablespoons of the sugar in a small pan over medium heat. When the milk comes to the boil, stir in the cornflour mixture. Cook until the milk is thickened and forms into a custard (about 2 minutes). Let it cool thoroughly. Stir in the mango pulp and mix well. (Both the mango pulp and the custard may be prepared ahead and refrigerated for up to 2 days, separately or mixed together.)

3 Whip the double cream until it forms definite peaks. Stir in the almond extract and the remaining tablespoon of sugar. Cover, and refrigerate until the final assembly.

4 To assemble, stir the brandy and lemon juice into the mango and custard mixture. Fold in the whipped cream. Spoon the dessert into 8 individual dishes. (Or fold in only half the whipped cream, and spread the remainder over the mango mixture in a thin layer, covering it totally.) Garnish with a piece of mango. Chill thoroughly before serving.

NOTE The Mango Fool may be prepared 2 hours before serving.

SWEETMEATS AND BEVERAGES

◆

All Indians seem to be born with a sweet tooth; they crave sweets not because they love sugar but because Indian sweets are absolutely irresistible. Hundreds of varieties of Indian sweetmeats can be made with fresh and dried fruits, nuts, vegetables, and pulses. Frequently milk fudge (*khoya*) is folded in to provide richness, body, and texture. Sweetmeats can be flavoured with saffron, cardamom, rose or screwpine water, and decorated with silver foil (*vark*), chopped nuts, and sugar glazes. Since most sweetmeats are cooked to a fudgelike consistency, they keep well for a long time.

To moderate the sweetness and wash them down smoothly, sweetmeats are generally eaten with a beverage. Often a savoury snack like Savoury Pastries with Spicy Potato Filling (p. 105) is eaten simultaneously to balance flavours. Snacking in this yin and yang way — a sweet with a savoury plus a beverage — is a favourite Indian pastime. Indians eat snacks when they are hungry — and that could be at any time of day.

SWEETMEATS

MITHAI

◆

FUDGE

BARFI

◆

Barfi can be made with several ingredients — nuts, vegetables, fruits, lentils, flour, and milk. The ground ingredients are cooked with sugar and, sometimes, fat, until they reduce to a fudge-like consistency. The fudge is then flavoured with spices, perfumed with flower essences, and poured onto a greased plate. When slightly cool, it is decorated with silver foil (*vark*) and cut into neat diamond-shaped or square pieces.

Barfi made with nuts is generally less sweet than the other kinds. The following recipes show three distinct ways of cooking *barfi*. The first one is prepared with a heavy sugar syrup; the second is made with a light syrup and yields a soft fudge; the third contains milk. All three are delicious and extremely simple to make.

FOAMY COCONUT FUDGE

NARIAL BARFI

◆

This coconut fudge, with its light, foamy texture, is an exquisite creation. Its special crumbly texture is achieved by adding toasted coconut to a very thick bubbling syrup, a technique popular in the south of India.

NOTE Use only freshly grated coconut. Dry flaked coconut simply does not taste as good. For a combination flavour, add two tablespoons of roasted unsalted chopped cashew nuts with the coconut.

MAKES ABOUT 3 DOZEN PIECES

◆

10 oz/300 g freshly grated coconut
12 oz/375 g sugar
Pinch of cream of tartar (optional)
¼ teaspoon ground cardamom
2 tablespoons usli ghee *(p. 52), or light vegetable oil*

1 Grease a 9 in/22.5 cm square or 6 × 12 in/15 × 30 cm baking tray.

2 Heat a large heavy-bottomed pan with non-stick surface over medium-high heat for 1 minute. Add the grated coconut and fry, stirring constantly, until it looks dry and flaky but is still snow white (about 5-7 minutes). Transfer the coconut to a bowl.

3 Add sugar, cream of tartar if you are using it, and 8 fl oz/25 cl cold water to the pan, and bring to the boil, stirring. Let the syrup boil over medium-high heat, uncovered, for 7-10 minutes or until the syrup is thickened and looks frothy and full of bubbles. Add the coconut and cardamom powder, and cook for 2-5 minutes, stirring rapidly and vigorously. Stir in the *ghee*, and continue cooking until the mixture begins to foam and stick to the bottom of the pan (about 1 minute). *Do not stop stirring the fudge during this last critical minute, for any reason whatsoever,* or you may end up with crystals instead of the desired flaky-textured fudge.

4 Immediately pour the mixture into the greased tray and working deftly and quickly, spread the fudge to form an even layer, patting it gently with a flat spatula. (Do not pack too much or the fudge will become dense. The fudge should be light and foamy, filled with air pockets.) Let it cool for 5 minutes. Then cut into neat 1½ in/4 cm squares.

NOTE This fudge keeps well for several months if stored tightly sealed.

CASHEW NUT FUDGE

KAJOO BARFI

◆

This fudge is made with cashew nuts that have been soaked in water. The nuts are drained, ground to a paste, and cooked with sugar until the mixture reaches a fudge consistency. This technique, popular with Maharashtrians in south-western India, produces a soft, chewy fudge with a grainy texture.

NOTE Almonds, pistachios, or walnuts may be substituted for the cashews.

MAKES ABOUT 3 DOZEN PIECES

◆

8 oz/250 g raw cashew nuts
5 oz/150 g sugar
1 tablespoon butter
2 teaspoons rose water
3 in/7.5 cm square pieces of silver foil (vark – optional)

1 Place the cashew nuts in a bowl. Pour boiling water over them to cover, and soak for 1 hour. Drain the nuts, put them in the container of an electric blender or food processor, and reduce them to a fine paste (adding a little milk or water if the paste begins to clog).
2 Grease a 9 in/22.5 cm square baking tray.
3 Heat a non-stick frying pan (at least 9 in/22.5 cm in diameter) over medium heat for 2 minutes. Add the nut paste and the sugar. Reduce heat to medium-low and cook, stirring and scraping the side and bottom of the pan constantly with a flat spatula for 20 minutes or until the fudge is thick and sticky. Stir in the butter.
4 Pour the fudge into the greased tray. Spread it evenly by patting it gently with the spatula. Let it cool thoroughly.
5 When cool, brush the top with the rose water, and let it dry briefly. Press the silver foil over the fudge, and cut 1½ in/4 cm square or diamond-shaped pieces, using a knife dipped in cold water.

NOTE This fudge keeps well, if stored tightly sealed, at room temperature for 3 weeks and for several months in the refrigerator.

ALMOND MILK FUDGE

BADAAM BARFI

◆

MAKES ABOUT 4 DOZEN PIECES

◆

1 lb/500 g blanched almonds
1 pint/60 cl milk
5 oz/150 g sugar
2 tablespoons usli ghee (p. 52), or Indian vegetable shortening, or butter
2 × 3 in/7.5 cm square pieces of silver foil (vark – optional)

1 Put the almonds in the container of an electric blender or food processor, and powder them finely. Set aside until needed.

2 Mark and grease a 8 in/20 cm square on a baking sheet, or on a sheet of greaseproof paper placed on the work surface.

3 Bring the milk to the boil in a heavy-bottomed non-stick pan. Cook over high heat, uncovered, for 10 minutes or until it has thickened to the consistency of a cream soup, stirring constantly to prevent burning.

4 Reduce heat to medium, add sugar, and cook for an additional 2 minutes or until all the sugar has dissolved. Add the powdered almonds and *ghee*. Stir vigorously and constantly as the mixture begins to lump up and stick to the spoon. Release the fudge from the spoon by scraping it off with a knife or a teaspoon. Continue cooking the mixture for 3 minutes.

5 Pour the fudge on the centre of the greased square, and working deftly and quickly, flatten and spread it to an even thickness within the square. If you are using the silver foil, place it over the fudge, and gently press it to make it adhere. While the fudge is still warm, cut it into neat 1 × 2 in/2.5 × 5 cm diamond-shaped pieces, using a sharp knife dipped in cold water.

NOTE This fudge keeps well if stored, tightly sealed, at room temperature for 3 weeks, and for several months in the refrigerator.

CHEESE DELIGHTS

GOKUL KE PEDE

◆

Peda is generally made with milk fudge – *khoya* – which is fried and mixed with sugar, nuts, and flavourings. Made with Indian cheese (*chenna*), this dessert is a refreshingly different addition to any table. This *peda*, a speciality of Uttar Pradesh, has a coarse, grainy texture and is very light.

MAKES ABOUT 2 DOZEN PIECES

◆

3 pints/2 litres milk
3 tablespoons vinegar, mixed with 3 tablespoons water
3 oz/90 g sugar
⅛ teaspoon ground cardamom
2 oz/60 g icing sugar
2-3 teaspoons milk
1 teaspoon usli ghee (p. 52), or light vegetable oil
2 tablespoons finely chopped or ground unsalted pistachio nuts

1 Make cheese (*chenna*) with the milk and vinegar water mixture, following instructions on page 53.
2 Place the cheese in a large shallow bowl, and knead with the palm of your hand until it becomes a smooth dough. Add the sugar, and knead again for a few minutes to mix well. Set aside.
3 Heat a non-stick frying pan over medium heat for 1 minute. Add the cheese (the cheese will melt and become a thick paste) and bring to the boil. Cook the bubbling paste, stirring constantly to prevent sticking, for 5 minutes or until it begins to dry and starts to look crumbly. Reduce heat to medium-low, and continue cooking for an additional 3 minutes or until the mixture looks very dry and grainy.
4 Return the mixture to the bowl, and sprinkle the icing sugar and cardamom powder over it. When cool enough to handle, knead vigorously, using the heels of your hands to crush and break the cheese grains. As you knead, sprinkle in the milk to moisten the mixture. Add only enough milk to make the mixture adhere together and hold its shape when pressed into patties.

5 Wash your hands thoroughly, wipe dry, and grease them with the *ghee* or oil to prevent the cheese mixture from sticking to your fingers. Take out 1 tablespoon of the mixture, and roll it into a smooth ball. Press the ball between your palms to form a 1½ in/4 cm patty. Press the edges with your fingers to smooth them. (You may use a small greased biscuit-mould to press and mould the cheese mixture.) Make a gentle depression in the centre of the patty, and place a pinch of chopped nuts in it. Press it slightly to ensure that the nuts adhere to the patty. Lay the shaped patty on a platter, and continue with the rest of the cheese mixture the same way.

NOTE These patties store well, if sealed, at room temperature for 3 weeks, and for several months in the refrigerator.

SESAME CRUNCH

GAJJAK

◆

This is a simple and popular sweet, sesame crunch, known as *Gajjak* in India. I like to use natural, unroasted sesame seeds because they impart a lovely flavour and make the sweet slightly chewy.

MAKES ABOUT 6 DOZEN PIECES

◆

6 oz/ 175 g raw sesame seeds
1 tablespoon water
1 tablespoon sweet butter
3 oz/ 90 g sugar
½ teaspoon lemon juice

1 Grind the sesame seeds to a fine powder, using either a coffee grinder or an electric blender.
2 Grease a section, about 9 in/22.5 cm square, of a marble or wooden board. Cut a 9 in/22.5 cm square piece of greaseproof paper, grease it thoroughly, and set aside.
3 Heat the water and butter in an enamel pan over medium-low heat. When the butter melts, add the sugar, and cook until it melts and turns a butterscotch colour (about 10-15 minutes), stirring constantly to prevent burning.

4 Add the lemon juice, and stir rapidly for 5 seconds (the melted sugar will sizzle), and then add the sesame powder. Mix vigorously for 15 seconds, and immediately pour the mixture on the greased surface. Place the greaseproof paper (greased side down) over the sesame mixture, and using a rolling pin, roll into a ⅛ in/3 mm thick sheet. Working quickly, while the mixture is still warm, peel off the greaseproof paper, and using a sharp knife, cut it into 1 in/2.5 cm squares or diamond-shaped pieces (*The entire process – from pouring the sesame mixture onto the greased board through cutting the shapes – must be done very quickly, without interruption, because once the mixture cools it becomes brittle and impossible to handle.*)

5 When cool, separate the pieces. Wrap each one in decorative silver paper, or simply store them in an airtight container. *Gajjak* keeps indefinitely.

BEVERAGES

THANDA-GARAM

◆

Indian beverages are in a class by themselves. They are fragrant drinks, filled with nutritives, laced with such aromatic spices as cinnamon and cardamom, or herbs such as basil, or essences like rose and sandalwood. There is no tradition of serving a beverage after an Indian meal. Beverages are served at any time of day. They always accompany sweetmeats and savoury snacks.

SPICED TEA

MASALA CHAH

◆

Indians like to aromatize everything they eat and drink, and tea is no exception. Generally, cinnamon, cardamom, and cloves are added to give tea a spicy fragrance, but the addition of black pepper, ginger root, coriander, and fennel is not uncommon. The people in the cooler parts of India have traditionally added spices to their tea, not just for flavouring but also to induce heat in the body. Spiced teas are particularly welcome after an Indian meal; they provide a gentle ending to the intricately spiced Indian dishes.

The recipe below produces a wonderfully fragrant tea, richly accented with the flavour of cinnamon.

FOR 8 PERSONS

◆

2½ pints/ 1.5 litres cold water
5 tablespoons milk, or to taste
1 stick cinnamon, 3 in/ 7.5 cm long
6 green cardamoms
4 whole cloves
12 black peppercorns (optional)
12 teaspoons sugar, or to taste
6 teaspoons leaf tea (orange pekoe)

1 Combine water and milk in a deep pan, and bring to the boil. Add the spices and sugar. Stir to blend, and turn off the heat. Cover the pan, and let the spices soak for at least 10 minutes.

2 Add the tea leaves or bags, and bring the water to a second boil. Reduce heat and simmer, covered, for 5 minutes. Uncover, check the colour and taste, and if desired add more milk and sugar. Strain the tea into a warm teapot, and serve immediately.

This is the way the traditional spiced tea is made. You may, however, omit the milk or sugar, or both, in which case reduce the quantity of tea to 2 teaspoons.

CARDAMOM TEA

ILAICHI CHAH

◆

This tea is mellower than *masala* tea. It is flavoured only with pods of green cardamom, which lend a tasty sweetness.

FOR 8 PERSONS

◆

2½ pints/ 1.5 litres cold water
12 green cardamom pods
6 teaspoons leaf tea (orange pekoe)
Small piece of lemon, lime, or orange peel
Scalded milk and sugar, to be served on the side

1 Combine water and cardamom pods in a deep saucepan, and bring to the boil. Reduce heat and simmer, covered, for 5 minutes. Turn off heat, and let soak, covered, for 10 minutes.

2 While the cardamom is soaking, rinse the teapot with boiling water. Add the tea leaves or bags and the peel to the pot.

3 Bring the cardamom water to a full boil, and pour it, pods and all, into the teapot. Let the tea brew for 2-3 minutes before serving. Pass the scalded milk and sugar on the side.

This is the way Indians enjoy cardamom tea. You may, if you wish, omit the milk and sugar altogether, in which case reduce the tea to 2 teaspoons or else the brewed tea will be too strong and bitter.

ROSE-FLAVOURED YOGURT DRINK

LASSI

◆

A familiar sound in the streets of Delhi in the summer months is the rhythmic juggling of liquid and ice from one jug (*loota*) to another. What is being prepared is the heavenly yogurt drink called *lassi*. This foamy and frothy liquid, besides being so tasty, is perhaps the most healthy and nutritious drink in the world.

For a classic *lassi*, the quality of the yogurt is of prime importance. It should be slightly sour, so that when it is diluted it still retains a strong yogurt flavour. Also, it is essential that the yogurt be rich and creamy, or else the *lassi* will taste watery. If your yogurt lacks the right creaminess, you will need to add a little cream to enrich it.

FOR 2 PERSONS

◆

12 oz/375 g plain yogurt
3 tablespoons double cream
1 tablespoon rose water
6 tablespoons sugar
9-10 ice cubes

Put yogurt, cream, rose water, and sugar in the container of an electric blender, and blend for ½ minute or until the sugar is fully dissolved. Add ice cubes, and continue blending for another ½ minute or until the yogurt drink is frothy (the ice cubes will not disintegrate fully). Pour the drink, with the ice cubes, into 2 tall glasses, and serve.

MINTY YOGURT REFRESHER

MATTHA

◆

Mattha, literally translated, means buttermilk. Indian buttermilk is more like skimmed milk, and has a buttery-yogurt flavour. *Mattha* is frequently served just by itself, though it is quite common to add a little salt, crushed cumin, and a few fragrant herbs. For the best flavour, the yogurt should be a little tangy.

FOR 2 PERSONS

◆

8 oz/250 g plain yogurt
6 fl oz/20 cl cold water
12 mint leaves
½ teaspoon ground roasted cumin seeds (p. 62)
½ teaspoon salt
8-9 ice cubes

1 Put yogurt, water, and 8 mint leaves in the container of an electric blender, and blend for ½ minute or until the mint is finely chopped.
2 Add cumin, salt, and ice cubes, and continue blending for an additional ½ minute or until the yogurt drink is frothy (the ice cubes will not disintegrate fully). Pour the drink with the ice cubes into 2 tall glasses. Squeeze the 4 remaining mint leaves slightly in your fingers, to release the fragrance, and place them on top. Serve immediately.

INDIAN SUMMER PUNCH

THANDAI

◆

Writing about *thandai* brings back sweet memories of my childhood in Kanpur. Summer vacation was always a very special time of the year; that was when various sweetmeats and pickles were prepared and different spice blends ground and mixed. Every day a fresh beverage was made especially for us while we played in the yard with the sun beating down. The most delicious of all these was a cardamom-scented almond drink called *thandai*. It is a speciality of Uttar Pradesh and its preparation was, I remember, a long drawn-out process. First, different nuts and seeds were carefully measured. Then each was cleaned and blanched. Then the nuts were mixed and ground to a paste, with a little milk or water, on an Indian stone grinder. This paste was then blended into milk, sweetened with sugar, and poured into tall glasses filled with crushed ice.

Thandai can be made quite effortlessly, in a fraction of the time it takes by the traditional method, by using an electric blender. The results are very good. This beverage is perfect for warm, sultry days. It is a particularly good nonalcoholic drink to serve at cocktail time.

NOTE It isn't necessary to make *thandai* with milk – you can use cold water instead, as is often done – though the milk tends to mellow the spices, giving the drink a more delicate taste.

MAKES 1½ pints/1 litre OF *THANDAI* CONCENTRATE

◆

2 tablespoons fennel seeds
Seeds from 8 green cardamom pods
6 whole cloves
12 peppercorns
4 oz/125 g blanched almonds
6 oz/175 g raw seeds (such as sunflower, pumpkin, or papaya)
boiling water
6 oz/175 g sugar
1½ pints/1 litre milk or water

1 Grind fennel, cardamom, cloves, and peppercorns into a fine powder, using a coffee grinder or a mortar and pestle. Set aside.

2 Place almonds and raw seeds in a bowl, add boiling water to cover, and let soak for ½ hour. Drain.

3 Put the soaked almonds and seeds, along with ½ pint/30 cl of boiling water, in the container of an electric blender, and blend until the almonds and seeds are reduced to a fine paste. Add sugar, and spice mixture, and continue blending until sugar is thoroughly dissolved (about ½ minute).

4 Pour the punch mixture into a bowl. Add ½ pint/30 cl of boiling water to the blender, and run it through briefly to release any paste clinging to the sides. Add this to the punch mixture, and stir to blend.

5 Strain the punch mixture through 3 layers of muslin, squeezing to extract as much liquid as possible. (The pulp may be saved and used in nut fudges.) Transfer the concentrate to a bottle or pitcher, and chill thoroughly.

To make individual drinks, pour 4 fl oz/12.5 cl of *thandai* concentrate into a tall glass. Add 4 fl oz/12.5 cl milk or water, stir well, add 3 or 4 ice cubes, and then serve.

GLOSSARY

◆ A ◆

Aam	ripe mango fruit
Aata	flour; wholemeal flour
Achar	pickle
Adrak	fresh ginger root, also known as green ginger
Agni	God of fire worshipped by Vedic Indians
A-himsa	nonviolence; the doctrine of refraining from the killing of animals or insects
Ajwain	carom seeds, also known as lovage
Akhroot	walnut
Aloo	potato
Amchoor	mango powder made from raw sour mangoes
Anardana	dried edible seedlike fruit of the pomegranate
Anda	egg
Appalam	lentil wafers
Arbi	Indian starchy root vegetable
Arhar Dal	lentils
Arwa Chawal	long grain rice

◆ B ◆

Badaam	almond
Badaami	meat or chicken, cooked with ground almonds and spices
Bade	small doughnut-shaped fried bean dumplings
Badi Elaichi	black cardamom pods
Badshahi	emperor's
Bag Bazaar	famous market in Calcutta
Bagda Jheengari	giant prawns
Baghar	spice-perfumed butter used for flavouring *dal*, yogurt salads, vegetables, relishes, and some meat and poultry
Baigan	aubergine
Bakara or bakari	goat
Bakare ka Gosht	goat's meat

Bandh Gobhi	cabbage
Bara Jheenga	lobster
Barfi	fudge
Barista	crisp fried onion shreds used in Moslem cooking
Barra Kabab	thin strips of boneless loin or rib meat, marinated, skewered, and grilled
Bartan Maanj-hane Wali	paid worker who cleans dishes and pans twice a day
Basoondi	dessert made with *rabadi*, sweetened with honey or sugar, and garnished with nuts
Basmati	generic name of a variety of Indian long grain rice
Beans	green beans
Besan	chick-pea flour
Bhara	stuffed
Bharta	smoked aubergine fried with onions, tomatoes, and herbs
Bharva	same as *Bhara*
Bhatoora	leavened dough made of yogurt, potatoes and white flour, rolled into circles and deep fried
Bhindi	okra
Bhojia	vegetables stir-fried with spices and seasonings
Bhona	fried
Bhonao	the technique of frying onions, and meat
Bhone Piaz ke lachee	crisp fried onion shreds used as garnish for pilafs
Bhorji	scramble, generally applied to scramble of eggs
Biriyani	an elaborate pilaf made by cooking meat or chicken separately as *korma* and then folding fragrant rice into it. Lamb *biriyani* is generally flavoured with saffron and screw-pine essence, and garnished with nuts and silver foil
Biswa Tulsi	sweet basil
Bombil, or *Bombay Duck*	small transparent fish (found along the western coast of India), sun-dried, and sold as a wafer
Boti Kabab	boneless pieces of meat, marinated, skewered, and grilled
Brahma	the supreme Hindu God, the creator of the universe
Brahmin	priestly class, or person belonging to priestly class – the topmost of the four Hindu castes, others being, in order of importance, *kshatryas* (the warrior class), *vaishya* (trader), and *shudra* (cultivator or artisan). Untouchables are outcastes, and include *chamaar* (leather worker), *bhangi* (sweeper), and *dhobi* (laundryman)

✦ C ✦

Chah	tea
Chakki	grain mill
Chakko	knife
Chakla	marble or wooden board for rolling bread
Chalni	strainer, sieve, sifter
Channa	dried chick-peas; also cooked chick-pea dish with spices
Channa Dal	yellow split peas
Chapati	thin griddle-baked wholemeal bread
Chapli Kabab	minced meat mixed with spices, herbs, and seasonings, shaped into patties and shallow fried
Chat	a cold dish made with vegetables, fruits, and spices, eaten as a snack or appetizer
Chaunk	same as *baghar*
Chaunk Gobhi	Brussels sprout
Chawal	rice
Chenna	Indian cheese
Chimta	tongs
Choolha	coal- or wood-burning Indian mud stove
Chota Piaz	shallot
Choti Elaichi	green cardamom; also white bleached cardamom
Chotoo Jheengari	large shrimp or prawn
Chukandar	beetroot

✦ D ✦

Dahi Bhalle	fried bean dumplings in spice- and herb-laced yogurt, speciality of Punjab State
Dal	pulses (lentils and dried peas and beans)
Dalchini	cinnamon
Deghi Mirch	Indian paprika made from mild Kashmiri peppers
Dhakkan	lid
Dhania	coriander
Dhan-sak Masala	spice blend used for making *Dhan-sak*, a chicken, lentil, and vegetable stew
Dhooli Urad	white split gram bean
Doodh	milk
Doodhwala	milkman

Do-piaza	literally translated, means meat, chicken, or shellfish, cooked in double its weight of onions
Ducan	shop
Dum	Indian technique of pot-roasting
Durga Pooja	festival during the months of September and October to worship the Goddess Durga, also known as Kali or Parvati, the consort of Lord Shiva

◆ E ◆

Elaichi	cardamom
Eleesh	fatty fish found in Hoogli river in Calcutta, Bengal

◆ F ◆

Firni	pudding made with rice flour, almonds, and creamy milk

◆ G ◆

Gajar	carrot
Gajjak	sesame brittle
Ganth Gobhi	kohlrabi
Garam	warm, hot
Garam Masala	aromatic blend of roasted spices used in cooking of North India
Geela Masala Bhoonana	brown-frying onion, garlic, and ginger root
Geela Masala Tay-yar Karana	preparing onion, garlic, and ginger root for cooking
Ghara	pottery or metal jug for storing water
Ghat	meaning 'steps', generally applied to the chain of hills along the western coast of India which rise sharply on the East and slope gradually toward the coast
Ghee	fat
Gingelly	light sesame oil
Gobhi or *Phool Gobhi*	cauliflower

Gochian	black beehive-shaped mushrooms from Kashmir region, similar to morels
Gol	round
Golda Jheengari	lobster
Gosht	meat
Ground Nut Oil	peanut oil
Gujjia	crescent-shaped sweet pastries filled with nuts and coconut
Gulab	rose
Gulab Jal	rose water
Gulkand	rose petals preserved in heavy sugar syrup

◆ H ◆

Haldi	turmeric
Halwa	vegetables, lentils, nuts and fruits, cooked with sugar and *ghee* to the consistency of plum pudding
Halwai	pastry chef
Halwai ki Ducan	pastry shop
Hara Dhania	fresh coriander leaves
Hara Piaz	spring onion
Hari Chutney ka Pullao	pilaf made with fresh mint, coconut, and spices – a speciality of Andra Pradesh
Hari Gobhi	broccoli
Hari Mirch or *Simla Mirch*	green pepper
Heeng	asafetida
Hindi	the most widely spoken Indo-European language in India, originally from Uttar Pradesh
Hindu	follower of Hindu religion, with Brahma as the supreme God, and worshipping the God Vishnu or the God Shiva
Hussaini Kabab	minced meat shaped into thin sausages, stuffed with nuts and raisins, and fried or grilled

◆ I ◆

Imli	tamarind

◆ J ◆

Jain	follower of Jain religion (primarily centred in the state of Gujrat), founded by Mahavira (599-527 B.C.) with *Agamas* as their sacred scriptures
Jaiphul	nutmeg
Jal Toori	literally translated, cucumber of the sea — a fish
Javitri	mace
Jeera	cumin
Jheenga or Jheengari	shrimp or prawn

◆ K ◆

Kabab	kebab
Kabab Masala	spice blend used for making kebabs
Kabadiwala	person who buys used clothes and gives in return new stainless steel utensils
Kacha	raw
Kachauri	fried puffy bread stuffed with spicy bean mixture
Kachoomar	chopped or sliced onions, tomatoes, and green pepper, flavoured with lemon juice
Kaddoo-kas	vegetable grater
Kadhi	dumplings made with chick-pea flour and simmered in yogurt with spices and vegetables
Kadhai	Indian cooking utensil similar to Chinese wok, used for frying food
Kajoo	cashew nut
Kala	black
Kala Channa	small black chick-peas that also yield chick pea flour (*besan*)
Kala Namak	black salt
Kalaiwala	person who lines or recoats copper and brass utensils
Kalaunji	onion seeds
Kali Dal	rich dish of black whole gram bean (*sabat urad*) cooked with butter, spices, and fresh herbs
Kali Mirch	black pepper
Karchi	stirring spoon
Kari	curry; also, sweet aromatic leaves of the kari plant
Kari Podi	curry powder
Kashmirir Pandit	Hindu from the state of Kashmir

Kasoori Mathari	savoury biscuits made with rich dough and dry fenugreek leaves
Kasoori Methi	dry fenugreek leaves
Katch	lamb
Katoori	small metal bowls for serving individual portions of dishes
Keema	minced meat; also the gravy dish cooked with the ground meat
Kekada	crab
Kesar	saffron
Kewra	screw pine
Khansaama	cook, chef
Khara	plain, unelaborate, with few spices
Khas-khas	white poppy seeds
Khasa	special
Khatte	sour
Kheer	pudding, rice pudding
Kheera	cucumber
Khichari	a porridge made with rice, yellow split mung beans, and spice-perfumed butter
Khoobani	apricot
Khoshboo	aroma
Khoya	milk cooked down to fudgelike consistency
Kofta	minced meatballs simmered in sauce with spices
Koosmali	relish made with raw grated carrots and fried black mustard seeds
Korma	braising, braised, to braise
Kulcha	leavened white-flour dough shaped into rounds and baked in the *tandoor*
Kulfi	Indian ice cream made with cooked-down milk, frozen in special conical moulds called *Kulfi ka saancha*

◆ L ◆

Lobhia	black-eyed peas
Lal Mirch	red pepper
Lassan	garlic
Lassi	yogurt thinned with water, sweetened, and flavoured with rose essence or rose water
Laung	clove

◆ M ◆

Maalik/Maalkin	master/mistress
Maan Dal	black whole gram bean
Maanz	meat
Maharaj/ Maharajin	male Brahmin cook/female Brahmin cook
Machi	fish
Makhan	butter
Makhani Murgh	cooked *Tandoori* chicken pieces simmered in creamy tomato sauce with butter and spices and flavoured with fresh coriander leaves
Malai	cream
Malai Kofta	meatballs simmered in creamy, buttery tomato sauce with spices
Malpoora	sweet wholemeal pancakes flavoured with crushed fennel
Masala	spice, spices, spice blend, blend of seasonings and spices
Masala Bhoonana	roasting spices
Masala Musulana	crushing spices
Masala Peesana	grinding spices
Masalchi	cook's assistant
Masar Dal	pink lentils
Masoor Dal	same as *Masar Dal*
Matar	peas, chick-peas
Matar Shufta	vegetarian counterpart of *Keema Matar* (the gravy dish of minced meat and green peas) made with fried milk-fudge grains, a speciality from the state of Kashmir
Mattha	yogurt drink flavoured with salt, roasted cumin, and fresh mint leaves
Meetha	sweet
Mithai	sweetmeat, sweets
Meethe Neam ke Patte	kari leaves
Methi	fenugreek seeds, fenugreek greens
Mirchi ka Achar	fresh hot chilies, slit, stuffed with spices, and pickled in mustard oil
Mirchi ki Bhaji	mild green chilies cooked in butter with molasses, tomatoes, and spices, a speciality of Rajasthan State
Moolee	in coconut sauce

Moong Badian	fried mung bean dumplings made with puréed yellow mung beans and spinach
Moong Dal	yellow split mung beans
Mughal	Moghul – Turks, Mongol by origin and Moslem by religion, brought Persian culture, food, cooking techniques, and garnishes to India in the sixteenth century
Mughal Garam Masala	classic blend of highly fragrant and mild-tasting spices used for flavouring dishes of Moghul origin
Mughalai	in the Moghul tradition
Muharram	the day of observation of Saint Hussain's death
Mullagatanni	*Mullaga* (black pepper) *tanni* (water or broth), the origin of Mulligatawny Soup
Mungaude ki Bhaji	*Moong Badian* simmered with tomatoes, seasonings, and spices
Murgh or *Murghi*	Chicken
Musalmaan	Moslem – follower of Islamic religion with Mohammad (A.D. 570–632) as prophet

◆ N ◆

Namak	salt
Namaste, Namaskaar	Indian word of greeting
Nan	teardrop-shaped bread made with leavened dough and baked in the *tandoor*
Nandi	sacred bull – carrier of Lord Shiva
Nargisi Kofta	meatballs stuffed with whole eggs, fried, cut in half to expose the egg, and simmered in onion gravy
Narial	coconut
Narial-kas	coconut grater
Naukar/Naukarani	male servant/female servant
Nimboo	lemon, lime

◆ O ◆

Obla	boiled
Oobalana	to boil, boiling
Op-phul	by-products

◆ P ◆

Paan	leaves of the betel pepper plant (*piper betle*); also the digestive preparation made with betel leaf (*paan ka patta*), lime paste (*choona*), catechu (*kattha*), and betel nut (*sopari*), which may also contain coconut flakes, fennel, clove, cardamom, tobacco and *gulkand*, and be covered with silver foil
Paani	water
Pachadi	yogurt salad made with raw vegetables and yogurt, flavoured with fried black mustard seeds
Pakode	fritters
Palak	spinach greens
Paneer	*Chenna* compressed into a cake and cut into small pieces
Papad	lentil wafers
Papeeta	papaya
Paraath	large high-rimmed platter used for mixing and kneading dough, cleaning *dal* or *basmati* rice, and preparing and cutting vegetables
Paratha	griddle-fried wholemeal flaky bread
Parsee	follower of the Persian Zoroastrian religion (primarily centred at Bombay in the state of Maharashtra), with Zoroaster as prophet. Parsees fled from their Persian homeland between the eighth and twelfth centuries to escape religious persecution by Moslem rulers
Pasanda Kabab	same as *Barra Kabab*
Pateela	handleless saucepan used for general cooking
Payasam	pudding made with yellow mung beans, split peas, and coconut milk, a speciality of the southern regions
Peda/Pede	milk fudge moulded into small pillows and garnished with pistachio nuts
Peela	yellow
Phool Badi	tapioca or sago wafers; rice wafers
Phool Gobhi	cauliflower
Phulka	baked wholemeal puffed bread
Piaz	onion
Pista	pistachio
Pitthi	spicy bean stuffing used in *Kachauri*
Podina	mint
Pomfret	non-oily firm-fleshed fish similar to flounder

Poori	deep-fried puffy bread
Pullao	pilaf – *basmati* rice cooked in *ghee* or oil with spices, meat, chicken, or vegetables
Punch-phoron	spice blend used for flavouring vegetables in the eastern regions of India
Puppadam	puffy lentil wafers, a speciality of Malabar in South India

◆ R ◆

Rabadi	thickened milk sauce made by cooking down milk
Rabadi Dooth	milk enriched with *rabadi*
Rai	mustard
Raita	raw or cooked vegetables or fruits mixed with seasoned yogurt
Raja	king
Rajma	red kidney beans
Ram Tulsi	white basil
Rang	colour
Ras Malai	dessert of cheese dumplings in pistachio-flecked cream sauce
Rasam	spicy lentil broth, a speciality of the South
Rasedar	vegetables in thin gravy
Rasooi	kitchen
Rogan Josh	lamb braised in yogurt and cream with Moghul spices, a Kashmiri speciality
Rogani Gosht	rice meat dish made with cream, *usli ghee*, and spices
Roi	a local fish sold in *Bag Bazaar* in Calcutta
Roti	bread
Ruh	essence

◆ S ◆

Sabat Moong	green whole mung beans
Sabat Urad	black whole gram beans
Sabzi	vegetables; also, stir-fried vegetable preparation from North India
Sabziwala	vegetable seller
Sada	plain

Safaid	white
Saag	greens
Salan	spicy gravy
Sambaar	vegetable and lentil stew with tamarind, flavoured with spices
Sambaar Podi	blend of hot spices used for flavouring *sambaar*
Sambhar Namak	white salt, table salt
Samosa	triangular savoury pastries filled with potatoes or meat
Sarsoon	mustard greens
Saunf	fennel; anise
Seek Kabab	thin sausage-shaped kebabs of grilled minced meat and fresh herbs
Selha Chawal	rice
Sem	beans
Sendha Namak	coarse salt
Shahi	royal
Shamme Kabab	minced meat and yellow split peas, flavoured with mint, ginger root, and spices, shaped into small patties and fried
Sharbat	fruit punch
Shorva	soup
Shiva	the God of destruction or power
Sikh	bearded and turbanned follower of Sikh religion (primarily centred in the state of Punjab), founded by Guru Nanak (A.D. 1469–1538), with *Granth Sahip* as principal scripture
Sil-batta	grinding stone
Sonth	dry ginger powder
Sookha Dhania	coriander seeds
Sookha Masala Bhoonana	frying spices
Sooji	semolina, farina
Sopari	betel nut
Srikhand	dessert made with drained yogurt, sugar, nuts, and saffron

◆ T ◆

Tadka	same as *Baghar*
Tahari	spicy rice-and-peas dish with turmeric and herbs

Tala	deep-fried
Talna	deep frying
Tamatar	tomato
Tandoor	Indian clay oven
Tandoori	food cooked in a *tandoor*
Tandoori Masala	spice mix used for flavouring *Tandoori* chicken
Tari	gravy
Tava	handleless iron griddle
Tej Patta	bay leaf
Tel	oil
Thal	metal platter
Thali	metal dinner plate
Thandai	summer punch made with ground seeds, almonds, spices, sugar, and whole milk
Tikka	cutlet
Toor Dal	red lentils
Toovar Dal	same as *toor dal*
Topshe	a local fish sold in *Bag Bazaar* in Calcutta

◆ U ◆

Urad Dal	white split gram bean
Usli Ghee	Indian clarified butter

◆ V ◆

Vanaspati Ghee	vegetable shortening
Vark	silver foil
Veda	literature of the ancient Indians, compiled between 1500 and 500 B.C.
Vedic	referring to the period of the *veda*
Vendaloo	Goanese hot and pungent curry
Vishnu	the God of preservation

◆ Y ◆

Yakhni	meat broth
Yerra	same as *Jheenga*

◆ Z ◆

Zaffran	saffron
Zarda	sweet saffron pilaf, traditionally made on *Muharram*

ACKNOWLEDGEMENTS

♦

When I think of all the people who taught me to cook, shared their secret formulas for various cooking techniques, divulged prized recipes, or helped in any small way in the preparation of this book, I am overcome by a sudden burst of emotion. My love and gratitude for all they have done are boundless and shall remain forever.

It seems best to start at the beginning. First I thank my mother, who in an unconscious yet powerful way influenced my senses, my palate and my judgement. She took painstaking care in getting information on various ingredients and sending it to me. My mother-in-law gave me the precious gift of wisdom by reminding me that loving, living, and eating are inseparable and the essence of life. She generously shared many of her treasured family recipes, which have since become my own family favourites and are included in this book. And I thank my family's resident cook, who poured all her love and affection into the food, who filled my life with sweet memories of delicacies, and who taught me many basic skills involved in Indian cooking — including making perfect puffy breads. I would also like to mention my husband's and my own grandmothers, aunts, sisters, and fathers for their advice and help.

I am grateful to Mrs Moinuddin and Mrs Salamatullah for their recipe for *Shamme Kabab*. Mrs Puri and Mrs Bakshi for their *Channa* recipes. Karim for sharing his family's technique of making *Keema* and *Hussaini Kabab*. Mrs Uppal for her *Peele Chawal*. And Mrs Bhatnagar for the *Meetha Sabat Nimboo Achar* recipe. I am indebted to Mrs B. Singh for showing me the *korma* techniques and exquisite *biriyani* garnishes. Pares Bhattacharji for introducing me to the glorious wealth of fish and shellfish of Bengal, and the many marvellous ways of cooking it. Nazir Mir for giving me insights into the Kashmiri cooking traditions. Asha Vyas for her perceptions about Gujrati food and the general cooking of North India. Saleem Ali of Spice and Sweet Mahal for generously taking time to discuss the food of Pakistan and its various special ingredients. Asha Gokhale for her recipe for *Kajoo Barfi*. And Mrs Khosla for discussing *Imli Chutney*. I am also grateful to the New York Botanical Garden; Cornell University Cooperative Extension, Ithaca; the United States Department of Agriculture; Adriana Kleiman; and Ruth Schwartz, for their help in researching information on spices and grains.

I am thankful to my students for the experience they gave me. Their innumerable questions proved very useful in the writing of this book. I am also grateful to Patricia Wells and Florence Fabricant for their interest, encouragement, and efforts in publicizing my cooking. I would also like to make special mention of Rayna Skolnik, a student and a dear friend, who took time from her very busy schedule to read the manuscript and make constructive suggestions. Betsy Cenedella for her careful and tireless copy editing, for remaining patient and smiling when changes were made in certain recipes. And Molly Finn for her support and expert advice.

Finally, I wish to thank my American editor, Maria Guarnaschelli, who laboured over the book with an energy and passion beyond words. For her enthusiastic support and wise guidance all through the book, for her numerous valuable suggestions, superb editing, and for giving form to the book, I express my gratitude and affection forever.

INDEX